crossing borders activating spaces

grenzen überschreiten räume aktivieren

·

crossing borders activating spaces

grenzen überschreiten räume aktivieren

Editor Herausgeber: Internationales Doktorandenkolleg „Forschungslabor Raum"

jovis

CROSSING BORDERS ...
GRENZEN ÜBERSCHREITEN ...

...ACTIVATING SPACES

What topic is currently so relevant in the planning and design disciplines that the International Doctoral College (IDK) "Spatial Research Lab" should address it intensely for three years? This was the question asked in the early summer 2016 by those professors who had been concerned since 2007 with the development of European metropolitan regions (IDK I) and urban transformation landscapes (IDK II), because they were determined to put together a third curriculum (IDK III) for the years 2017 to 2020 to promote a new generation of highly qualified young scientists.

The arrival of more than a million asylum seekers from the war and crisis zones around Europe had been dominating daily media and political events for some time in 2016. Public debates had flared up about the security of Europe's external borders, as well as about maintaining open internal European borders. Despite emphatic calls for greater solidarity, an increasingly strong renationalization was emerging in Europe, not only in immigration and asylum policies. In June 2016 in the United Kingdom, an EU membership referendum initiated the exit process from the European Union—a bitter disappointment for the scientific community in Europe. Just a few years before, there had been an intense focus on a greater outward opening of the EU as part of globalization. To ensure better internal European networking, the planning of efficient infrastructure corridors beyond national borders had been driven forward together. Now, however, populist calls for the closing of borders, the defence of nationalist sovereignty, and the turning away of migrants were setting a delimiting tone. In view of this, the professors responsible for the doctoral college decided consciously to set a positive signal for constructive togetherness as well as for cross-border teaching and research in Europe with the theme "Crossing Borders—Activating Spaces".

"The fundamental idea behind the doctoral college is to support the up-and-coming generation of planners and designers in 'venturing into the unknown' beyond the boundaries of universities and disciplines," Bernd Scholl emphasized in his farewell lecture at ETH Zurich 2018. The setting of the theme was therefore intended to encourage especially the bold cross-border commuters among the young researchers to apply for one of the thirty places at IDK III. Many made use of this opportunity. Young colleagues were selected on the basis of their outlined doctoral topics, if the focus of their research questions was the consideration of national, spatial, or landscape borders. Furthermore, the initiators of the college from the beginning pursued the

Welches Thema ist aktuell in den planenden und entwerfenden Disziplinen so relevant, dass sich das Internationale Doktorandenkolleg (IDK) „Forschungslabor Raum" drei Jahre lang damit intensiv befassen sollte? Diese Frage stellte sich im Frühsommer 2016 jenen Professoren, die sich seit 2007 mit der Entwicklung europäischer Metropolregionen (IDK I) und urbanen Transformationslandschaften (IDK II) auseinandergesetzt hatten, denn sie waren fest dazu entschlossen, für die Jahre 2017 bis 2020 ein drittes Curriculum (IDK III) zur Förderung von wissenschaftlich hochqualifiziertem Nachwuchs aufzulegen.

Die Ankunft von mehr als einer Million Asylsuchenden aus den Kriegs- und Krisengebieten rund um Europa beherrschte 2016 bereits seit einiger Zeit das mediale und politische Tagesgeschehen. Die öffentlichen Debatten um die Sicherheit der europäischen Außengrenzen sowie um die Wahrung der Offenheit europäischer Binnengrenzen war voll entbrannt. Trotz eindringlicher Mahnungen zu mehr Solidarität zeichnete sich eine immer stärkere Re-Nationalisierung in Europa ab, nicht nur in der Migrations- und Asylpolitik. Im Juni 2016 hatte man im Vereinigten Königreich mit einem EU-Mitgliedschaftsreferendum den Austrittsprozess aus der europäischen Staatengemeinschaft angestoßen – eine herbe Enttäuschung für die wissenschaftliche Gemeinschaft in Europa. Noch wenige Jahre zuvor war man intensiv damit befasst, die EU im Zuge der Globalisierung stärker nach außen zu öffnen. Um eine bessere innereuropäische Vernetzung zu gewährleisten, hatte man die Planung leistungsfähiger Infrastrukturkorridore über nationale Grenzen hinweg gemeinsam vorangetrieben. Jetzt aber setzten populistische Rufe nach der Schließung von Grenzen, der Verteidigung nationalstaatlicher Souveränität und der Abwehr von Migrant*innen abgrenzende Akzente. Vor diesem Hintergrund entschieden sich die Verantwortlichen des Doktorandenkollegs bewusst dazu, mit dem Thema „Grenzen überscheiten – Räume aktivieren" ein positives Signal für ein konstruktives Miteinander sowie grenzüberschreitendes Lehren und Forschen in Europa zu setzen.

„Grundgedanke des Doktorandenkollegs ist es, förderungswürdigen Nachwuchs beim ‚Eindringen in Unbekanntes' über die Grenzen von Universitäten und Disziplinen zu begleiten", betonte Bernd Scholl in seiner Abschiedsvorlesung an der ETH Zürich 2018. Daher sollten mit der Themensetzung gerade die mutigen Grenzgänger*innen unter den Nachwuchsforscher*innen

aim of crossing both disciplinary and scientific theory borders in the open discourse. Under the title "Understanding of research at the International Doctoral College 'Spatial Research Lab'", the participating professors reinforce their shared basic stance in this publication and thereby contribute to the discussion, even beyond their collegial circle, about viable future science systems. The attributes empirical, interdisciplinary, reflexive, dialogical, multilocational, and geospatial are of decisive importance in this context and defined the transdisciplinary discussions during seven doctoral symposia and five flying visits to various border regions in Europe.

Jonas Bellingrodt, the coordinator of the doctoral college, explains in this book the frame conditions of the cooperation between doctoral students and lecturers. Of course, digital communication and information technologies offer many advantages for the creation of knowledge, especially in times of crisis in which direct meetings among project partners are restricted. However, at the doctoral college the importance of the direct, personal, and live exchange of thoughts between all participants became evident. If one wishes to be successful in the adventure of transdisciplinary research and gain insights that are relevant for the improvement of living conditions for man and nature, then this is only possible through direct communication and personal encounters. IDK offered a sheltered space for precisely this, for open discussions, with plenty of time for confidential consulting and numerous excursions to development regions and action areas. Over the course of three years, not only were the center and surrounding regions of the university towns Berlin, Dortmund, Karlsruhe, Munich, Vienna, and Zurich explored but valuable insights and experiences were gathered around the cities Patras, Belgrade, Casablanca, Copenhagen and Strasbourg, always accompanied by planning experts with local and specialist knowledge.

"Working with people from diverse backgrounds is valuable, but that doesn't mean it's easy," write the pioneers of the innovation method "Design Thinking," Tom and David Kelley. "It can lead to 'creative abrasion.' But as you work through conflicting opinions and points of view, new ideas can emerge. … To maximize the creativity of your team, keep in mind the principles …: (1) Know each other's strengths, (2) Leverage diversity, (3) Get personal, (4) Put the 'relationship' back in 'working relationship,' (5) Craft your team experience in advance and (6) Have fun!"[1] All the authors of this publication can confirm how fitting these observations and principles were for the doctoral college, in which creative confidence played a key role. An exchange beyond disciplines is tiring and in some cases leads to friction, sometimes even slows down the progress of a dissertation. However, this process also leads to the development of new ideas and to a more founded view of complex problems from a wide variety of perspectives. It is hopefully evident in this book that research in a community also promotes strengths, cultivates diversity, activates personalities, deepens working relationships, fosters foresight and, last but not least, is fun.

All the participating authors know, of course, that the wealth of impressions and experiences gathered during three years of cooperation can scarcely

dazu ermuntert werden, sich auf einen der 30 Plätze im IDK III zu bewerben. Diese Chance nutzten viele. Ausgewählt wurden junge Kolleg*innen aufgrund ihrer skizzierten Promotionsthemen, wenn im Fokus ihrer Forschungsfragen die Auseinandersetzung mit nationalen, räumlichen oder landschaftlichen Grenzen stand. Zudem verfolgten die Initiator*innen des Kollegs von Anfang an das Ziel, im offenen Diskurs sowohl fachdisziplinäre als auch wissenschaftstheoretische Grenzen zu überschreiten. Unter der Überschrift „Forschungsverständnis im Internationalen Doktorandenkolleg ‚Forschungslabor Raum'" bekräftigen die beteiligten Professor*innen in dieser Publikation ihre gemeinsame Grundhaltung und leisten damit auch über ihren kollegialen Zirkels hinaus ihren Beitrag zur Diskussion über zukunftsfähige Wissenschaftssysteme. Die Attribute empirisch, interdisziplinär, reflexiv, dialogisch, multilokal und raumbezogen sind in diesem Zusammenhang von entscheidender Bedeutung und prägten in sieben Doktorandenwochen und fünf Stippvisiten in verschiedenen Grenzregionen Europas die disziplinübergreifenden Diskurse.

Jonas Bellingrodt, Koordinator des Doktorandenkollegs, schildert in diesem Buch die Rahmenbedingungen der Zusammenarbeit zwischen Promovierenden und Dozierenden. Natürlich bieten die digitalen Kommunikations- und Informationstechnologien viele Vorteile bei der Wissensgenerierung, gerade in Krisenzeiten, in denen die unmittelbare Begegnung zwischen den Projektpartner*innen stark eingeschränkt ist. Doch im Doktorandenkolleg wurde erfahrbar, wie essenziell der unmittelbare, am realen Ort stattfindende persönliche Gedankenaustausch zwischen allen Beteiligten ist. Wenn man das Abenteuer transdisziplinärer Forschung erfolgreich bestehen und Erkenntnisse gewinnen möchte, die für die Verbesserung der Lebensbedingungen für Mensch und Natur relevant sind, dann ist das nur in direkter Kommunikation und persönlichen Begegnungen möglich. Genau dafür bot das IDK geschützten Raum für offene Diskussionen, viel Zeit für vertrauliche Beratungsgespräche und zahlreiche Exkursionen in Entwicklungsregionen und Aktionsräume. Im Laufe von drei Jahren erkundete man nicht nur die Zentren und angrenzenden Regionen der Universitätsstädte Berlin, Dortmund, Karlsruhe, München, Wien und Zürich, sondern sammelte auch wertvolle Erkenntnisse und Erfahrungen rund um die Städten Patras, Belgrad, Casablanca, Kopenhagen und Straßburg, stets in Begleitung von orts- und fachkundigen Planungsexpert*innen.

„Working with people from diverse backgrounds is valuable, but that doesn't mean it's easy", schreiben die Wegbereiter der Innovationsmethode „Design Thinking", Tom und David Kelley. „It can lead to ‚creative abrasion'. But as you work through conflicting opinions and points of view, new ideas can emerge. [...] To maximize the creativity of your team, keep in mind the principles [...]: (1) Know each other's strengths, (2) Leverage diversity, (3) Get personal, (4) Put the ‚relationship' back in ‚working relationship', (5) Craft your team experience in advance and (6) Have fun!"[1] Alle Autor*innen dieser Publikation können bestätigen, wie zutreffend diese Beobachtungen und Prinzipien auch für das Doktorandenkolleg waren, in dem *creative confidence*,

find adequate space between the two covers of a book. However, the doctoral college decided to issue once again a publication at the end of the third curriculum, aiming to achieve three objectives.

Firstly, this is also a type of logbook similar to the first publication by the college, in which the route of a research expedition is documented and the important course decisions, navigation and anchor points, as well as the impressions gathered on the tour, are described.[2] All travel companions are therefore offered the opportunity to consider at leisure what has been experienced and to reflect on what has been achieved or not achieved. In an ideal case, looking back allows insights to be gained that might prove valuable for personal progress. However, one of course can simply enjoy the good memories of a special expedition while reading and be happy to have been part of it. Secondly, this publication is intended to encourage others to embark on the adventure of transdisciplinary design with doctoral symposia and to adopt the methods of the doctoral college. These have been constantly adapted and developed further since 2007 but have been proven effective in principle for supporting up-and-coming young scientists, accompanying them on their way through the world of complex spatial problems. Thirdly and possibly the most important objective of this book is the free sharing of research insights gained over the years with other colleagues, to engage in open academic discourse and promote scientific progress.

In this sense, this book may very well be understood as a friendly invitation to engage in constructive discussions. It would be particularly pleasing if the cross-border workers in the (spatial) scientific sphere accepted this invitation because it is currently important once again to put up greater resistance to the global forces of delineation and exclusion in society, science and the economy. Borders must be crossed to activate spaces, especially to protect them as open spaces of thinking against harmful restrictions.

Finally, we take the opportunity here to cordially express our gratitude for the excellent cooperation and support. The college received financial support not only from the participating universities but also especially from the Professor Albert Speer Foundation, which facilitated the research work by the doctoral students with generous subsidies and scholarships. Many experts voluntarily accompanied the excursions to provide knowledgeable guidance through cities and regions. We owe to the guest professors and teaching staff, including highly esteemed colleagues and successful graduates of the doctoral colleges I and II, as well as the coordinator of the college, exceptionally instructive and inspirational expert impulses as well as a smooth organization of the complex three-year program.

Last not least we especially thank the doctoral students, who significantly contributed to the success of the college with great enthusiasm and dedication.

Professor Dr. Udo Weilacher
Speaker of IDK III on behalf of professor Undine Giseke and the professors Markus Neppl, Bernd Scholl, Stefan Siedentop, and Andreas Voigt

also kreatives Selbstvertrauen, eine Schlüsselrolle spielte. Ein Austausch über die Disziplinen hinweg ist anstrengend und führt zeitweise zu Abrieb, ja entschleunigt gelegentlich sogar den Fortschritt einer Dissertation. Aber dieser Prozess führt auch zur Entfaltung neuer Ideen und zur fundierteren Betrachtung komplexer Problemstellungen aus unterschiedlichsten Perspektiven. Dass Forschen in der Gemeinschaft aber auch Stärken fördert, Diversität kultiviert, Persönlichkeiten aktiviert, Arbeitsbeziehungen vertieft, Voraussicht begünstigt und last not least viel Spaß macht, wird in diesem Buch hoffentlich spürbar.

Alle beteiligten Autor*innen wissen natürlich, dass die Vielfalt der gesammelten Eindrücke und Erfahrungen aus drei Jahren Zusammenarbeit nur schwerlich zwischen zwei Buchdeckeln ausreichend Platz findet. Das Doktorandenkolleg hat sich dennoch dazu entschieden, am Ende des dritten Curriculums wieder eine Publikation zu veröffentlichen, weil drei Ziele damit erreicht werden sollen. Erstens ist auch dies, wie bereits die erste Veröffentlichung des Kollegs, eine Art Logbuch[2], in dem die Route einer Forschungsreise dokumentiert wird und die wesentlichen Kursentscheidungen, Navigations- und Ankerpunkte sowie die auf der Tour gesammelten Eindrücke beschrieben werden. Allen Reisegefährt*innen bietet sich somit die Möglichkeit, nochmals in Ruhe das Erfahrene nachzuvollziehen und über Erreichtes, aber auch Unerreichtes zu reflektieren. Im Idealfall lassen sich aus dem Rückblick Erkenntnisse gewinnen, die sich für den persönlichen Fortschritt als wertvoll erweisen könnten. Natürlich kann man bei der Lektüre aber auch einfach nur die guten Erinnerungen an eine besondere Expedition genießen und sich darüber freuen, dabei gewesen zu sein. Zweitens soll diese Publikation auch andere dazu ermutigen, sich mit Doktorandenkollegien auf das Abenteuer transdisziplinärer Forschung einzulassen und die Methodik des Kollegs zu übernehmen. Die wurde seit 2007 zwar immer wieder ein wenig verändert und weiterentwickelt, hat sich aber grundsätzlich hervorragend bewährt, um junge Nachwuchswissenschaftler*innen zu fördern und auf ihrem Weg durch die Welt der komplexen Probleme im Raum zu begleiten. Drittes und wichtigstes Ziel dieses Buches ist es aber, die im Laufe der Jahre gewonnenen Forschungserkenntnisse mit anderen Fachkolleg*innen freimütig zu teilen, um miteinander in den offenen fachlichen Austausch zu kommen und den wissenschaftlichen Fortschritt zu fördern. In diesem Sinne darf dieses Buch sehr gerne als Einladung zu konstruktiven Gesprächen verstanden werden. Besonders erfreulich wäre es, wenn die Grenzgänger*innen im (raum-)wissenschaftlichen Umfeld diese Einladung annehmen würden, denn aktuell gilt es wieder einmal, sich verstärkt gegen global wirksame Ab- und Ausgrenzungskräfte in Gesellschaft, Wissenschaft und Wirtschaft mutig zur Wehr zu setzen. Es müssen Grenzen überschritten werden, um Räume zu aktivieren, auch und gerade, um sie als Freiräume des Denkens vor negativen Einschränkungen zu schützen.

Zu guter Letzt bietet sich hier die Gelegenheit, sich herzlich für hervorragende Zusammenarbeit und Förderung zu bedanken. Finanzielle Unterstützung erfuhr das Kolleg nicht nur durch die beteiligten Hochschulen,

sondern vor allem auch durch die Professor Albert Speer – Stiftung, die den Promovierenden mit großzügigen Zuschüssen und Abschlussstipendien ihre Forschungsarbeiten erleichterte. Viele Fachexpert*innen waren bei den Exkursionen bereitwillig zur Stelle, um kenntnisreich durch Städte und Regionen zu führen. Den Gastprofessor*innen und Lehrbeauftragten, darunter hoch geschätzte Kolleg*innen und erfolgreiche Absolvent*innen der Doktorandenkollegien I und II, sowie dem Koordinator des Kollegs verdanken wir überaus lehrreiche und inspirierende Fachimpulse sowie eine reibungslose Organisation des aufwendigen Dreijahresprogramms.

Wir danken vor allem aber auch den Promovierenden, die mit großem Enthusiasmus und viel Engagement maßgeblich zum Erfolg des Kollegs beigetragen haben.

Professor Dr. Udo Weilacher
Sprecher des IDK III im Namen von Professorin Undine Giseke und den Professoren Markus Neppl, Bernd Scholl, Stefan Siedentop und Andreas Voigt

UNDERSTANDING OF RESEARCH AT THE INTERNATIONAL DOCTORAL COLLEGE "SPATIAL RESEARCH LAB"

Starting points

In 2007, six professors in space-related specialist fields from Germany, Austria, and Switzerland took the initiative and founded the International Doctoral College (IDK) "Spatial Research Lab." In the opinion of the participating professors, particularly at the doctoral level there was a need for additional impulses to extend the subject and personal horizons of up-and-coming academics worth being promoted. As the resources for corresponding programs and seminars are not available at many universities, the cooperation opens up new possibilities beyond university boundaries. To carry out the doctoral college, it is very important for the involved professors to have a shared understanding of research. The critical and precise reflection on different thought patterns and methodological approaches to research questions is in our view an elementary part of higher education.

Among the most important starting points for the doctoral college and also for establishing a shared understanding of research are difficult unsolved spatial development tasks. The attempt to solve spatial problems leads to the generation of knowledge for the clarification and answering of academic research. The aim is to find answers (solutions) or rather temporary answers (hypotheses/assumptions). The exploration and testing methods used for finding and testing solutions to problems can result in valuable insights and principles, but they rarely replace real space as a laboratory. This applies in particular to the understanding of social, legal, and political interactions.

The viability of assumptions and hypotheses (and their empirical content) must be established through critical discussion. This represents a particular challenge in the field of the spatial planning and spatial design disciplines, because contrary to the exact sciences there are no sets of rules independent of human perceptions and interpretations. To a far greater extent than in other disciplines, research means theoretically and methodically addressing the nonrepeatability of experiments and the acceptance of individual cases as a starting point for research.

At best, patterns of spatial development can be recognized and used as a starting hypothesis for future developments. The outlining of leading academic questions, as well as the development and especially the testing of subsequent hypotheses, require a culture of academic discourse.

The curriculum for higher studies is therefore also concerned with ensuring an ongoing critical discourse about the seminar's understanding of research and individual topics through an accomplished intentionally realized dramaturgy of situations and constellations. For the working atmosphere of the doctoral college it is decisive to spark academic curiosity

FORSCHUNGSVERSTÄNDNIS IM INTERNATIONALEN DOKTORANDENKOLLEG „FORSCHUNGSLABOR RAUM"

Ausgangspunkte

2007 haben sechs Professoren raumrelevanter Fachrichtungen aus Deutschland, Österreich und der Schweiz die Initiative ergriffen und das Internationale Doktorandenkolleg (IDK) „Forschungslabor Raum" gegründet. Namentlich auf der Stufe des Doktorats bedurfte es aus Sicht der beteiligten Professoren zusätzlicher Impulse zur Erweiterung des fachlichen und persönlichen Horizonts des förderungswürdigen wissenschaftlichen Nachwuchses. Da in vielen Universitäten für entsprechende Programme und Kollegs die Ressourcen nicht vorhanden sind, eröffnet die Zusammenarbeit über die Hochschulgrenzen hinaus neue Spielräume. Für die Durchführung des Doktorandenkollegs ist die Annäherung an ein gemeinsames Forschungsverständnis der aktuell beteiligten Professor*innen von großer Bedeutung. Auch die kritische und präzise Reflexion unterschiedlicher Denkmuster und methodischer Annäherungen an Fragestellungen gehört nach unserer Auffassung zum elementaren Bestandteil der höheren Ausbildung.

Zu den wichtigen Ausgangspunkten des Doktorandenkollegs und damit auch der Entwicklung des gemeinsamen Forschungsverständnisses zählen schwierige ungelöste Aufgaben der räumlichen Entwicklung. Aus dem Versuch, raumrelevante Probleme zu lösen, erschließt sich das zur Klärung und Beantwortung wissenschaftlicher Fragen vorhandene und zu generierende Wissen. Ziel ist es, Antworten (Lösungen) oder besser vorläufige Antworten (Hypothesen/Vermutungen) zu finden. Die für das Auffinden und Prüfen von Problemlösungen verwendbaren Methoden des Erkundens und des Testens können wertvolle Einsichten und Grundlagen ergeben, doch sie ersetzen selten den realen Raum als Labor. Das gilt insbesondere für das Verständnis der sozialen, rechtlichen und politischen Interaktionen. Dabei muss die Tauglichkeit von Annahmen und Hypothesen (und ihres empirischen Gehalts) im kritischen Diskurs überprüft werden. Dies ist im Bereich der raumplanenden und raumgestaltenden Disziplinen eine besondere Herausforderung, weil – anders als in den exakten Wissenschaften – keine von menschlichen Wahrnehmungen und Deutungen unabhängigen Gesetzmäßigkeiten existieren. Viel stärker als in anderen Disziplinen heißt Forschung, sich theoretisch und methodisch mit der Nicht-Wiederholbarkeit des Experiments und der Akzeptanz des Einzelfalls als Ausgangpunkt der Forschung auseinanderzusetzen. Allenfalls lassen sich Regelmäßigkeiten räumlicher Entwicklungen erkennen und als Ausgangshypothese für zukünftige Entwicklungen verwenden. Das Eingrenzen der wissenschaftlichen Leitfragen, das Entwickeln und besonders das Prüfen weiterführender Hypothesen erfordern eine Kultur des akademischen Diskurses.

among all the participants and then, through the pros and cons of critical arguments, to consolidate and hone the respective work and ultimately get to the heart of the matter.

To ensure that this succeeds, the targeted sequencing of these offers (situations and constellations) plays a central role. It was clear to us that a too rigid framework can be overwhelming for all participants. The framework was therefore to open up possibilities and allow flexibility in the organization of the doctoral college.

Maxims

We were guided by a few maxims for the development of the curricula. These also serve the purpose of developing a shared understanding of research:

- At the center is the discourse between doctoral students and professors, as well as among the doctoral students, as part of the biannual doctoral symposia, supplemented by two additional excursions abroad per year ("flying visits").
- The starting points are real, difficult, and unsolved tasks (problems) of spatial development and social change manifested at specific locations. The intention is for participants to take their own observations as the basis for an understanding of problem situations and rules of spatial circumstances.
- Without hypotheses (assumptions) that are individually formulated by the participants, there can be no qualified criticism, and without initial assumptions there are no reference points for explorative spatial research.
- Knowledge about important topics, methods, and ways of thinking is to be conveyed and acquired in a series of several passages.
- Communication plays an important role from the beginning and should be trained and reflected on through the involvement of qualified specialists.
- The widening of cooperation beyond university boundaries should be encouraged.
- Intensive phases of exchange should be followed by a longer individual consideration of the selected topic.
- For the maturing of a shared understanding, the development of precise research points and hypotheses that are independently and individually formulated by participants, as well as for continuous critical discourse, participation in the joint doctoral symposia is obligatory.

These maxims have been proven effective once again after carrying out the third curriculum. Through the introduction of so-called flying visits, which are brief joint research stays at the university towns and abroad, the program was enriched with an interesting format for considering problematic situations and possible solutions. It also served the purpose of presenting the research results of the participating professors in the doctoral college for discussion. This also led to the emergence of deeper layers in the understanding of research. With the following explanation of our shared

Im Curriculum höherer Studien geht es deshalb auch darum, den einmal begonnenen kritischen Diskurs zum Forschungsverständnis und zu einzelnen Themenfeldern durch eine geschickte Dramaturgie von Situationen und Konstellationen in Gang zu halten. Für das Arbeitsklima des Doktorandenkollegs ist es entscheidend, für möglichst alle Teilnehmer*innen das Feuer der wissenschaftlichen Neugier zu entfachen und dann, im Für und Wider kritischer Argumente, die jeweilige Arbeit zu fundieren, zu schärfen und am Ende auf den Punkt zu bringen.

Damit dies gelingt, spielt die zweckmäßige Abfolge dieser Angebote (Situationen und Konstellationen) eine zentrale Rolle. Klar war uns, dass ein zu starrer Rahmen alle Beteiligten überfordern kann. Der Rahmen sollte folglich im wahrsten Sinne des Wortes Spielräume eröffnen und Beweglichkeit in der Organisation des Doktorandenkollegs erlauben.

Maximen

Wir haben uns bei der Gestaltung der Curricula von einigen wenigen Maximen leiten lassen. Sie dienen auch der Heranbildung eines gemeinsamen Forschungsverständnisses:

-   Im Zentrum steht der gemeinsame Diskurs der Promovierenden mit den Dozierenden sowie der Promovierenden untereinander im Rahmen der halbjährlich stattfindenden Doktorandenwochen, ergänzt durch zwei zusätzliche Auslandexkursionen pro Jahr (Stippvisiten).
-   Ausgangspunkt sind reale, ebenso schwierige wie ungelöste Aufgaben (Probleme) der räumlichen Entwicklung und gesellschaftlicher Veränderungen, die sich im Raum manifestieren. Durch eigene Anschauung soll das Verständnis für Problemsituationen und Regelmäßigkeiten räumlicher Verhältnisse gefördert werden.
-   Ohne eigene Hypothesen (Vermutungen) kann es keine qualifizierte Kritik, ohne erste Annahmen keine Anhaltspunkte für explorative Raumforschung geben.
-   Wissen zu wichtigen Themenfeldern, methodischen und Denkmusterfragen soll in mehreren Durchgängen vermittelt und erworben werden können.
-   Kommunikation spielt von Anfang an eine wichtige Rolle und soll durch Mitwirkung ausgewiesener Fachpersönlichkeiten trainiert und reflektiert werden.
-   Die Zusammenarbeit über Hochschulgrenzen hinaus soll zunehmend gefördert werden.
-   Auf intensive Phasen des Austausches soll jeweils eine länger dauernde individuelle Beschäftigung mit dem gewählten Thema folgen.
-   Für das Reifen des gemeinsamen Verständnisses, der Entwicklung präziser Forschungsfragestellungen und eigener Hypothesen, ebenso wie für den kontinuierlichen kritischen Diskurs, ist die Teilnahme an den gemeinsamen Doktorandenwochen Pflicht.

Diese Maximen haben sich auch nach Durchführung des dritten Curriculums bewährt. Durch die Einführung der sogenannten Stippvisiten, kurze

understanding of research, we would like to present the status of our considerations for discussion.

The IDK's understanding of research

Within the IDK, we feel obliged to pursue an interdisciplinary rather than sectoral understanding of planning, as well as a research approach that is open to a variety of theories and methods as well as to alternative, novel planning and design methods. The practical application of these methods is intended to serve the purpose of solving concrete spatial problems and of generating spatial knowledge—new knowledge about the space, the actors in this space and the need for change. In addition, methods beyond the applicable standardized, economized norms, such as of a creative-experimental nature, are to be developed further and applied in order to grasp and explore complex spatial phenomena that elude established academic approach methods.

The IDK faces the challenges of complex spatial developments and concrete planning tasks through interdisciplinary design and through dialogue, by holding discussions about spatial planning, city planning, architecture, regional and municipal development, and landscape architecture and environmental planning, in addition to initiating cooperative, solution-oriented approaches to research.

Empirical—interdisciplinary—reflexive—dialogical—multilocal—space-related

The IDK research lab is focused on the interrelations of science, society, technology and space. Our research objects are spatiosocial: the spatial and social are inextricably entertwined. The ways we work are:

1) *empirical:* Whether the topic is urban restructuring, new forms of spatial appropriation, urban mobility, or energy transition—we research empirically and also base our dialogue on empirical research. We pursue a broad concept of empiricism: statistics and space-related models as well as qualitative analyses of documents or observations, all play a part. What is crucial is that theoretically formulated assumptions lead to the systematic assessment, explanation, and examination of the research object. However, we are open to inductive research strategies in which new theoretical knowledge can be gained from observations made in case studies.

2) *inter- und transdisciplinary:* Whether we are planners, designers or researchers—we have an inter- and transdisciplinary approach that is based on empirical research and direct experiences from planning practice. We are aware of the opportunities and challenges of collaborative research, publishing, and communicating together. A closer cooperation between architecture, landscape architecture, urban development, spatial planning, social sciences, and engineering, as well as scientists and practitioners, is of central importance for the solution of spatial and urban problems.

gemeinsame Forschungsaufenthalte im In- und Ausland, konnte das Programm mit einem für die Anschauung von Problemsituationen und Lösungsansätzen interessanten Format bereichert werden. Es diente auch dazu, Forschungsresultate beteiligter Professuren des Doktorandenkollegs zur Diskussion zu stellen. Auch dabei traten tiefer liegende Schichten des Forschungsverständnisses zu Tage.

Mit der folgenden Darlegung unseres gemeinsamen Forschungsverständnisses wollen wir den Stand unserer Überlegungen zur Diskussion stellen.

Forschungsverständnis

Innerhalb des IDK fühlen wir uns einem interdisziplinären, nicht sektoral ausgerichteten Planungsverständnis ebenso verpflichtet wie einem Forschungsansatz, der für verschiedenartige Theorien und Methoden, auch für alternative, neuartige Planungs- und Entwurfsmethoden, offen ist. Die praktische Anwendung dieser Methoden soll zur Lösung konkreter Probleme im Raum führen und der Generierung von Raumwissen – von neuem Wissen über den Raum, die Akteur*innen und den Veränderungsbedarf im Raum – dienen. Dabei sollen auch Methoden jenseits geltender standardisierter, ökonomisierter Normen, zum Beispiel entwerferisch-experimenteller Art, weiterentwickelt und eingesetzt werden, um komplexe Raumphänomene zu erfassen und zu erkunden, die sich gängigen wissenschaftlichen Erfassungsmethoden entziehen.

Den Herausforderungen komplexer Raumentwicklungen und konkreter Planungsaufgaben stellt sich das IDK in interdisziplinärer Forschung und im Dialog, indem es Raumplanung, Stadtplanung, Architektur, Landes- und Stadtentwicklung sowie Landschaftsarchitektur und Umweltplanung ins Gespräch bringt und kooperative, lösungsorientierte Forschungsansätze initiiert.

Empirisch – interdisziplinär – reflexiv – dialogisch – multilokal – raumbezogen

Im IDK Forschungslabor Raum geht es um die Wechselwirkungen von Wissenschaft, Gesellschaft, Technologie und Raum. Unsere Forschungsgegenstände sind räumlich-sozial: Räumliches und Soziales sind untrennbar miteinander verbunden. Dazu arbeiten wir:

1) *empirisch*: Ob Stadtumbau, neue Formen der Raumaneignung, urbane Mobilität oder Energiewende – wir forschen empirisch und gründen den Dialog auch auf empirische Forschung. Wir pflegen einen breiten Begriff von Empirie: Statistiken, raumbezogene Modelle, aber auch qualitative Analysen von Dokumenten oder Beobachtungen zählen dazu. Entscheidend ist, dass theoretisch formulierte Annahmen und Vermutungen zur systematischen Erfassung, Erklärung und Überprüfung des Forschungsgegenstandes führen. Wir sind aber auch offen für induktive Forschungsstrategien, bei denen aus Beobachtungen in Fallstudien neues theoretisches Wissen gewonnen werden kann.

3) *reflexive:* Whether the questions concern sustainable water management, landscape transformation or the effects of controversial technical knowledge—every object is of interest in both directions: What are the expected positive or negative consequences of this development? And what are the social conditions (e.g., cultural habits or political target conflicts) that contribute to shaping it? How do these transform space?

4) *dialogical:* Whether in test planning, parametric design, or digital information transmission—we try to engage in dialogue in a suitable manner with our doctoral students as well as with the public, local experts, politicians, or companies, and we employ dialogue to work through research-based potential solutions and strategies. We make use of the whole variety of publication and communication media.

5) *multilocal:* Whether in Zurich or Berlin, Copenhagen or Munich, Vienna, Dortmund, or Karlsruhe—we are aware of the diversity of social, economic, and ecological contexts and perceive the problems in all their local specificity. However, we are also seeking patterns to be able to derive the general from individual cases (an inductive method). Knowledge gained in this way about rules of spatial development is intended to ensure the concrete ability to act in other locations and in different contexts.

6) *Space-related:* Whether the problems are on a large or small scale—what is crucial for our research approach is the relevance for the development of concrete spatial systems and associated living environments. The material components play just as an important role as the subject-related and social components of a space.

The main objective of the IDK is to gain a better understanding of the complex spatial systems in the interest of our society and to shape them accordingly.

Outlook

Meanwhile over eighty doctoral students have taken part in the three IDK curricula. More than half of them successfully completed their research project with a doctorate. Many works are about to be completed or are in progress.

At the meetings across the curricula, an *esprit de corps* developed among those participating in the doctoral college. Exchanges confirmed that alongside the subject qualifications related to the dissertation, the possibility of individual considerations of the topic as well as professional *and* private challenges are appreciated—in view of the fact that the majority of the doctoral students were not able to focus exclusively on their dissertation during the curriculum. This situation pushes the boundaries for many doctoral students and leads to certain dilemmas. Creating enough opportunities for academic work besides all other obligations is no doubt among the biggest personal challenges. Mastering this is also part of the maturation

2) *inter- und transdisziplinär:* Ob Planende, Entwerfende oder Forschende – wir arbeiten inter- und transdisziplinär sowie auf der Basis von empirischer Forschung und unmittelbarer Erfahrungen aus der Planungspraxis. Wir sind uns der Chancen wie auch der Herausforderungen des kollaborativen Forschens, Publizierens und Miteinander-Kommunizierens bewusst. Eine verstärkte Zusammenarbeit von Architektur, Landschaftsarchitektur, Städtebau, Raumplanung, Sozialwissenschaften und den Ingenieurwissenschaften sowie von Wissenschaftler*innen und Praktiker*innen ist von zentraler Bedeutung für die Lösung räumlicher und urbaner Probleme.

3) *reflexiv:* Ob nachhaltiges Wassermanagement, Landschaftstransformation oder die Effekte kontroversen technischen Wissens – jeder Gegenstand interessiert in beide Richtungen: Welches sind die erwarteten positiven oder negativen Folgen seiner Entwicklung? Und welches sind die gesellschaftlichen Bedingungen (z. B. kulturelle Gewohnheiten oder politische Zielkonflikte), die ihn mitprägen? Wie verändern diese Raum?

4) *dialogisch:* Ob Testplanung, parametrisches Entwerfen oder digitale Informationsvermittlung – wir versuchen auf geeignete Weise, mit unseren Promovierenden, aber auch mit der Öffentlichkeit, lokalen Expert*innen, der Politik oder mit Unternehmen in den Dialog zu treten und erarbeiten im Dialog forschungsbasierte Lösungsansätze und -strategien. Dabei nutzen wir die ganze Diversität von Publikations- und Kommunikationsmedien.

5) *multilokal:* Ob Zürich oder Berlin, Kopenhagen oder München, Wien, Dortmund oder Karlsruhe – wir sind uns der Verschiedenartigkeit der sozialen, ökonomischen und ökologischen Kontexte bewusst, nehmen die Problemstellungen in ihrer lokalen Einzigartigkeit wahr. Wir sind auf der Suche nach Mustern, um vom Besonderen, vom Einzelfall auf das Allgemeine (induktiv) schließen zu können. Derart entwickeltes Wissen über Regelmäßigkeiten der räumlichen Entwicklung soll die konkrete Handlungsfähigkeit an anderen Orten und in anderen Kontexten gewährleisten.

6) *raumbezogen:* Ob groß- oder kleinmaßstäbliche Problemstellungen – entscheidend für unsere Forschungsansätze ist die Relevanz für die Entwicklung konkreter Raumsysteme und damit verbundener Lebensräume. Dabei spielen die materiellen Komponenten eine ebenso große Rolle wie die subjektbezogenen und gesellschaftlichen Komponenten des Raumes.

Leitziel des IDK ist, die komplexen Raumsysteme im Interesse unserer Gesellschaft besser zu verstehen und zu gestalten!

Ausblick

Mittlerweile haben über 80 Doktorand*innen an den drei Curricula des IDK teilgenommen. Mehr als die Hälfte von ihnen hat das jeweilige

process. Concentrating enough focus and attention on what is essential for a professional career in life is one of the most significant experiences. We view the reflected handling of this challenge as a central condition for being able to take initiatives at a high professional level and to assume responsibility. This is particularly important at a time in which the frame conditions that were believed to be certain can change rapidly: these include, for example, the stability of states with a democratic constitution, uncertainties about the future of Europe and the European Union, and the increasing visible signs of climate change. Since the foundation of the doctoral college in the year 2007, the global economic crisis of 2008, and the nuclear reactor accident at Fukushima at the beginning of 2011, as well as the coronavirus COVID-19 pandemic that broke out in the spring of 2020, have had far-reaching consequences, also for spatial development. Affordable housing in municipal areas is currently a priority topic, as is the drifting apart of urban and rural areas. The reduction of greenhouse gases alongside the abolishment in some countries of coal and nuclear power places a focus on questions regarding energy generation, handling, and distribution.

These include more energy-efficient settlement development and mobility. The International Doctoral College "Spatial Research Laboratory" has made important contributions to the associated research tasks. We would be delighted if the initiative continued to bear fruit in future.

Forschungsvorhaben mit einer Promotion erfolgreich abgeschlossen. Viele Arbeiten stehen vor dem Abschluss oder sind noch im Entstehen.

Bei den curriculaübergreifenden Treffen ist ein *esprit des corps* unter den Mitwirkenden des Doktorandenkollegs entstanden. Im Austausch wurde bestätigt, dass neben der fachlichen Qualifikation im Rahmen der Dissertation die Möglichkeit zur individuellen Reife am Thema und auch den beruflichen *und* privaten Herausforderungen geschätzt wird – dies vor dem Hintergrund, dass die überwiegende Zahl der Promovierenden sich während des Curriculums nicht ausschließlich mit der eigenen Dissertation beschäftigen konnte. Diese für viele Promovierende an Grenzen führende Situation führt zu einigen Dilemmata. Sich für wissenschaftliches Arbeiten Frei- und Spielraum verschaffen zu können, gehört dabei wohl zu den größten persönlichen Herausforderungen. Diese zu meistern, ist ebenfalls Teil des Reifeprozesses. Trotz allem ist die Konzentration der Kräfte auf das für eine berufliche Lebensphase Wesentliche eine der prägendsten Erfahrungen. Wir sehen den reflektierten Umgang damit als zentrale Voraussetzung, um in gehobenen Positionen Initiativen ergreifen und Verantwortung wahrnehmen zu können.

Dies ist von besonderer Bedeutung in einer Zeit, in der sich sicher geglaubte Rahmenbedingungen rasch ändern können: Dazu gehören beispielsweise die Stabilität demokratisch verfasster Staaten, Unsicherheiten über die Zukunft Europas und der Europäischen Union und die sich mehrenden sichtbaren Zeichen des Klimawandels. Seit Gründung des Doktorandenkollegs im Jahr 2007 erzeugten die globale Wirtschaftskrise von 2008, der Reaktorunfall von Fukushima Anfang 2011 und die im Frühjahr 2020 ausgebrochene Pandemie infolge des Corona Virus COVID-19 Zäsuren mit weitreichenden Konsequenzen, auch für die räumliche Entwicklung. Bezahlbarer Wohnraum in städtischen Gebieten gehört aktuell zu den prioritären Themen, ebenso wie das Auseinanderdriften von Stadt und Land. Die Reduktion der Treibhausgase bei gleichzeitigem Ausstieg einiger Länder aus Kohle und Atomkraft rückt Fragen des Umgangs mit Energie, der Energieerzeugung und -verteilung ins Zentrum. Dazu gehören auch die energieeffizientere Siedlungsentwicklung und Mobilität. Das Internationale Doktorandenkolleg „Forschungskolleg Raum" hat zu damit verbundenen Forschungsaufgaben wichtige Beiträge geleistet. Wir freuen uns, wenn die Initiative auch in Zukunft reiche Früchte trägt.

At their 2018 summer retreat in the ETH Zurich guest house, the Villa Garbald in Castasegna, professors and teaching staff discussed their shared understanding of research and future research strategies in the doctoral college.

Professor*innen und Lehrbeauftragte berieten auf ihrer Sommer-Klausur 2018 im Gästehaus der ETH Zürich, der Villa Garbald in Castasegna, über das gemeinsame Forschungsverständnis und zukünftige Forschungsstrategien im Doktorandenkolleg.

METHODOLOGIES OF THE DOCTORAL COLLEGE

METHODIK IM DOKTORANDENKOLLEG

ORGANIZATION OF AN INTERNATIONAL DOCTORAL COLLEGE

JONAS BELLINGRODT

The International Doctoral College (IDK) "Spatial Research Lab" started in 2006 as an experiment by a learning organization and has continued to develop and establish itself up until today—not least through the dedication of the professorships of six different institutions, who participate actively every week and are open to implementing improvements and suggestions during the ongoing process. The result of this process is more than a network of experts. It is suitably described in the chapter "Understanding of Research" as an *esprit de corps* that always has a focus on acquiring scientific knowledge across spatial and institutional borders and beyond subject-specific boundaries. This format was put to the test when two professors within the college changed. Established routines were questioned, and new specialist input enriched the third curriculum. The following organizational tools are the result of an exploratory journey in the Spatial Research Lab that has already been ongoing for fourteen years.

The central task of the coordinator of the third IDK was to ensure that events ran smoothly. The lessons of the two previous curricula proved to be helpful for this purpose: support over the course of IDK 1 (2009–2012) in setting up the penultimate working week, and participation in IDK 2 (2013–2016). Insights into the specialist discussions and debates already emerged when the first college was hosted at TU Munich just before the 2012 graduation. The way professors and those graduating discussed respectfully with each other was impressive—not primarily waiting to be able to advance one's own point of view but always listening to each other in order to work out solutions to complex problems in spatial development. The teaching staff did not give the impression of having conferred in advance; on the contrary: the opinions that were discussed, whether complementary or contradictory, were presented openly and debated argumentatively. The wide subject portfolio enriched the dissertation projects in this college format, as the approaches to work were illuminated from a variety of perspectives with a focus on their relevance, consistency of argumentation, and innovation potential. What then is the secret recipe for carrying out a graduate college whose aim is not only to move various doctoral theses along but also to intensify their subject matter? Apart from the constellation of the right mix of active parties, certain central organizational challenges present themselves. To engage in open specialist exchanges as quickly as possible, it is important to establish trust among the participants.

JONAS BELLINGRODT

Das Internationale Doktorandenkolleg (IDK) „Forschungslabor Raum" wurde 2006 als Experiment einer lernenden Organisation begonnen und hat sich bis heute weiterentwickelt und gut etabliert – nicht zuletzt durch das Engagement der Professor*innen sechs unterschiedlicher Institutionen, die jede Woche aktiv mitgestalten und offen sind, im laufenden Prozess Verbesserungen und Anregungen umzusetzen. Das Ergebnis dieses Prozesses ist mehr als ein Expertennetzwerk. Es ist im Kapitel „Forschungsverständnis" passend beschrieben als *esprit des corps*, der über räumliche und institutionelle Grenzen hinweg und über fachliche Grenzen hinaus den wissenschaftlichen Erkenntnisgewinn immer im Fokus hat. Auf den Prüfstand wurde dieses Format gestellt, als ein Wechsel von zwei Professor*innen innerhalb des Kollegs stattfand. Erarbeitete Routinen wurden hinterfragt und neue fachliche Inputs bereicherten das dritte Curriculum. Folgende organisatorische Instrumente sind das Ergebnis einer bereits 14 Jahre andauernden Erkundungsreise im „Forschungslabor Raum".

Zentrale Aufgabe des Koordinators des dritten IDK war es, den reibungslosen Ablauf der Veranstaltungen zu gewährleisten. Hilfreich waren dabei die Einblicke in die beiden vorherigen Curricula: Unterstützung im Zuge des IDK 1 (2009–2012) bei der Ausrichtung der vorletzten Arbeitswoche, Teilnahme am IDK 2 (2013–2016). Bereits als das erste Kolleg kurz vor Abschluss 2012 an der TU München zu Gast war, ergaben sich Einblicke in die Fachgespräche und Debatten. Beeindruckend war die Art und Weise wie Professor*innen und Promovierende respektvoll miteinander diskutierten; nicht primär darauf wartend, die eigene Position verbreiten zu können, sondern einander zuhörend, um der Lösung komplexer Probleme bei der Entwicklung des Raumes auf die Spur zu kommen. Die Lehrkräfte machten nicht den Eindruck, als hätten sie sich zuvor abgestimmt, im Gegenteil: Die zur Diskussion gestellten, sich teilweise ergänzenden und sich widersprechenden Meinungen wurden offen präsentiert und argumentativ erörtert. Das breite Fachportfolio bereichert in diesem Kollegformat die Dissertationsvorhaben, da die Arbeitsansätze aus unterschiedlichen Blickwinkeln beleuchtet und auf Relevanz, Konsistenz in der Argumentation und Innovationspotenzial hin geprüft werden.

Was ist also das Geheimrezept für die Durchführung eines Graduiertenkollegs, dessen Ziel es ist, unterschiedliche Promotionsvorhaben nicht nur zu beschleunigen, sondern auch fachlich zu intensivieren? Neben der Zusammensetzung der richtigen Mischung an Agierenden stellen sich einige zentrale organisatorische Herausforderungen. Um möglichst schnell

IDK pack of cards

Through the extent of the traveling over three years, the participants got to know each other very well. However, it is not easy for all doctoral students to present their own dissertation, during its development process, to such a wide specialist panel with the prescribed openness. In order to take account of this emotional factor in the college and to speed up the process of getting to know each other, a pack of cards was produced consisting of a collection of unusual business cards of the participants. As this network brings together a wide range of specialist competences, all the doctoral students added a content statement on the back of their respective card. All the participants in the college, including the professors and teaching staff, were asked in advance to take a stance regarding the framework theme "Crossing Borders—Activating Spaces" and to complete the sentence "For me, crossing borders means …"

A suitable meaningful photo was added as support. Via the set of cards, all the participants had a complete overview of all contact details from the beginning and, via the statements and associated reference photos, they also had first concrete indications of with whom they would be working over the next three years. The decisive side effect, however, was that each card set was part of an interactive game, through an uncomplicated contribution that was visible for all those involved and contained a personal statement.

miteinander in den offenen fachlichen Austausch zu kommen, ist es wichtig, Vertrauen unter den Teilnehmenden herzustellen.

IDK-Quartett

Durch die vielen Reisen innerhalb der drei Jahre lernen sich die Teilnehmenden sehr gut kennen. Aber die eigene Dissertation im Entstehungsprozess einem solch breiten fachlichen Gremium vorzustellen, in einer Offenheit, wie sie in diesem Kolleg Voraussetzung ist, fällt nicht allen Promovierenden leicht. Um diesem emotionalen Faktor im Kolleg Rechnung zu tragen und den Prozess des Kennenlernens zu beschleunigen, wurde ein Kartenset produziert. Ähnlich einem Quartett besteht es aus einer Sammlung ungewöhnlicher Visitenkarten der Teilnehmenden. Da dieses Netzwerk die unterschiedlichsten Fachkompetenzen vereint, ergänzten alle Promovierenden auf der Rückseite ihrer jeweiligen Karte ein inhaltliches Statement. Alle Teilnehmenden des Kollegs einschließlich der Professor*innen und Lehrbeauftragten waren gefordert, vorab zum Rahmenthema „Grenzen überschreiten – Räume aktivieren" Stellung zu beziehen und den Satz „Grenzen zu überschreiten, bedeutet für mich, …" zu vervollständigen.
Unterstützend wurde ein passendes, aussagekräftiges Foto hinzugefügt. Durch das Kartenset hatten alle Teilnehmenden von Beginn an einen kompletten Überblick über alle Kontaktdaten und durch die Thesen sowie passenden Referenzbilder auch erste fachliche Hinweise darauf, mit wem man die kommenden drei Jahre zusammenarbeiten würde. Der entscheidende Nebeneffekt aber war, dass man vom ersten Tage an durch einen unkomplizierten Beitrag Teil eines (Zusammen-)Spiels war, mit einem persönlichen Statement sichtbar für alle Beteiligten.

Workshop-Charakter

Während der Doktorandenwochen, in denen sich alle intensiv dem Fortschritt ihrer Dissertationen widmeten, waren keine externen Zuhörer*innen erlaubt. Erst die vertrauensvolle Zusammenarbeit innerhalb des Kollegs und der *Closed-circle*-Charakter ermöglichten es, offen und frei jedwede Themen anzusprechen. Der wesentliche Faktor des offenen fachlichen Austausches ist die vertrauensvolle Kommunikation innerhalb des Kollegs. Die gemeinsamen Forschungsreisen und Arbeitswochen, in denen der persönliche Austausch im Vordergrund steht, bilden hierfür das Fundament. Die drei bis vier Treffen pro Jahr wechselten sich ab mit Arbeitsphasen, die jeder individuell vor- und nachbereitete. So diente ein Server als Plattform für den gemeinsamen Datenaustausch, wo die Meilensteine für die jeweiligen Arbeiten vermerkt und verbindlich die im Verlauf des Kollegs vereinbarten Textbausteine hochzuladen waren. Aber auch Grundlagentexte und sonstige Inputs wurden hier zur Verfügung gestellt.
Im ersten Jahr waren alle Promovierenden aufgefordert, einen Forschungsplan zu präsentieren, der die wesentliche Eingrenzung der Thematik in räumlicher, zeitlicher und sachlicher Hinsicht darstellt. Im zweiten Jahr war ein Schlüsselkapitel zu verfassen und vorzustellen, gefolgt von der

Workshop character

During the doctoral symposia, in which everyone dedicated themselves intensively to the progress of their dissertations, no external audience was allowed. It was only the trusting cooperation within the college and the *closed-circle* character that made it possible to address any topic openly and freely. The key factor of open subject-related exchanges is trusting communication within the college. The joint research trips and working weeks in which personal exchanges are in the foreground form the foundation for this. The three to four meetings per year alternated with work phases that everyone prepared and followed up on individually. A server provided a platform for shared data exchanges, where the milestones for the respective works were recorded and where it was mandatory to upload the agreed text components over the course of the college. Basic texts and other input were also made available here.

During the first year, all the doctoral students were requested to present a research plan that presented the basic parameters of the subject in spatial, scheduling, and factual terms. During the second year, a key chapter was to be compiled and presented, following by the presentation of a detailed draft in the third year, in which the initial findings were examined thoroughly. This obligatory procedure and mandatory participation in all the events are the only irrevocable rules of this college. As it is a vocational format alongside work, the conditions for the individual participants vary greatly. For the joint research process, it is essential for everyone to contribute continuously. The moderation of the discussions among professors and doctoral students was taken on by the coordinator, ensuring equal content input from all the students. To ensure the follow-up and processing of the subject-specific discussion, all the presentations and discussions were recorded and then provided to the doctoral students. The recordings also served the coaching by Dr. Eva Ritter. As a communication coach and medical doctor, she was involved from the start of the first curriculum and made a significant contribution to establishing effective communication processes within the college. As an external expert, she made sure of generally understandable language—a simple requirement that nevertheless represents a fundamental basis for bringing together so many different specialist competences. She was the internal consultant for the doctoral students as well as the professors and teaching staff. Apart from factual input on communication skills and negotiating strategies for the doctoral students, important guidelines were imparted to the teaching staff through the anonymized account of interpersonal challenges.

Content procedure

Regular routines are a further guarantee of a successful procedure. Each doctoral symposium had a fixed basic structure: the kick-off was a joint aperitif that was dedicated to the local particularities of the location as well as of the cuisine. The following three days were dedicated to the presentation of the progress of the dissertations. The doctoral students gave a twenty-minute

HARDWARE, SOFTWARE, ORGWARE: EIN RAUMTHEORETISCHER ZUGANG ZUM GROßRÄUMIGEN ENTWERFEN

JULIAN PETRIN

Scheren im Kopf – *form follows function follows form*

Es mag abgegriffen klingen, die Suche nach dem Wesen des großräumigen Entwerfens im 21. Jahrhundert mit einem Zitat des Entwurfsverständnisses der Design-Moderne zu beginnen. Aber die in der Planung noch immer tief verankerte Formel, dass die Form der Funktion zu folgen habe, soll mein Ausgangspunkt sein, um auszuloten, was das Entwerfen auf der regionalen Maßstabsebene ausmacht. Bei dieser Suche geht es nicht darum, die Zeiten des altväterlichen entwerfenden Genius wieder heraufzubeschwören. Es geht darum, das Weiterdenken großer Raumkontexte im Sinne des Entwerfens als Disziplin zu stärken und zugleich die Komplexität des Entwurfsbegriffs auf der großräumigen Maßstabsebene zu erfassen.

Meine Suche beginnt mit dem Mantra der Moderne, weil in ihm ein streng lineares Entwurfsverständnis eingeschrieben ist, demzufolge die *Form* ihre Legitimität alleine aus der *Funktion* bezieht. Es ist nur allzu nachvollziehbar, dass eine großräumige Planung, die diese Linearität tief verinnerlicht hat, vor dem Entwerfen im Sinne eines Andersdenkens physischer Strukturen des Raumes zurückschreckt. Wo das Programm so komplex und so abhängig von unübersichtlich vielen endogenen wie exogenen Faktoren erscheint, wie sollte man da eine Form aus der Funktion ableiten? Selbst in Prozessen, in denen die kommunale Ebene das Neudenken räumlicher Strukturen erlaubt (die letztlich ihre Planungshoheit berühren), gibt es diese Hemmung. Kein Wunder, dass viele Raumbilder auf regionaler Ebene deskriptiv bleiben und sich großräumige Leitbilder oder Konzepte meist auf politische Impulse zurückziehen – häufig auf beschreibende Pfeile, Sechsecke und Diagramme. Damit negiert die Raumplanung die Macht der räumlichen Setzung, gerade in einem frühen Stadium des Politikzyklus. Denn ist es in der Realität nicht auch andersherum? Folgt die Funktion – verstanden als das räumliche Programm – nicht auch der Form, gerade auch auf der Ebene des Weiterdenkens großmaßstäblicher Raumkontexte? Kann das spekulative Ausloten von Entwicklungsoptionen nicht auch erst die Spielräume des Denkens eröffnen, oder gar seine eigenen Realitäten schaffen?

Man denke an die Grenzziehungen der vergangenen 150 Jahre, von den willkürlichen Durchschneidungen sozialer und kultureller Räume in der Zeit der Kolonialisierung bis hin zu den mitunter dysfunktionalen Resultaten der Gebietsreformen in den vergangenen 50 Jahren. Sie lassen sich auch als brutale Akte des Entwerfens lesen: Sie haben eine neue Form eingeführt, die sich jeder funktionalen Logik widersetzte und der die Funktion schließlich folgen musste, mit noch heute nachklingenden Folgen. Bei näherem Hinsehen gilt

function to reorient itself—in line with Giddens' duality of structure and action, which determine each other mutually in a cycle.[1] This is not intended as a call for design brutality, but a circular, nonlinear understanding of the interaction of form and function could be the basis for a design stance that takes a significantly more confident approach to large-scale contexts and dares to think in conscious interventions and disruptions, wherever it may seem necessary.

Even so, the conundrum remains in the mind: which of the thin lines on the plans on a scale of 1:50,000 will in fact ever become reality? Must not every attempt to rethink settlement structures, to cast green nets across the region, or to courageously invent new infrastructure corridors and spatial relationships falter at the all too complex interests of the involved parties and the reality of the processes on location? This draws attention to the level of governance and places the limitedness of a classical-modern design understanding in the foreground. Because actually it should be: *form follows function—and politics*. At the latest at this point the question arises: Where must we start when we design on a large scale? Can it be that the actual problem is a still too one-dimensional spatial concept?

If one wants to examine the essence of large-scale design, one cannot avoid the sociological spatial theory discourse that has been circling for about twenty years around the question of what we are actually talking about when we design space—thereby offering an important indication of a more differentiated attitude to large-scale design.

A model suggestion: Three levels of design and a cycle—
form follows function follows politics

To clarify at the outset: if one follows a sociological understanding of space, the duality of form and function (or physical space and program) is by far not adequate for describing the design "attacks" on a large space. The dual view of design negates the probably decisive aspect of space: that of norms, regulations, and power mechanisms that must also be part of the design process. If one looks at spatial theory models, this level almost always plays a decisive role.

One of the reference points of this spatial theory discourse is the spatial concept of Henri Lefebvre, originally published under the title *La production d'espace*.[2] Lefebvre puts forward a spatial model composed of three mutually overlapping levels: *spatial practice*, *representations of space*, and *representational spaces, experienced space*. With his model, he indicates the interdependence of material structures and norms and values expressed through representations, as well as individual practices, which is repeatedly a subject of the sociological discourse on space.

This interdependence is taken up by Dieter Läpple in his concept of the of the self-producing social "matrix space."[3] Läpple distinguishes four levels that determine each other mutually:

dies für jedwede Veränderung großräumiger Strukturen, seien sie mensch-gemacht oder nicht. Die neue Form, die einer veränderten Funktion (oder einem politischen Willensakt oder einer Naturkraft) gefolgt ist, zwingt ihrer-seits wiederum die Funktion dazu, sich neu auszurichten – ganz im Sinne der Gidden'schen Dualität von Struktur und Handlung, die sich in einem Kreis-lauf gegenseitig bedingen.[1] Dies soll kein Aufruf zur entwerferischen Bruta-lität sein. Aber ein zirkuläres, nicht lineares Verständnis der Interaktion von Form und Funktion könnte Grundlage einer entwerferischen Haltung sein, die sich großräumigen Kontexten deutlich selbstbewusster nähert und sich traut, in bewussten Interventionen und Disruptionen zu denken, wo es nötig sein mag.

Dennoch bleibt die Schere im Kopf bestehen: Welche der dürren Linien auf den Plänen im Maßstab 1:50.000 werden tatsächlich jemals Realität werden? Muss nicht jeder Versuch, Siedlungsstrukturen neu zu denken, grüne Netze über die Region zu werfen oder mutig neue Infrastrukturkorridore und Raum-bezüge zu erfinden, an allzu komplexen Akteursinteressen und der Realität der Prozesse vor Ort scheitern? Damit rückt die Ebene der Governance den Blick und die Beschränktheit eines klassisch-modernen Entwurfsverständ-nisses in den Vordergrund. Denn eigentlich müsste es heißen: *form follows function – and politics*. Spätestens hier stellt sich die Frage: Wo müssen wir an-setzen, wenn wir großräumig entwerfen? Kann es sein, dass das eigentliche Problem ein immer noch zu eindimensionaler Raumbegriff ist? Will man dem Wesen des großräumigen Entwerfens auf den Grund gehen, kommt man nicht um den soziologischen Raumtheoriediskurs herum, der sich seit etwa 20 Jahren um folgende Frage herum entspannt hat, wovon wir eigentlich sprechen, wenn wir Raum gestalten – und damit einen wichtigen Fingerzeig für eine differenziertere Haltung gegenüber großräumigem Entwerfen bietet.

Ein Modellvorschlag: drei Ebenen des Entwerfens und ein Kreislauf – *form follows function follows politics*

Um es vorwegzunehmen: Folgt man einem soziologischen Verständnis von Raum, reicht die Dualität von Form und Funktion (oder physischem Raum und Programm) bei Weitem nicht aus, um die entwerferischen „Angriffsebenen" auf den großen Raum zu beschreiben. Die duale Sicht auf das Entwerfen ne-giert die wahrscheinlich entscheidende Ebene des Raumes: die der Normen, Regeln und Machtmechanismen, die ebenfalls Teil des Entwurfsprozesses sein müssen. Blickt man auf raumtheoretische Modelle, spielt diese Ebene fast immer eine entscheidende Rolle.

Einer der Bezugspunkte dieses Raumtheoriediskurses ist das Raumkonzept von Henri Lefebvre, ursprünglich erschienen unter dem Titel *La production d'espace*.[2] Lefebvre entwirft ein Raummodell aus drei sich gegenseitig über-lagernden Ebenen: *räumliche Praxis, Raumrepräsentationen* und *Repräsentations-räume, erlebter Raum*. Mit seinem Modell weist er auf die im raumsoziolo-gischen Diskurs immer wieder thematisierte Interdependenz von materiellen Strukturen mit durch Repräsentationen ausgedrückten Normen und Wer-ten sowie individuellen Praktiken hin. Diese Interdependenz greift Dieter

1. The material-physical substrate of social circumstances, consisting of artifacts, material usage structures, culturally formed nature, and the people in their physical-spatial corporeality
2. The social interaction and action structures that relate to the material substrate—action structures and material substrate find their equivalent in Lefebvre's "spatial practice"
3. An institutionalized and normative regulation system, consisting of forms of ownership, power and control relationships, and legal regulations, as well as social and aesthetic norms
4. A spatial, symbol and representation system associated with the material substrate that indicates the social functions of the artifacts that structure space

These levels work together in the process of spatial production—the continual creation, appropriation, reformation, and reappropriation of space that is a complex interaction of practices, structures, norms, and interventions. For the two mentioned spatial theory reference points for large-scale design, what appears decisive to me is the emergence of the complex of regulations, norms, values, and power mechanisms that allows practices (*function*) in the first place and determines the special structures (*form*) doubly—through the direct setting of frameworks and indirectly through the influence of spatial practices with all their formative effects. This level that can also be described as "spatial regime" plays a decisive role on the large-scale level, which always brings an overlapping of different governance systems. It must be considered during the designing process, or rather designed along with it.

Three levels of large-scale design thus emerge, which each require their own tools and approaches, but which must be closely interlinked:

1) The level of *hardware*—the physical structures that are, on the one hand, the trigger or the "guiding grooves" and at the same time also the reflection and consequence of the spatial practices and functions as well as of the spatial regime
2) The level of *software*—the spatial practices and functions that can also be described as informational and material "flows"[4]
3) The level of *orgware* (selected in reference to the term from information technology)—of the constellations of involved parties, power mechanisms, regulations, and values that compose the spatial regime and delineate the framework of spatial development

Which level is at the starting point that the formation influences have on the space is pointless to ask, because all levels are in multiple circular interdependence.

Especially because of this interdependence, large-scale designing must comprise the questioning, further thinking, and intervening on all three levels: it must sound out and design possible new practices, usages, and functional

Läpple in seinem Konzept des sich selbst hervorbringenden gesellschaftlichen „Matrix-Raums" auf.[3] Läpple unterscheidet vier Ebenen, die sich gegenseitig bedingen:

1. das materiell-physische Substrat gesellschaftlicher Verhältnisse, bestehend aus Artefakten, materiellen Nutzungsstrukturen, kulturell überformter Natur und den Menschen in ihrer körperlich-räumlichen Leiblichkeit;
2. die gesellschaftlichen Interaktions- und Handlungsstrukturen, die sich auf das materielle Substrat beziehen – Handlungsstrukturen und materielles Substrat finden ihre Entsprechung in Lefebvres „spatial practice";
3. ein institutionalisiertes und normatives Regulationssystem, bestehend aus Eigentumsformen, Macht- und Kontrollbeziehungen, rechtlichen Regelungen sowie sozialen und ästhetischen Normen;
4. ein mit dem materiellen Substrat verbundenes räumliches Zeichen-, Symbol- und Repräsentationssystem, das auf die sozialen Funktionen der raumstrukturierenden Artefakte hindeutet.

Diese Ebenen wirken im Prozess der Raumproduktion zusammen, der immerwährenden Herstellung, Aneignung, Neuformierung und Wiederaneignung von Raum, die eine komplexe Interaktion aus Praktiken, Strukturen, Normen und Interventionen ist.

Entscheidend erscheint mir bei beiden genannten raumtheoretischen Bezugspunkten für das großräumige Entwerfen das Hervortreten des Komplexes aus Regeln, Normen, Werten und Machtmechanismen, der Praktiken (*function*) überhaupt zulässt und die räumlichen Strukturen (*form*) doppelt determiniert – ganz unmittelbar durch direkte Rahmensetzung und indirekt durch den Einfluss auf die räumlichen Praktiken mit all ihren formativen Wirkungen. Diese auch als „räumliches Regime" beschreibbare Ebene spielt auf der großräumigen Ebene, die immer auch eine Überlagerung unterschiedlicher Governance-Systeme mit sich bringt, eine entscheidende Rolle. Sie muss beim Entwerfen mitgedacht werden, mehr noch: mitentworfen werden.

Letztlich treten damit drei Ebenen des großräumigen Entwerfens hervor, die jeweils eigenständige Werkzeuge und Herangehensweisen erfordern, aber eng miteinander verzahnt sein müssen:

a) die Ebene der *Hardware* – der physischen Strukturen, die einerseits Trigger beziehungsweise „Spurrillen" und zugleich auch Abbild und Folge der räumlichen Praktiken und Funktionen sowie des räumlichen Regimes sind;
b) die Ebene der *Software* – der räumlichen Praktiken und Funktionen, die sich auch als informationelle und materielle „Flows" beschreiben lassen;[4]
c) die Ebene der *Orgware* (gewählt in Anlehnung an den Begriff aus der Informationstechnologie) – der Akteurskonstellationen, Machtmechanismen, Regeln und Werte, die sich zum räumlichen Regime zusammensetzen und den Rahmen der Raumentwicklung abstecken.

requirements (software level)—alongside corresponding physical-spatial interventions and structures (hardware level)—that trigger and enable the new practices. And there must be answers to which funding, rules, values, and process structures are necessary to enable the hardware and software.

At the latest at this point it becomes clear: large-scale design is far more than acting on the level of form. In the sociological sense, it is the attempt at targeted influencing of the process of spatial production on all spatial levels.

Such a view of design has effects not only on the approach in the practical processes of modeling and developing space, but also on design theory. After the architectural focus on the morphological-urban development figure, despite certain rollbacks following the Düsseldorf declaration that have been overcome in most teaching plans, with orgware, a new level of design theory is coming to the fore: the design of processes, regulations, networks of involved parties, and financing models that ultimately enable spatial development. It is only when designers are also competent on these levels that they acquire the authority that a bold further consideration of large spatial contexts requires.

1 The three levels of large-scale design and their interdependencies
1 Die drei Ebenen des großräumigen Entwerfens und ihre Interpendenzen

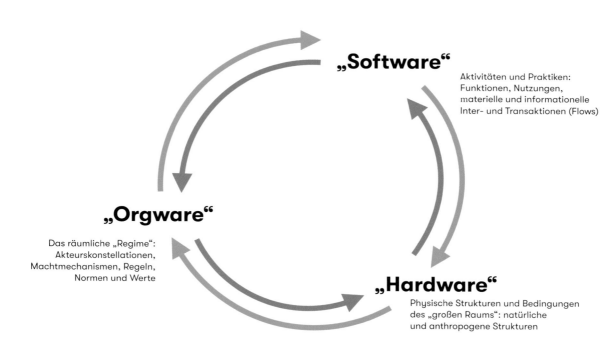

„Software"

Aktivitäten und Praktiken:
Funktionen, Nutzungen,
materielle und informationelle
Inter- und Transaktionen (Flows)

„Orgware"

Das räumliche „Regime":
Akteurskonstellationen,
Machtmechanismen, Regeln,
Normen und Werte

„Hardware"

Physische Strukturen und Bedingungen
des „großen Raums": natürliche
und anthropogene Strukturen

Welche Ebene dabei am Ausgangspunkt der Formationskräfte auf den Raum steht, ist müßig zu fragen, denn alle freien Ebenen befinden in mehrfachen zirkulären Interdependenzen.

Gerade wegen dieser Interdependenz muss das großräumige Entwerfen das Infragestellen, Weiterdenken und Intervenieren auf allen drei Ebenen umfassen: Es muss mögliche neue Praktiken, Nutzungen, funktionale Anforderungen ausloten und entwerfen (Ebene der Software) – im Zusammenspiel mit entsprechenden physisch-räumlichen Interventionen und Strukturen (Ebene der Hardware), die die neuen Praktiken triggern und ermöglichen. Und es muss Antworten geben, welche Trägerschaften, Regeln, Werte und Prozessstrukturen notwendig sind, um Hardware wie Software zu ermöglichen. Spätestens hier wird deutlich: Großräumiges Entwerfen ist weit mehr als das Agieren auf der Ebene der Form. Im soziologischen Sinn ist es der Versuch der zielgerichteten Einflussnahme auf den Prozess der Raumproduktion auf allen Ebenen des Raumes.

Eine solche Sicht auf das Entwerfen hat Auswirkungen nicht nur auf die Herangehensweise in praktischen Leitbild- und Raumbildprozessen, sondern auch auf die Entwurfslehre. Nachdem die baumeisterliche Fokussierung auf die morphologisch-städtebauliche Figur trotz manchem Rollback in Folge der Düsseldorfer Erklärung in den meisten Lehrplänen überwunden wurde, rückt mit der Orgware eine neue Ebene der Entwurfslehre in den Blick: das Design von Prozessen, Regelwerken, Akteursnetzen und Finanzierungsmodellen, die eine Raumentwicklung letztlich ermöglichen. Erst wenn Entwerfende auch auf diesen Ebenen kompetent sind, gewinnen sie die Souveränität, die ein mutiges Weiterdenken großer Raumkontexte erfordert.

DESIGNING/METHOD(S)

MARKUS NOLLERT

Eureka!

Tristan and I have already mulled over the Cologne-Bonn region the whole day.[1] We have discussed and rejected approaches, and told each other a multitude of design stories that came to nothing. And it all started so well: instead of an initial draft, we put together, in a dossier, findings and hypotheses about the state of the region. We made it clear that established modes of behavior in the region lead to a situation that causes increasing spatial problems and is no longer viable in the long term. With the dossier, we defied the guidelines but evidently touched a nerve. And now this: we are stuck and are gradually coming to the end of our energy. Then Julian comes by, spies the mountains of tracing paper, listens to our situation and then says: "How about the 'Rhenish ladder'?"[2] He means a system of transport connections and settlement hubs around the cities of Cologne and Bonn, with two "side supports" in a north-south direction and several

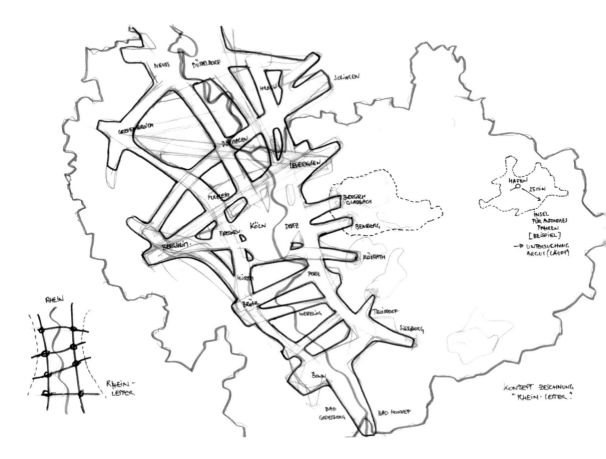

MARKUS NOLLERT

Heureka!

Den ganzen Tag schon haben Tristan[1] und ich über der Region Köln-Bonn gebrütet. Wir haben Ansätze diskutiert und verworfen, haben uns gegenseitig Entwurfsgeschichten erzählt, die reihenweise ins Stocken geraten sind. Dabei hatten wir einen so guten Start: Statt eines ersten Entwurfes haben wir Befunde und Hypothesen zum Zustand der Region in einem Dossier zusammengestellt. Wir haben klargemacht, dass eingespielte Verhaltensweisen in der Region zu einer Situation führten, die immer größere räumliche Probleme verursacht und langfristig nicht mehr tragbar ist. Mit dem Dossier haben wir uns über die Vorgaben hinweggesetzt, aber scheinbar den Nerv getroffen. Und jetzt das: Wir kommen nicht weiter und sind langsam am Ende unserer Kräfte. Da kommt Julian[2] vorbei, sichtet die Transparentpapierberge, hört sich unsere Situation an und sagt dann: „Wie wäre es mit der ‚Rheinischen Leiter'?" Er meint ein System aus Verkehrsverbindungen und

1 The "Rhenian ladder" as a sketch and end product. Contribution to the agglomeration concept Cologne-Bonn, 2018.
1 Die „Rheinische Leiter" als Skizze und Endprodukt. Beitrag zum Agglomerationskonzept Köln-Bonn, 2018.

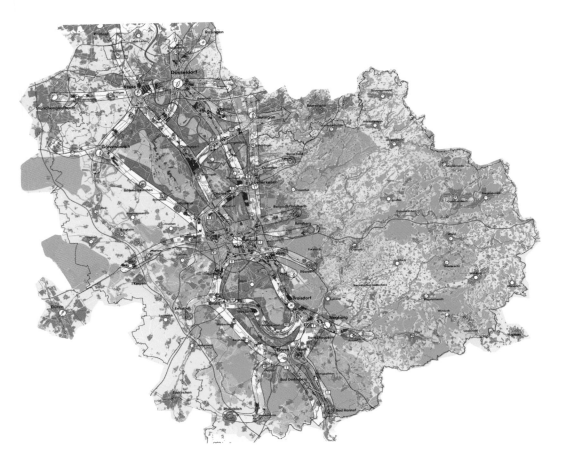

traversing "rungs." Tristan and I cannot believe that Julian solved our Gordian knot in passing. Eureka! Eight months and many discussions later, the design is ready, with a slightly reinvented name—the "Rhenian Ladder." When we think about designing in spatial disciplines, for many of us, Eureka moments such as these initially go through our minds: the intuitive idea of one or several persons which—developed further—represents the solution to a complex situation. But the glimpse into a design workshop recounted here also shows other aspects of designing as a method that are increasing in importance: that one can and should approach large-scale problem situations of spatial development, as well, with a complex design; that it is precisely the cul-de-sacs of a design process that generate valuable knowledge; that a history and arguments are part of a design; and that one's own exploration of the problems to be solved is a design and research act at the same time. It also shows implicitly that research about the methods of design must cross borders and requires a perspective that often only becomes possible through one's own contribution to a design task.

Designing/method(s)

The consideration of designing as a method as part of the third International Doctoral College "Spatial Research Lab" (IDK) is based on the understanding of a spatial planning design that addresses the clarification of complex problem situations in multiple actor networks.[3] Following this understanding, designing is viewed as an "explorative activity" that "attempts through bringing forth, selecting and formulating the essence and structure of an element to provide a satisfactory answer to a specific question." The product, the design, is "to be understood as a proven [but hypothetical] discussion basis on which to build a clarification process about the further procedure in the matter to be handled."

This design understanding is based on the question of to what extent and how designing can contribute to the generation of (action) knowledge. In complex problem situations, this action knowledge consists not only of the development of conceptual suggestions but also of a contribution to the exploration of the actual task as a "wicked problem," as well as the exploration of possibilities of reaching joint decisions in the context of the existing actor networks and their interests.[4] This understanding, which is also evident in the approach of "spatial design" of Jef van den Broek,[5] therefore brings together various movements of the design discussion: the addressing of complexity as a design subject and of the interplay between intuition and intellect;[6] the discussion about the incorporation of actors into the design activity[7] and the associated negotiation processes; and questions about the methodology of design and the significance of the examination of tricky and complex starting situations.[8]

Regarding the question of viable methods within such a design understanding, in Hille von Seggern's words "one cannot reckon that design processes cannot be fully objectivized," as the situation described above also shows.[9] Which path ultimately leads to the destination cannot be foreseen. Whether

Siedlungsschwerpunkten um die Städte Köln und Bonn, mit zwei „Holmen"
in Nord-Süd-Richtung und mehreren querenden „Sprossen". Tristan und
ich können nicht glauben, dass Julian im Vorbeigehen unseren gordischen
Knoten gelöst hat. Heureka! Acht Monate und viele Diskussionen später ist
sie fertig entworfen – die „Rheinische Leiter".

Wenn wir über Entwerfen in räumlichen Disziplinen nachdenken, gehen
vielen von uns zunächst Heureka-Momente wie dieser durch den Kopf: der
intuitive Einfall einer oder mehrerer Personen, der – ausgearbeitet – die
Lösung einer verzwickten Situation darstellt. Doch der geschilderte Blick
in eine Entwurfswerkstatt zeigt noch weitere Aspekte des Entwerfens als
Methode auf, die mehr und mehr an Bedeutung gewinnen: dass man sich
entwerferisch komplexen und auch großmaßstäblichen Problemsituationen
der Raumentwicklung nähern kann und soll; dass gerade die Sackgassen
eines Entwurfsprozesses wertvolles Wissen generieren; dass zu einem Entwurf auch eine Geschichte und Argumente gehören; und dass die eigene
Erkundung der zu lösenden Probleme ein entwerferischer und forschender
Akt zugleich ist. Er zeigt aber implizit auch, dass das Forschen über die Methoden des Entwerfens Grenzen überschreiten muss und eine Perspektive
erfordert, die häufig nur durch die eigene Mitarbeit an der Entwurfsaufgabe
möglich wird.

Entwerfen/Methode(n)

Die Beschäftigung mit dem Entwerfen als Methode im Zuge des dritten
Internationalen Doktorandenkollegs (IDK) „Forschungslabor Raum" basiert
auf dem Entwurfsverständnis des raumplanerischen Entwerfens, welches
sich mit der Klärung komplexer Problemsituationen in Multi-Akteursnetz-
werken auseinandersetzt.[3] In diesem Verständnis wird Entwerfen als „explorative Tätigkeit" verstanden, „welche durch das Hervorbringen, Auswählen
und Formulieren von Gestalt und Beschaffenheit eines Elements versucht,
für eine bestimmte Fragestellung eine zufriedenstellende Antwort zu liefern".
Das Produkt, der Entwurf, ist als eine „geprüfte[, aber hypothetische] Dis-
kussionsgrundlage zu verstehen, auf deren Basis ein Klärungsprozess über
das weitere Vorgehen in der zu behandelnden Frage aufbauen kann".[4]

Diesem Entwurfsverständnis liegt die Frage zugrunde, inwiefern und wie
Entwerfen zur Generierung von (Handlungs-)Wissen beitragen kann. Dieses
Handlungswissen besteht in komplexen Problemsituationen eben nicht nur
aus der Entwicklung konzeptioneller Vorschläge, sondern auch in einem
Beitrag zur Erkundung der eigentlichen Aufgabe als „verzwicktes Problem"[5];
sowie zur Erkundung von Möglichkeiten, im Kontext der bestehenden
Akteursnetzwerke und ihrer Interessen zu gemeinsam getragenen Entscheidungen zu kommen. Dieses Verständnis, welches auch im Ansatz des
„spatial design" von Jef van den Broek[6] sichtbar wird, vereint damit mehrere
Strömungen der Entwurfsdiskussion: die Auseinandersetzung mit der Komplexität als Entwurfsgegenstand und mit dem Zusammenspiel zwischen Intuition und Intellekt;[7] die Diskussion um den Einbezug von Akteur*innen in
die Entwurfstätigkeit[8] und die damit verbundenen Aushandlungsprozesse;

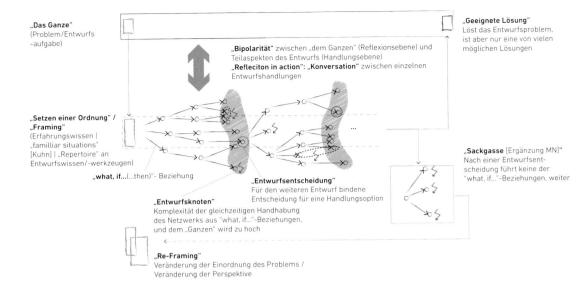

the image of the "Rhenian ladder" would also have emerged at another point in time and without the temporary failure of several attempts and the resulting insights, I cannot even say even myself as someone involved in the process. Instead, the design actions are like *puzzling over something*, which alludes fittingly not only to putting together individual parts into a whole but also a long and serious consideration of an object or a person with the aim of understanding it or them.[10] However, a viable lead for explaining significant elements of such a design process is provided by the reflexive practice of Donald Schön, which Martin Prominski attributed to his "metatheory of complex landscape design" with an interplay of unpredictability, processuality, and relationality."[11]

By establishing an initial order from known situations, a process starts in which designers build up networks of "what if …" relationships. Regarding these relationships and the overall design subject, they then confer until they can no longer afford this oscillation due to too many dependencies. At one of these so-called decision-making hubs, a decision must be made for one of the designed options, to have capacities once again for new networks of "what if…" relationships. The result of this process is either a suitable solution or failing—and an associated reinterpretation or *reframing* of the task.[12]

Problem seeking, partly baked ideas, and speculation collective

The oscillating between individual parts of the network of individual design considerations and the whole—i.e., the design task—gains a special significance, because it is only hanging in the balance of individual design components that provides the virtual experimentation with transformation possibilities and therefore new insights. An increasingly complex design

2 Attempt at an illustration of reflexive practice according to Schön.
2 Versuch einer Illustration der reflexiven Praxis nach Schön.

Erweiterung der reflexiven Praxis und auch des Entwerfens selbst lassen sich besonders gut mit dem Begriff des Spekulationskollektivs beschreiben, den J. D. Bernal im Buch *The scientist speculates – an anthology of partly baked ideas* geprägt hat. „Wollen wir nicht versagen, muss die Idee von einsamen Denkern [oder auch Entwerfenden, Anm. Nollert] durch etwas ersetzt werden, was wir ‚Spekulationskollektive‘ nennen können. Mit anderen Worten, wir müssen zurückgehen zu den ältesten und wertvollsten Formen wissenschaftlichen Denkens, zur Dialektik [...]“.[16] Das Prinzip der Rede und Gegenrede und die Arbeit an und mit Argumenten wird so zu einem zentralen Bestandteil des Entwurfsprozesses.

Der anfängliche Blick in die Entwurfswerkstatt der „Rheinischen Leiter“ zeigt eine Ebene dieser Spekulationskollektive im Sinne des gemeinsamen Entwerfens interdisziplinärer Teams. Doch erst die kritische Diskussion dieser *partly baked idea* mit den Akteur*innen und Expert*innen im Rahmen der Kupplungen des Agglomerationskonzepts Köln-Bonn ermöglichte die Schärfung und Anreicherung der Idee zu einem Konzept. Dieses Konzept ist zwar immer noch hoch spekulativ, stellt aber einen möglichen Ansatz zur Entwicklung dieser Region dar.

Entwerfend forschen – Entwerfen erforschen

Auch das Doktorandenkolleg kann als ein Spekulationskollektiv verstanden werden und jede der Dissertationen als Entwurfsprozess. Die Diskussion über das Entwerfen führte daher häufig auch zu einer Debatte um dessen Eignung als wissensgenerierende Methode. Diese ist zwar durch die Abhängigkeit von Lösung und Problem als Eigenschaft „verzwickter“ Probleme[17] mehr oder weniger unumstritten, jedoch bleibt die methodische Begründung von Entwürfen als Teil der Forschung eine Herausforderung. Denn das aktive Verändern der Situation und die Reflexion des eigenen Tuns haben es weiterhin schwer, als wissenschaftliche Handlungen anerkannt zu werden – auch wenn Ansätze wie die Aktionsforschung[18] mittlerweile Möglichkeiten dazu eröffnen.

Das Modell der Entwurfsforschung Jürgen Weidingers[19] zeigt dies auch für die Erforschung des Entwerfens. Die Singularität und Kontextbezogenheit eines einzelnen Entwurfs ist mit dem heute geltenden Wissenschaftsverständnis nicht vereinbar. Erst eine Serie von Entwurfsergebnissen einer Autorenschaft eröffnet die Möglichkeit, Regelmäßigkeiten und Unterschiede zu erkennen, Erkenntnisse zu formulieren und den wissenschaftlichen Diskurs mit anderen Disziplinen zu fördern.

Es bleibt eine Herausforderung und wichtige Aufgabe, entwerfend zu forschen und das Entwerfen zu erforschen – insbesondere was die Methoden angeht, denn noch immer bestimmen die Entwurfsergebnisse die Diskussion. Conditio sine qua non ist und bleibt aber die Reflexion des eigenen und fremden Tuns, denn ohne sie ist das Entwerfen einfach nur eine Methode, aber keine Forschung.

PROJECTING—MODELING—VISUALIZING: A DISCUSSION ABOUT METHODS

ANDREAS NÜTTEN

The third International Doctoral College "Spatial Research Lab" (IDK) has always been accompanied by the question of how design methods, which in some cases are based on very intuitive decision-making processes, can be embedded in a scientific context. Or to put it differently: how can scientific standards be complied with and how can they be construed without losing the intuitive character of design?[1]

The exemplary illustrations from the ongoing dissertation *Landschafts-metropole* (Landscape metropolis) show possible structural and illustrative-methodological design steps as primarily conceptual interpretations of space on a spatial planning scale.

Projection

Projecting is a method of analytical design in architecture and urban development that makes it possible to see the spatial or structural starting situation in a new light through layering with familiar spatial structures (usually on the same scale) or reference projects. In urban development this is usually on the level of the structural plan, which prominently shows development structures, conspicuous individual buildings, and the various open space types. As a rule, prominent historical urban structures are projected, whose dimensions and special constellations are known and can be evaluated as a qualified comparison.

Supplementing the structural plan, further information (function or usage diagrams, infrastructures, exploration results, etc.) can be projected, or a whole series of different spaces can be projected to draw conclusions from the comparison. The projection of current projects can in turn bring innovative and inspiring structural concepts and programming into the design discussion.

The knowledge acquisition value of projecting is evident: what is still unknown is confronted with what is already known and can be evaluated. The "blank sheet," following intuitive assumptions, is filled with something that is complete within itself, which can be expedient but also deformed, distorted, scaled, or rejected. Projecting brings measurable and rateable search figures as placeholders in a discovery process, which can be "modeled" in well-founded and comprehensible steps. This tests possible interpretations and conceptions and allows the identification of new possibilities, as well as further questions.

As a concrete example, the polycentric study area Hannover-Braunschweig-Göttingen-Wolfsburg can be overlayered structurally with various metropolises, to test how the metropolitan region can be read and interpreted in comparison.

PROJIZIEREN – MODELLIEREN – VISUALISIEREN: EINE METHODENDISKUSSION

ANDREAS NÜTTEN

Das dritte Internationale Doktorandenkolleg (IDK) „Forschungslabor Raum"
war stets von der Frage begleitet, wie sich entwerferische Methoden, die
teils auf sehr intuitiven Entscheidungsprozessen beruhen, in einen wissenschaftlichen Kontext einbetten lassen. Oder anders ausgedrückt: Wie sind
wissenschaftliche Standards einhaltbar beziehungsweise wie können sie
ausgelegt werden, ohne die intuitive Prägnanz des Entwerfens zu verlieren?[1]
Die beispielhaft aufgezeigten Grafiken aus der eigenen laufenden Dissertation *Landschaftsmetropole* veranschaulichen mögliche strukturelle und
bildhaft-methodische Schritte des Entwerfens als zunächst konzeptionelle
Lesarten des Raumes im raumplanerischen Maßstab.

Projizieren

Das Projizieren ist eine Methode des analytischen Entwerfens in Architektur
und Städtebau, die es erlaubt, die räumliche oder strukturelle Ausgangslage
durch das Überlagern mit (meist maßstabsgleichen) bekannten räumlichen
Strukturen oder Referenzprojekten in einem neuen Licht zu sehen. Im Städtebau geschieht dies meist auf Ebene des Strukturplanes (Schwarzplan), wel-
cher Bebauungsstrukturen, auffällige Einzelbauten und die verschiedenen
Freiraumtypen prägnant hervortreten lässt. Dabei werden in der Regel pro-
minente historische städtebauliche Strukturen projiziert, deren Dimensionen und besonderen Konstellationen bekannt sind und die sich im Vergleich
qualifiziert bewerten lassen.

Den Strukturplan ergänzend, können weitere Informationen (Funktions- oder
Nutzungsdiagramme, Infrastrukturen, Erkundungsergebnisse etc.) projiziert werden, oder es kann eine ganze Serie an unterschiedlichen Räumen
projiziert werden, um Erkenntnisse aus dem Vergleich zu ziehen. Das Projizieren aktueller Projekte wiederum kann innovative Strukturkonzepte und
Programmierungen inspirierend in die Entwurfsdiskussion einbringen.

Der erkenntnisbringende Wert des Projizierens liegt auf der Hand: Noch
Unbekanntes wird mit bereits Bekanntem und Bewertbarem konfrontiert.
Das noch „weiße Blatt" wird intuitiven Vermutungen folgend mit etwas in
sich Vollständigem gefüllt, das zielführend sein kann, aber auch verformt,
verzerrt, skaliert oder verworfen werden kann. Das Projizieren führt messbare und bewertbare Suchfiguren als Platzhalter in einen Findungsprozess
ein, die in begründeten und nachvollziehbaren Schritten „modelliert" werden können. Dies testet mögliche räumliche Lesarten und Konzeptionen
und lässt neue Möglichkeiten, aber auch weitere Fragen erkennen.

Im konkreten Beispiel wird der polyzentrische Untersuchungsraum Hannover-Braunschweig-Göttingen-Wolfsburg mit verschiedenen Metropolen

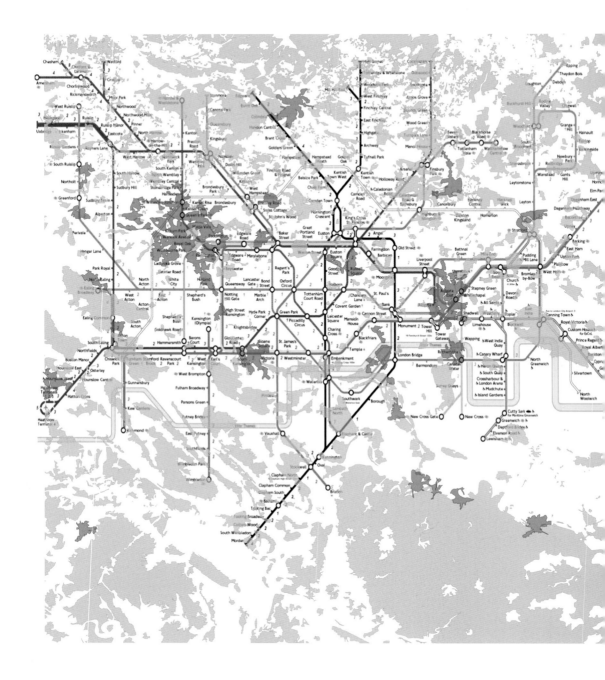

London serves as a first object of comparison, as a classical monocentric and economically significant metropolis. While the spatial extent of the study area is significantly larger (fig. 1), in the spatiotemporal comparison it is noticeable that the accessibility between the core cities is comparable with the accessibility of various urban poles and institutions within London in terms of the travel times of the underground (fig. 2).

1 *The spatial expanse of the metropolis of London.* **1** *Die räumliche Ausdehnung der Metropole London.*

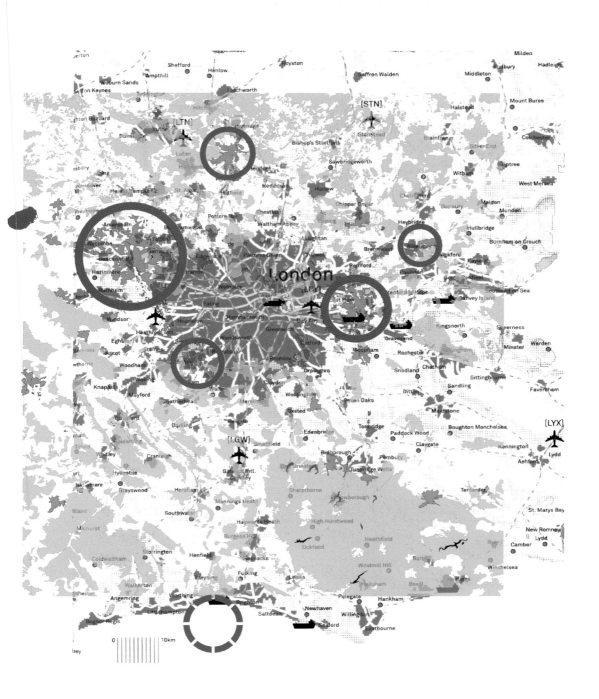

2 *Spatiotemporal comparison of the metropolis of London.*
2 *Raumzeitlicher Vergleich der Metropole London.*

strukturell überlagert, um zu testen, wie die Metropolregion im Vergleich gelesen und interpretiert werden kann. Als erstes Vergleichsobjekt dient London als klassische monozentrische und ökonomisch bedeutsame Metropole. Während die räumliche Ausdehnung des Untersuchungsraumes deutlich größer ist (Abb. 1), fällt beim raumzeitlichen Vergleich auf, dass die Erreichbarkeit der Kernstädte untereinander vergleichbar ist mit der

On the basis of this discovery, various hypotheses can be formed: the Hannover study area can be understood as a metropolis with its own accessibility-based polycentric urbanity for around 2.5 million inhabitants. The comparison brings forth many further questions about this that require the special metropolis typology to be specified more precisely. In this regard, projecting opens up the very demonstrative possibility of "argument and counterargument,"[2] whether it is through a type of reflexive self-dialogue of the designer or the public discussion of participation procedures.

Modeling

Forming models is a traditional scientific as well as artistic method. Modeling is to be understood as a process that, starting from an original, creates one or more models through various simplification, depiction, or supplementation steps, which in turn can generate a prototypical model as a starting point for something new that can be generally applied to comparable starting situations.

For this modeling process from the original to a model or to models, Herbert Stachowiak defines two types of "attributes" in his publication of 1973 about general model theory. Today one would rather speak of features displayed by the original and model(s) that can be added or discarded during modeling. Only the "depiction area," as it is called, remains constant between the original and model(s) (fig. 3).[3]

Disregarded attributes, according to his definition, are consciously omitted attributes of the model. "This corresponds to the simplifying, 'abbreviating' essential characteristic of the model, also to the 'pragmatic,' geared towards a purpose."[4] Abundant attributes, on the other hand, according to Stachowiak's definition, are consciously added attributes of the model. "They have a 'bridging theory' function, can be 'fabricated or freely invented or even vaguely assumed attributes,' which give rise to

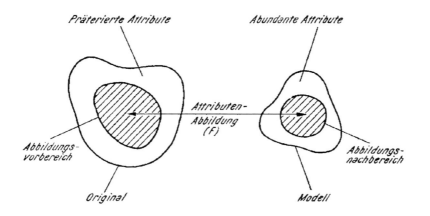

3 *The original model representation according to Stachowiak.*
3 *Die originale Modellabbildung nach Stachowiak.*

Erreichbarkeit verschiedener urbaner Pole und Institutionen innerhalb Londons bezogen auf die Fahrzeiten der Untergrundbahn (Abb. 2).

Auf Basis dieser Entdeckung lassen sich verschiedene Hypothesen bilden: Der Untersuchungsraum Hannover kann als Metropole mit einer eigenen, für circa 2,5 Millionen Einwohner*innen bestehenden, erreichbarkeitsbasierten polyzentrischen Urbanität verstanden werden. Der Vergleich wirft hierzu viele weitere Fragen auf, die auffordern, den besonderen Typus Metropole genauer zu spezifizieren. Hierzu eröffnet das Projizieren auf sehr anschauliche Weise die Möglichkeit von „Rede und Gegenrede"[2], sei es in einer Art reflexivem Selbstdialog des Entwerfenden oder im öffentlichen Diskurs von Beteiligungsverfahren.

Modellieren

Modelle zu bilden, ist eine klassische wissenschaftliche wie auch künstlerische Methode. Das Modellieren ist dabei als Prozess zu verstehen, der von einem Original ausgehend über verschiedene Vereinfachungs-, Abbildungs- oder Anreicherungsschritte ein oder mehrere Modelle erschafft, die wiederum ein prototypisches Modell als Ausgangspunkt für etwas Neues generieren können, das auf vergleichbare Ausgangslagen allgemein übertragbar ist.

Für diesen Modellierungsprozess vom Original zu(m) Modell(en) definiert Herbert Stachowiak in seiner 1973 erschienenen Publikation zur allgemeinen Modelltheorie zwei Arten von „Attributen"[3] (heute würde man eher von Merkmalen sprechen, die Original und Modell(e) aufweisen), die während des Modellierens hinzugefügt oder weggelassen werden. Nur der sogenannte Abbildungsbereich stimmt zwischen Original und Modell(en) überein (Abb. 3). Präterierte Attribute sind nach seiner Definition bewusst weggelassene Attribute des Modells. „Dies entspricht dem vereinfachenden ‚verkürzenden' Wesensmerkmal des Modells, ebenso dem ‚pragmatischen', auf einen Zweck ausgerichteten."[4] Abundante Attribute hingegen sind nach Stachowiaks Definition bewusst hinzugefügte Attribute des Modells. „Sie besitzen ‚überbrückungstheoretische' Funktion, können ‚fingierte bzw. frei erfundene oder auch vage vermutete Attribute' sein, die im Prozess der Modellbildung erkenntnisbildend sind und auch Rückschlüsse auf das Original zulassen."[5] Um besser verstehen und differenzieren zu können, was Modelle im wissenschaftlichen oder auch künstlerischen Kontext allgemein zu leisten vermögen, lohnt sich ein Blick auf Stachowiaks allgemeinen Modellbegriff und seine Behauptung, jedes Modell verfüge über ein Abbildungsmerkmal, ein Verkürzungsmerkmal und ein pragmatisches Merkmal:

1) Das Abbildungsmerkmal ist dadurch definiert, dass „Modelle stets Modelle von etwas sind, nämlich Abbildungen, Repräsentationen natürlicher oder künstlicher Originale, die selbst wieder Modelle sein können. Solche Originale können auf natürliche Weise entstanden, technisch hergestellt oder sonst wie gegeben sein."

knowledge in the process of model forming and also allow conclusions about the original."[5]

To be able to understand and differentiate better what models can generally achieve in a scientific or artistic context, it is worth taking a look at Stachowiak's general model concept and his claim that each model has a mapping, reduction, and pragmatism characteristic:

1) The mapping characteristic is defined by the fact that "models are always models of something, namely depictions, representations of natural or artistic originals, which can in turn be models themselves. Such originals may have been created naturally, produced technically or otherwise."

2) The reduction characteristic corresponds according to Stachowiak to the fact that "models in general do not feature all the attributes of the original they represent but only those that appear relevant to the respective model makers and/or users."[6]

4 *Spatial structure corresponding to Howard's Social Cities model.*
4 *Raumstruktur in Analogie zu Howards Modell der Social Cities.*

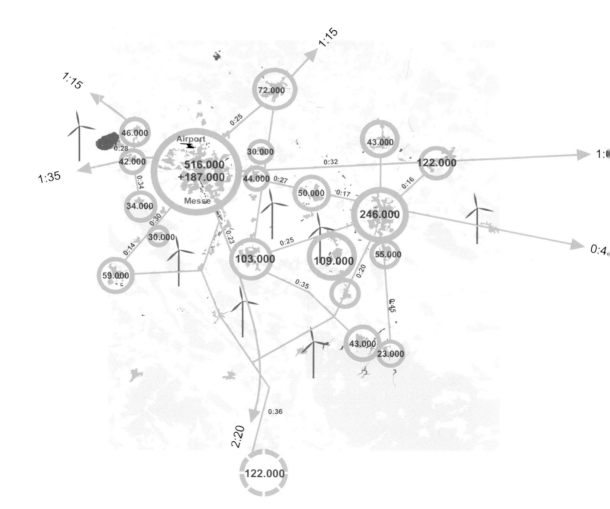

2)	Das Verkürzungsmerkmal entspricht nach Stachowiak der Tatsache, dass „Modelle im Allgemeinen nicht alle Attribute des durch sie repräsentierten Originals erfassen, sondern nur solche, die den jeweiligen Modellerschaffern und/oder Modellbenutzern relevant scheinen."[6] Und schließlich besitzen alle Modelle ein

3)	pragmatisches Merkmal, da „Modelle in ihren Originalen nicht per se eindeutig zugeordnet sind. Sie erfüllen ihre Ersetzungsfunktion a) für bestimmte – erkennende und/oder handelnde, modellbenutzende – Subjekte, b) innerhalb bestimmter Zeitintervalle und c) unter Einschränkung auf bestimmte gedankliche oder tatsächliche Operationen. [...] Modelle sind nicht nur Modelle von etwas. Sie sind auch Modelle für jemanden, einen Menschen oder einen künstlichen Modellbenutzer."[7]

Das Arbeiten mit Attributen (später vereinfacht Merkmale genannt) ermöglicht, den Prozess des analytischen Entwerfens analog zum Modellieren vorzunehmen. Das heißt, vom Untersuchungsraum als Original ausgehend, werden in Schritten einer bewussten Vereinfachung wesentliche Merkmale beschrieben, gefiltert und reduziert. Der gleiche Vorgang wird mit ausgewählten Stadtmodellen vorgenommen, die auf den Raum als mögliche konzeptionelle Lesarten projiziert werden, und durch die dem Originalraum neue Merkmale hinzugefügt werden. Die ausgewählten Merkmale sowohl des Originals wie auch der weiteren Stadtmodelle werden einer übersichtlichen Anzahl von Kategorien zugeordnet: ideelle, strukturelle, programmatische, soziale und umsetzungsstrategische Merkmale. In einer Matrix der Modellmerkmale werden sie organisiert und sichtbar gemacht. Der Erkenntnisgewinn besteht in einer übersichtlichen Darstellung von Information und der Möglichkeit, ein neues Stadtmodell zu generieren, das auf zielorientiert ausgewählten Merkmalen des Originals und der Beispielmodelle aufbaut.

Im konkreten Beispiel werden auf die polyzentrische Metropolregion Hannover-Braunschweig-Göttingen-Wolfsburg strukturelle Merkmale von Howards Modell der „Social Cities" projiziert und visualisiert (Abb. 4).

Gewisse vermutete Übereinstimmungen bestätigen sich, etwa das Verhältnis von Siedlungsfläche zu Landfläche bei Howards Modell von circa 1:6 und die polyzentrische Anordnung von „Stadt" als effizient vernetztes Städtenetz mittelgroßer Städte und eine durch Erreichbarkeit definierte gestaffelte Zentralität. Weitere Projektionen der programmatischen und ideellen Merkmale von Howards Modell auf den Untersuchungsraum eröffnen eine umfassende Modelldiskussion: ein Lernen von Howards Modell – Aktualität, aber auch die Grenzen der heutigen Anwendbarkeit testend.

Visualisieren

Visualisieren ist immanenter Teil des Entwerfens. Schon die Wahl der Darstellungsweisen ist eng mit einer bestimmten Intention oder der Zuspitzung von inhaltlichen Aussagen verbunden. So ist die Strukturkarte des Untersuchungsraumes eine eigentlich unmögliche Karte (Abb. 5), da sie sich für

3) And finally, all models have a pragmatic characteristic, as "models are not assigned clearly per se to their originals. They fulfil their replacement function a) for specific—cognitive and/or active, model-using— subjects, b) within certain time intervals and c) with restriction to certain theoretical or actual operations. … Models are not only models of something. They are also models for somebody, a person or an artificial model user."[7]

Working with attributes (which I will now call characteristics for simplicity) makes it possible to carry out the process of analytical design analogously to modeling. This means, starting from the original as a study area, essential characteristics are described, filtered, and reduced in conscious simplification steps. The same procedure is carried out with selected urban models that are projected onto the space as possible conceptual interpretations and through which new characteristics are added to the original area. The selected characteristics of both the original and the additional urban models are attributed to a defined number of categories: nonmaterial, structural, programmatic, social, and practical strategic characteristics. They are organized and presented in a matrix of model characteristics. The gaining of insights comes from a clear presentation of information and the possibility of generating a new urban model that builds on targeted selected characteristics of the original and the sample models.

As a concrete example, one sees here how structural characteristics of Howard's model of "social cities" are projected and visualized onto the polycentric metropolitan region Hannover-Braunschweig-Göttingen-Wolfsburg (fig. 4).

Certain supposed concordances are confirmed, for example, the ratio of settlement area to rural area in Howard's model of around 1:6 and the polycentric arrangement of "town" as an efficiently networked urban mesh of medium-sized towns and a staggered centrality defined by accessibility. Further projections of the programmatic and nonmaterial characteristics of Howard's model onto the studied area open up a comprehensive model discussion: a learning of Howard's model—currency but also testing the borders of present-day applicability.

Visualizing

Visualizing is an immanent part of designing. Even the choice of means of representation is closely linked to a certain intention or the emphasizing of content statements. The structural map of the examined space is actually an impossible map (fig. 5), as it makes use of the graphic elements of different meanings for the presentation of the three predominant landscape types of the overall area within one map.

By highlighting or leaving out various structural elements per individual area, the areas are strongly contrasted, which is represented with a conscious emphasis through a type of inverse graphics: forests as spatially structuring elements are black in the northern and southern area, while

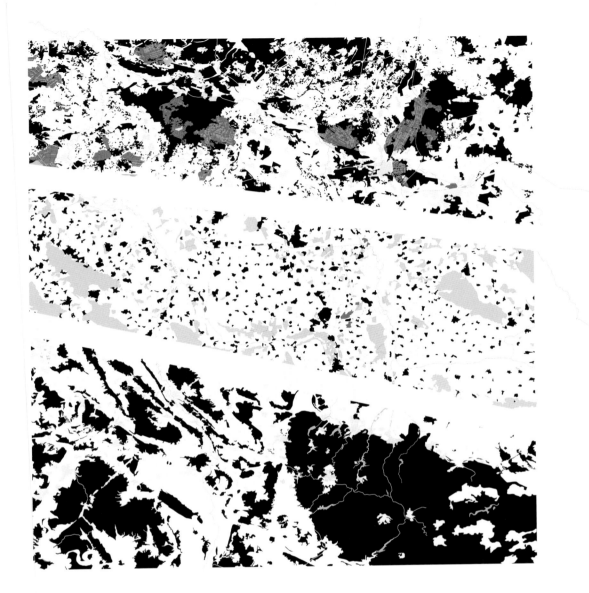

5 *Structural map for the three predominant landscape types.*
5 *Strukturkarte für die drei übergeordneten Landschaftstypen.*

die Darstellung der drei übergeordneten Landschaftstypen des Gesamtraumes innerhalb einer Karte unterschiedlicher Bedeutung der grafischen Elemente bedient.

Durch Hervorhebung oder Weglassen unterschiedlicher Strukturelemente pro Teilraum werden die Teilräume stark kontrastiert, was durch eine Art Inversgrafik bewusst überhöht dargestellt wird: Wälder als raumbildende Elemente sind im nördlichen und südlichen Teilraum schwarz, im zentralen Teilraum zugunsten der Offenheit und Weite des Raumes grau dargestellt. Hier sind die vernetzten Dörfer als prägende Struktur schwarz hervorgehoben. Die räumliche Kontraste hervorhebende Strukturkarte stellt die Ausgangslage für konkrete Raumerkundung und exemplarische „Tiefenbohrungen" vor Ort.

they are presented as grey in the central area in the interests of openness and expanse of space. Here the interlinked villages are highlighted in black as a defining structure. The structural map that highlights spatial contrasts places the starting situation for concrete spatial exploration and exemplary "deep probing" at the location.

A collage as a scenic spatial imagery of the landscape type 2 (fig. 6) can be the result of such a spatial exploration. It brings together aesthetic spatial characteristics, typical spatial activities, and atmospheric phenomena of the Börde landscape in an image, in this way showing concrete locational situations in wider contexts.

Projecting, modeling, and visualizing are part of designing as a knowledge-generating and iterative process. The methods shown here counter the standardization and normalization tendencies in planning with a more in-depth thinking about concrete contexts and qualities. This spatially aesthetic and experimental methodology is part of a reflexive, yet also deductive and inductive, process of knowledge generation.[8] Modeling, in particular, makes it possible to integrate designing advantageously into a scientific context and to open up a concrete scope for thoughts and possibilities.

6 Collage of scenic spatial imagery of the landscape type 2.
6 *Collage aus szenischem Raumbild des Landschaftstypus 2.*

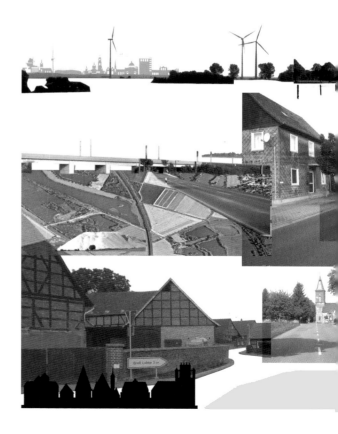

Eine Collage als szenisches Raumbild des Landschaftstypus 2 (Abb. 6) kann Ergebnis einer solchen Raumerkundung sein. Sie versammelt raumästhetische Merkmale, raumtypische Aktivitäten und atmosphärische Phänomene der Bördelandschaft in einem Bild und veranschaulicht auf diese Weise konkrete örtliche Situationen in größeren Kontexten.

Projizieren, Modellieren und Visualisieren sind Teil eines Entwerfens als erkenntnisgenerierender und iterativer Prozess. Die aufgezeigten Methoden stellen den Standardisierungs- und Normierungstendenzen in der Planung ein vertieftes Nachdenken über konkrete Kontexte und Qualitäten gegenüber. Diese raumästhetische und experimentelle Methodik ist Teil eines reflexiven, gleichzeitig deduktiven wie auch induktiven Prozesses der Wissensgenerierung.[8] Insbesondere das Modellieren erlaubt es, Entwerfen gewinnbringend in einen wissenschaftlichen Kontext zu integrieren und konkrete Denk- und Möglichkeitsräume zu eröffnen.

CROSSING BORDERS ONCE AGAIN

MICHAEL KOCH

Crossing borders—this was the impetus that led to the "invention" of the International Doctoral College "Spatial Research Lab" (IDK) around 2005 and the ensuing development of the first curriculum in 2007 to 2011: the program was to try to cross national, disciplinary, and planning culture borders together in a research process, which proved to be a challenge. The first two rounds of IDK have been documented;[1] here, we present the third volume. In volume 1, I had argued for a pragmatic use of new terms for urban design and research, because playful attempts at a probing reorientation of the urbanistic disciplines appeared helpful.[2]

In volume 2, I tried in the context of the discussions within the IDK to qualify our disciplinary border experiences in relation to the increasingly evident necessity, in view of the unsolved environmental and urban development problems, to cross the borders of existing knowledge, responsibilities, and methods. The postulations of the geological era of the Anthropoecene (Paul Critzen), as well as of a "transformative science"[3] prompted me at the time to postulate a "disciplinary reinvention"[4] of urbanistic disciplines.

With the following essay, I am building on this. My observation is that practice lags behind the lofty postulations of multidisciplinary, interdisciplinary, and transdisciplinary work. This causes me, against the background of some other "border experiences" parallel to the IDK, to advocate further experimental border-crossing urban practices.

Communication attempts

In 2016, my team at the HCU and I were able to organize an interdisciplinary symposium under the title "Crossing Disciplinary Boundaries: New Fields of Work in Urban Design and Urban Research," sponsored by the VW foundation.[5] Around 100 participants from around 30 different professions from the corresponding quite varied fields of urban practice and research worked together for three days. The exchanges of individual experiences culminated in communication about the necessities of new specialist qualifications to solve urban development problems. In view of such diverse professional origins, this communication process naturally proved to be a challenge: each participant put forward experiences and conclusions in their own professionally determined language.

Despite the multitude of voices, the shared finding was that new urban professional fields are not only apparent but have for a long time been a widespread reality—which raises the question as to which training procedures can convey the necessary content and qualifications for this and how one should proceed.

EINMAL MEHR
DIE GRENZEN ÜBERSCHREITEN

MICHAEL KOCH

Grenzen überschreiten – das war der Impetus, der zur „Erfindung" des Internationalen Doktorandenkollegs (IDK) „Forschungslabor Raum" um 2005 und der folgenden Ausschreibung des ersten Curriculums 2007–2011 führte: Zu versuchen, nationale, disziplinäre und planungskulturelle Grenzen gemeinsam forschend zu überschreiten, war Programm und erwies sich als Herausforderung. Die ersten beiden Durchgänge des IDK sind dokumentiert,[1] der dritte Band wird hiermit vorgelegt. In Band 1 hatte ich für eine pragmatische Verwendung neuer Begriffe für das städtebauliche Entwerfen und Forschen geworben, weil mir spielerische Versuche einer suchenden Neuorientierung der urbanistischen Disziplinen hilfreich erschienen.[2]

In Band 2 versuchte ich vor dem Hintergrund der Diskussionen im IDK, unsere disziplinären Grenzerfahrungen einzuordnen in die angesichts ungelöster Umwelt- und Stadtentwicklungsprobleme immer spürbarer werdende Notwendigkeit, die Grenzen von Wissensbeständen, Zuständigkeiten und Methoden zu überschreiten. Die Postulate vom eingetretenen Erdzeitalter des Anthropozän (Paul Crutzen) sowie zu einer „Transformativen Wissenschaft"[3] veranlassten mich damals, eine „Disziplinäre Wieder-Er-Findung"[4] von urbanistischen Disziplinen zu postulieren.

Mit dem folgenden Essay knüpfe ich daran an. Meine Beobachtung ist, dass die Praxis den hehren Postulaten zu multi-, inter- und transdisziplinärer Arbeit hinterherhinkt. Das veranlasst mich vor dem Hintergrund einiger anderer „Grenzerfahrungen" parallel zu den IDK für weitere experimentelle grenzüberschreitende urbane Praktiken zu werben.

Verständigungsversuche

2016 konnten mein Team an der HCU und ich ein von der VW-Stiftung gefördertes interdisziplinäres Symposium unter dem Titel „Crossing disciplinary boundaries. New fields of work in urban design and urban research" organisieren.[5] Etwa 100 Teilnehmende aus rund 30 unterschiedlichen Berufen mit entsprechend sehr verschiedenen urbanen Praxis- und Forschungsfeldern arbeiteten drei Tage zusammen. Der Austausch über eigene Erfahrungen mündete in eine Verständigung über Notwendigkeiten neuer fachlicher Qualifikationen zur Lösung urbaner Entwicklungsprobleme. Angesichts der so unterschiedlichen beruflichen Herkunft erwies sich dieser Verständigungsprozess nachvollziehbarer Weise als Herausforderung: Jede*r erläuterte in der eigenen, beruflich bedingten Sprache Erfahrungen und Schlussfolgerungen.

Bei aller Vielstimmigkeit war der gemeinsame Befund: Neue urbane Berufsfelder zeichnen sich nicht nur ab, sondern sind längst verbreitete Realität –

New fields of work

In 2018, we were able to summarize the experiences, points of view, and postulations of the symposium with numerous participants in a book with the title *New Urban Professions: A Journey through Practice and Theory*.[6] The questioning of one's own professional relevance and of sole responsibility proves by all means to also be a personal challenge: "But to organize and keep this process constructive, it requires a special trust base: the aim of new urban professions uniting our disciplinary knowledge stokes fear among the old urban professions of becoming less important."[7]

New fields of work of cooperative and coproductive urban change and urban design often move nowadays very far outside of the respective formalized planning routine and tools and thus do without the certainty and legal security that these promise. The give and take in the necessary negotiation processes places demands on the trust potential of all those involved and must be agreed reliably. Not only must the processes and procedures be thought out, but the planning tools must be reviewed, adjusted, and reinvented in view of the tasks to be solved. The new connection between work process and plan culminates among other things in the proposition of a "performative plan."[8]

Right to the city

Henri Lefebvre's postulation of a *Right to the City* (1968) as a right to participation in the shaping of the transforming urban everyday life also accompanies discussions in Latin America up until today. The resulting necessity of a disciplinary reorientation was also discussed from 2009 on as part of a cooperation between HCU and the University of São Paulo/São Carlos and other universities in the city.[9]

One of our Brazilian colleagues postulated later on this subject: "Challenged by huge urban problems in São Paulo, we discuss that urbanism must be seen not as a specialization but as a field of activity, where not only architects and town planners are involved, but economists, anthropologists, engineers, etc. also act. And especially in today's reality, real estate market agents, legislators, administrators and public managers." And: "To be successful, these different professionals must work together in a co-productive way: interpretations and urbanistic proposals can only be fostered in a manner consistent with the joint participation of representatives of the public administration, the private sector, and civil society."[10]

In February 2019, the Escola da Cidade (São Paulo) issued invitations to the XIV International Seminar under the title "Still the Right to the City?" In view of the increasing problems of the city and a flagrant fainting to counter them possible new urban approaches were discussed based on international examples.

Learning from …?

The current conditions of urban development in São Paulo and the responding search for disciplinary answers recall the disciplinary differentiation

was die Fragen aufwirft, welche Ausbildungsgänge die dafür notwendigen Inhalte und Qualifikationen vermitteln könnten und wie dies geschehen sollte.

Neue Arbeitsfelder

2018 konnten wir die Erfahrungen, Positionen und Postulate des Symposiums mit zahlreichen Teilnehmenden in einem Buch mit dem Titel *New urban Professions – A Journey through Practice and Theory*[6] zusammenfassen. Das Infragestellen der eigenen professionellen Relevanz und der alleinigen Zuständigkeit erweist sich durchaus auch als persönliche Herausforderung: „But to organize and keep this process constructive, it requires a special trust base: the aim of new urban professions uniting our disciplinary knowledge stokes fear among the old urban professions of becoming less important."[7]

Neue Arbeitsfelder der kooperativen und koproduktiven Stadtveränderung und Stadtgestaltung bewegen sich heute häufig sehr weit außerhalb der jeweiligen formalisierten Planungsroutine und -instrumente und entbehren damit der von diesen versprochenen Gewissheit und rechtlichen Sicherheit. Das Geben und Nehmen in den notwendigen Aushandlungsprozessen fordert das Vertrauenspotenzial aller Beteiligten heraus und muss verlässlich verabredet werden.

Nicht nur die Prozesse und Verfahren müssen überdacht werden, sondern auch die planerischen Instrumente sind im Hinblick auf die zu lösenden Aufgaben zu überdenken, neu zu justieren und auch neu zu erfinden. Der neue Zusammenhang von Arbeitsprozess und Plan mündet unter anderem in die These von einem „performativen Plan".[8]

Recht auf Stadt

Henri Lefebvres Postulat eines *Recht auf Stadt* (1968) als Recht auf Teilhabe am und Mitgestaltung vom sich transformierenden urbanen Alltag begleitet bis heute auch die Diskussionen in Lateinamerika. Die sich daraus ergebende Notwendigkeit einer disziplinären Neuorientierung diskutierten wir ab 2009 auch im Rahmen einer Kooperation zwischen der HCU und der Universität von São Paulo/Sao Carlos und weiteren Universitäten in der Stadt.[9]

Einer unserer brasilianischen Kolleg*innen postulierte dazu später: „Challenged by huge urban problems in São Paulo, we discuss that urbanism must be seen not as a specialization but as a field of activity, where not only architects and town planners are involved, but economists, anthropologists, engineers, etc. also act. And especially in today's reality, real estate market agents, legislators, administrators and public managers." Und: „To be sucessfull, these different professionals must work together in a coproductive way: interpretations and urbanistic proposals can only be forstered in a manner consistent with the joint participation of representatives of the public administration, the private sector, and civil society."[10]

Im Februar 2019 lud die Escola da Cidade (São Paulo) unter dem Titel „Still the Right to the City?" zum XIV. International-Seminar ein. Angesichts der

process in Europe. This ultimately culminated in the 1970s in the introduction of a wide variety of (city/space) planning study courses, which also resulted in a differentiation of planning management. And today various master's programs document the search for suitable urban answers to city development problems. The planning postulate of "inward development" is demanding once again in Europe that planning disciplines be rethought. "Inward development" means the consideration of structural, cultural and socioeconomic given urban circumstances. It requires situational targeted work and the productive incorporation of civil society into urban transformation processes in the interests of joint work processes of all relevant parties.

Learning from … the city as it is

Under this title, in October 2019 we (my colleague Bernd Kniess from HCU and I) organized, together with colleagues from various universities in São Paulo, under the lead of Renato Anelli USP São Carlos, a workshop with students as a contribution to the XII International Architecture Biennial held there, with the motto "Every Day." The workshop confronted once again the chasm between the visions and plans of the architects and planners, how the city should be developed and how it should look, and the evident persistent reality of the city. And within the boundaries of the disciplinary methods and tools, it sought to understand this reality and bring about lasting targeted change.

Of course, it continues to be necessary to work out scenarios, designs, and strategies for a city that is "better," i.e., sustainable in a wider sense. However, they must be developed in a new manner in connection with the everyday urban practice of the people living and working in the city. In the end, it is about a transformation process that can only succeed if one really understands the "city as it is," its inherent strengths. It sounds obvious, almost trite, but it appears to be difficult.

The excursions of students as part of the aforementioned workshop became astounding journeys of discovery. And they were confronted once again with the question of how to communicate successfully to understand and change the city. "In short, the challenge is to construct a transdisciplinary narrative to try to develop a capacity for cross-cutting articulation from this common field that is the city. A curiosity: in the face of this task, the question of language is, little by little, imposed as a central challenge."[11]

More experiments

Informal planning processes are undertakings full of conceptual, regulatory, and instrumental uncertainties. However, as experimental and situational special formats, they also have a high identification potential. Genius loci and "inherent logic" (Martina Löw) feed stories anchored in social space. These can nourish the necessary trust to navigate in the informal archipelago of uncertainty. Informal processes can become moments for breaking new ground in the realm of civil society. The integrity of urban

zunehmenden Probleme der Stadt und einer grassierenden Ohnmacht, ihnen zu begegnen, wurden anhand internationaler Beispiele mögliche neue urbanistische Ansatzpunkte diskutiert.

Lernen von …?

Die aktuellen Bedingungen der Stadtentwicklung in São Paulo und die darauf reagierende Suche nach disziplinären Antworten erinnern an den disziplinären Differenzierungsprozess in Europa. Dieser mündete in den 1970er Jahren schließlich in die Einführung unterschiedlichster (Stadt-/Raum-)Planungsstudiengänge, die sich auch in einer Ausdifferenzierung der Planungsverwaltungen niederschlugen. Und heute dokumentieren verschiedene Masterprogramme die Suche nach angemessenen urbanistischen Antworten auf die Stadtentwicklungsprobleme.

Das Planungspostulat der Innenentwicklung fordert in Europa erneut dazu heraus, die Planungsdisziplinen zu überdenken. Innenentwicklung bedeutet Auseinandersetzung mit baulichen, kulturellen und sozioökonomischen urbanen Beständen. Sie erfordert situative Maßarbeit und den produktiven Einbezug der Zivilgesellschaft in urbane Transformationsprozesse in Richtung gemeinsamer Arbeitsprozesse sämtlicher relevanter Akteur*innen.

Learning from … the city as it is

Unter diesem Titel organisierten wir (mein Kollege Bernd Kniess von der HCU und ich) zusammen mit Kolleg*innen verschiedener Universitäten in São Paulo unter Federführung von Renato Anelli USP São Carlos im Oktober 2019 einen Workshop mit Studierenden als Beitrag zur dortigen XII. Internationalen Architekturbiennale, die das Motto „Every Day" trug. Der Workshop konfrontierte erneut mit der Kluft zwischen den Visionen und Plänen der Architektenschaft und Planenden, wie die Stadt entwickelt werden und aussehen sollte, und der offensichtlich persistenten Realität der Stadt. Und er konfrontierte mit den Grenzen der disziplinären Methoden und Instrumente, diese Realität zu verstehen und gezielt dauerhaft zu verändern.

Selbstverständlich ist es nach wie vor notwendig, Szenarien, Entwürfe und Strategien für eine „bessere", also im umfassenden Sinne nachhaltige, Stadt zu erarbeiten. Aber sie müssen auf eine neue Art mit der alltäglichen urbanen Praxis der in der Stadt lebenden und arbeitenden Menschen verbunden beziehungsweise daraus entwickelt werden. Schließlich geht es um einen Transformationsprozess, der nur gelingen kann, wenn man die „Stadt, wie sie ist", die ihr innewohnenden Kräfte wirklich versteht. Klingt eigentlich selbstverständlich, fast banal, scheint aber schwer zu sein.

Die Exkursionen von Studierenden im Rahmen des oben erwähnten Workshops wurden zu erschütternden Entdeckungsreisen. Und sie konfrontierten erneut mit der Frage, wie uns die Verständigung beim Verstehen und bei der Veränderung der Stadt gelingen könnte: „In short, the challenge is to construct a transdiciplinary narrative to try to develop a capacity for crosscutting articulation from this common field that is the city. A curiosity:

practitioners is characterized by a recognizable attitude to communal and social values as well as by the ability to produce convincing sustainable work. These are personal competences that can only be acquired, developed further, and become relevant/effective in urban practice. Education must include the necessary links to practice so that the students can learn these competences.

When Georg Franck postulates the "urban commons," or if the commons are repeatedly brought up in urban discourse, then traditional social negotiation processes regarding the individual use of communal or public assets are discussed as possible references for future regulation processes in our urban societies.[12]

This evokes the utopia of the "free agreement" as a regulation mode of an anarchic society free of violence. The actions of the Situationists of the 1970s were inspired by this. Today a situational deregulation of obstructive regulations and a locally negotiated and agreed re-regulation could contribute to the creation of necessary laboratory and experience spaces—and thus show perspectives for the solution of concrete urban problems.

in the face of this task, the question of language is, little by little, imposed as a central challenge."[11]

Mehr Experimente

Informelle Planungsprozesse sind Unternehmungen voller konzeptioneller, regulativer und instrumenteller Ungewissheiten. Als experimentelle und situative Sonderformate besitzen sie aber auch ein hohes Identifikationspotenzial. Genius Loci und „Eigenlogik" (Martina Löw) speisen sozialräumlich verankerte Geschichten. Diese können das notwendige Vertrauen nähren, um im informellen Archipel der Ungewissheit zu navigieren. Informelle Prozesse können zu Momenten des Aufbruchs in zivilgesellschaftliche „Neuländer" werden. Die Integrität urbaner Praktiker*innen zeichnet sich ebenso durch eine erkennbare Haltung zu gemeinschaftlichen und gesellschaftlichen Werten aus wie durch die Fähigkeit, nachhaltige Überzeugungsarbeit zu leisten. Das sind persönliche Kompetenzen, die nur in der urbanen Praxis erworben, weiterentwickelt und relevant/wirksam werden können. Die Ausbildung muss die notwendigen Praxisbezüge aufweisen, damit die Studierenden diese Kompetenzen erlernen können.

Wenn Georg Franck die „urbane Allmende" postuliert oder im urbanistischen Diskurs immer wieder die *commons* beschworen werden, so werden damit tradierte gesellschaftliche Aushandlungsprozesse über die individuelle Nutzung und den Gebrauch gemeinschaftlicher oder öffentlicher Güter als mögliche Referenzen für zukünftige Regelungsprozesse in unseren Stadtgesellschaften diskutiert.[12]

Darin klingt die Utopie der „freien Vereinbarung" als Regelungsmodus einer gewaltfreien anarchistischen Gesellschaft an. Die Aktionen der Situationist*innen der 1970er Jahre waren davon beseelt. Heute könnte eine situative Deregulierung hinderlicher Vorschriften und eine vor Ort ausgehandelte und vereinbarte Re-Regulierung zur Schaffung notwendiger Labor- und Erfahrungsräume beitragen – und so Perspektiven zur Lösung konkreter urbaner Probleme aufzeigen.

Patras, November 2017

A PROPAEDEUTIC FOR THE INTERNATIONAL DOCTORAL COLLEGE?

WALTER SCHÖNWANDT

The International Doctoral College "Spatial Research Lab" has now completed several rounds. In light of this, the question has arisen: for which themes was a great deal of time regularly lost, so that for example a propaedeutic could help in future to "get to the point quicker"? As there is only space for 10,000 characters available for this section, the topic touched on here can only be an extract and discussed according to a few examples, so the subject is by no means exhaustive. The purpose is not to discuss the respective themes in detail in every dissertation. The task is more to include and emphasize what is necessary for the handling of one's own dissertation topic. The doctoral students should at least know what these topics harbor so that they do not embark "on the wrong track" in their argumentation.

In the following, the four topics of "planning," "difference between word and concept," "facts," and "architectural or physical determinism" are presented for discussion—as examples.

Planning

The question "What is spatial planning?" is the basic question about the core content of the entire profession. Explaining and reflecting on one's own planning concept—this means the thought patterns with which one approaches planning tasks—are often integral to a dissertation. What should such a planning concept include? It should show (i) which elements/components play a role in planning, (ii) how they are structurally connected, as well as what interrelations there are between them, (iii) how planning proceeds, and (iv) what relation all this has to its respective environment. It is important in this regard to emphasize that the striving for reflection is only possible if there is an explicit answer to the question "What is planning?" This means that the doctoral students are able to explicitly describe their specific answer to the question "What is planning?"—in other words, their respective planning concept (of which there could also be several). The benefit of this explicitness becomes clear if one considers that what is implicit is difficult to analyze, compare, test, improve, or communicate. This means that planning concepts that are only used intuitively but are not clearly formulated are not suitably for analysis and consequently for further development and improvement—precisely because they are only used subconsciously.

However, those who engage with the subject will establish that the current discourses in planning theory only help to a limited extent here: the

EIN PROPÄDEUTIKUM FÜR DAS INTERNATIONALE DOKTORANDENKOLLEG?

WALTER SCHÖNWANDT

Das Internationale Doktorandenkolleg (IDK) „Forschungslabor Raum" hat inzwischen mehrere Durchgänge absolviert. Vor diesem Hintergrund fragen manche: Bei welchen Themen wurde des Öfteren viel Zeit verloren, sodass beispielsweise ein Propädeutikum in Zukunft dabei helfen könnte, schneller auf den Punkt zu kommen? Da der für den vorliegenden Abschnitt zur Verfügung stehende Platz nur 10.000 Schriftzeichen umfasst, kann das hiermit angerissene Themenfeld nur ausschnittartig und anhand einiger Beispielthemen andiskutiert werden, die Themenliste ist also keinesfalls abschließend. Auch geht es nicht darum, in jeder Dissertation die nachfolgenden Themen ausführlich abzuhandeln. Die Aufgabe ist vielmehr, nur das, was für die Bearbeitung des eigenen Dissertationsthemas notwendig ist, zu durchdringen und aufzunehmen. Zumindest sollten die Promovierenden wissen, was es mit diesen Themen auf sich hat, damit sie argumentativ nicht auf ein „falsches Gleis" geraten.

Nachfolgend werden – als Beispiele – die vier Themen „Planung", „Unterschied zwischen Wort und Begriff", „Fakten" sowie „architektonischer bzw. physikalischer Determinismus" zur Diskussion gestellt.

Planung

Die Frage „Was ist räumliche Planung?" ist die grundlegende Frage nach dem inhaltlichen Kern der gesamten Profession. Den eigenen Planungsbegriff – damit sind die Denkmuster gemeint, mit denen man an Planungsaufgaben herangeht – zu erläutern und zu reflektieren, ist sehr oft Bestandteil einer Dissertation. Was sollte ein solcher Planungsbegriff enthalten? Er sollte aufzeigen, (i) welche Elemente/Komponenten beim Planen eine Rolle spielen, (ii) wie sie strukturell zusammenhängen sowie welche Wechselwirkungen zwischen ihnen bestehen, (iii) wie Planung abläuft und (iv) wie all dies in Beziehung zum jeweiligen Umfeld steht. Wesentlich in diesem Zusammenhang ist, hervorzuheben, dass die angestrebte Reflexion nur dann möglich ist, wenn es eine *explizite* Antwort auf die Frage „Was ist Planung?" gibt; das heißt, wenn die Promovierenden in der Lage sind, ihre spezifische Antwort auf die Frage „Was ist Planung?", also ihren jeweiligen Planungsbegriff (wobei es auch mehrere sein können), *explizit* zu beschreiben. Der Nutzen dieses Explizit-Machens wird klar, wenn man sich vergegenwärtigt, dass Implizites nur schwerlich analysiert, verglichen, getestet, verbessert oder kommuniziert werden kann. Das heißt, Planungsbegriffe, die nur intuitiv benutzt, aber nicht nachvollziehbar formuliert werden, sind – eben weil sie

"rational planning concept" (also referred to as "rational planning model") has long been considered outdated and standpoints such as "planning is communication" and "planning is strategy" emerge as too abstract and lacking in detail. Upon closer observation, it becomes evident that there are only very few explicit, structured planning concepts.

Consequently, some doctoral students are surprised when they realize that they—even if they often work very successfully in planning practice—do not have their own adequate, explicit, and structured planning concept.

Difference between word and concept

The fact that a definition is necessary for the stated term "planning"—needless to say not just for this one—is easier to understand if one considers one of the central postulations of semantics, which states that one must distinguish between a word (language/signs), for example the letter combination "p-l-a-n-n-i-n-g," and what is meant with the word, meaning the corresponding concept. What is important is that only what is meant, namely the concept, is the bearer of content, meaning, and substance, not the word itself. The consequence: only an explicit definition of a concept (this must have a defined core, without sharp edges) makes it clear and understandable and gives language—i.e., words—a meaning, content, and substance. Words alone and per se—without the explicit definition with the corresponding concept—are lacking in substance and meaning for the listener or reader in the sense that one does not grasp the definition of the concept that the speaker or author meant and intended. If listeners/readers nevertheless have the feeling that they have understood what the speaker/author wants to say in terms of content, this is because they themselves automatically and subconsciously attribute their own concept definition to the respective word. However, this own concept definition may not correspond to what the speaker/author actually means and wants to convey. This leads—once again virtually automatically—to many misunderstandings. Overall, this situation has something of the grotesque, because the substantial content is not generated by the speaker/author but by the listeners/readers—a topsy-turvy world, so to speak.

If a speaker/author is not capable, even on request, to define a certain concept, then in fact they do not know themselves what they are talking about, no matter how many words they utter in relation to it.

It is also important to note on the subject of concepts that it is not a "purely academic" playing with words. The relevance of this topic is evident in the fact that concepts are not only, as described above, the carriers of our knowledge but also guide as such our planning and actions.

This means: if the concepts are not adequately defined, listeners/readers can only speculate what a speaker/author may have meant with a certain concept. Consequently, discussions often drag on. In such cases, one should steer the discussion in another direction or else call it to a halt due to a lack of substance.

nur unbewusst angewandt werden – für eine Analyse und in der Folge für eine Weiterentwicklung und Verbesserung nicht zugänglich.

Doch wer sich mit diesem Thema befasst, stellt fest, dass die aktuellen Diskurse in der Planungstheorie hier nur bedingt weiterhelfen: Der „rationale Planungsbegriff" (er wird auch als „rationales Planungsmodell" bezeichnet) gilt seit Langem als veraltet, und Positionen wie „Planung ist Kommunikation" und „Planung ist Strategie" entpuppen sich als zu abstrakt und detailarm. Bei genauerer Betrachtung zeigt sich, dass es nur sehr wenige explizite, strukturierte Planungsbegriffe gibt.

Entsprechend sind manche Promovierenden überrascht, wenn sie erkennen, dass sie – auch wenn sie in der Planungspraxis oft sehr erfolgreich arbeiten – über keinen eigenen zureichenden, expliziten und strukturierten Planungsbegriff verfügen.

Unterschied zwischen Wort und Begriff

Dass es bei dem genannten Begriff „Planung" – aber selbstredend nicht nur bei diesem – etwas zu definieren gibt, ist leichter zu verstehen, wenn man sich eine der zentralen Thesen der Semantik vergegenwärtigt, die besagt, dass man zwischen einem Wort (Sprache/Zeichen), zum Beispiel der Buchstabenkombination „P-l-a-n-u-n-g", und dem mit diesem Wort Gemeinten, das heißt dem entsprechenden Begriff, unterscheiden muss. Wichtig ist, dass nur das Gemeinte, also der Begriff, Träger von Inhalt, Sinn und Substanz ist, nicht das Wort selbst. Die Folge: Erst eine explizite Definition eines Begriffs (dies geht nur kernprägnant, nie randscharf) macht selbigen klar und verständlich, und gibt der Sprache – also den Worten – Sinn, Inhalt und Substanz. Worte alleine und per se – ohne die explizite Definition des entsprechenden Begriffs – sind für Zuhörer*innen oder Leser*innen substanz- und sinnlos in dem Sinne, dass man die Definition des Begriffs nicht erfährt, die der oder die Redner*in oder Autor*in gemeint und zugrunde gelegt hat. Wenn Zuhörer*innen/Leser*innen trotzdem das Gefühl haben, sie hätten verstanden, was die Redner*innen/Autor*innen inhaltlich sagen wollen, so liegt dies daran, dass sie selbst dem entsprechenden Wort quasi automatisch und unbewusst *ihre eigene* Begriffsdefinition hinzufügen. Diese eigene Begriffsdefinition muss aber keineswegs derjenigen entsprechen, die der oder die Redner*in/Autor*in tatsächlich meint und übermitteln will. Auf diese Art und Weise entstehen – wiederum quasi automatisch – viele Missverständnisse. Insgesamt hat diese Situation freilich etwas Groteskes, weil die substantiellen Inhalte nicht von Redner*innen/Autor*innen erzeugt werden, sondern von den Zuhörer*innen/Leser*innen – verkehrte Welt sozusagen.

Wenn ein*e Redner*in/Autor*in auch auf Nachfragen nicht in der Lage ist, einen bestimmten Begriff zu definieren, dann weiß er/sie genaugenommen selbst nicht, wovon er/sie redet, egal, wie viele Worte er/sie im jeweiligen Zusammenhang äußert.

Wesentlich ist zudem, festzuhalten, dass es beim Thema Begriffe nicht um eine „rein akademische" Wortklauberei geht. Die Relevanz dieses Themenbereichs ergibt sich aus der Tatsache, dass Begriffe nicht nur, wie oben

In my experience, doctoral students are often irritated if one asks them what the key concepts they used actually specifically mean.

Facts

It is not rare for doctoral students to believe in "impartial, hard facts." This is scarcely surprising, after all, even at the "March for Science" in April 2017, posters were presented with the slogan "There are no alternatives to facts." Many therefore have difficulty with the realization that facts are not so straightforward. Scientific theory established a long time ago that, for example, the following sentence is not founded: "One can establish undeniable 'hard facts' in the world out there." The following sentence, on the other hand, gets to the heart of the problem: "It is impossible to ascertain states of affairs ('facts') independently of any valuation."

Often borne by false expectations in the beginning, doctoral students are often at a loss as to how they should handle these matters in their dissertation.

Architectural or physical determinism

Planners design physical-material spaces. As a rule, they do this to create advantageous environmental conditions for people/creatures. It is therefore no wonder that often among planners the idea of what is often called "architectural" or "physical determinism" emerges which, expressed in a simplified manner, is reflected in the following sentence: "If I design the physical-material space in such and such a fashion, I will directly achieve a certain intended effect on the person/user, namely in the form of a certain perception or a specific behavior." The underlying hypothesis "the physical-material situation X results in the perception/behavior Y among people" is, however, not very convincing. Instead it should be: "the physical-material situation X occasionally results in the perception/behavior Y among some people, but only in combination with other factors such as prior experiences, moods, etc. of the respective person, as well as in quite a specific environment and factors such as cultural or legal framework conditions, time budget, financial budget, etc. In addition, there are circumstantial constellations in which the physical-material situation X can also result in non-Y, in other words the opposite."

The following arguments go against "architectural" or "physical determinism." (i) There is no viable empirical evidence. (ii) From a theoretical perspective, there are also counterarguments, with Bunge reminding us in relation to the principle of cause and effect (causality) of the following: "The causal relation (or nexus) holds exclusively between events. Hence, to say that a thing causes another, or that it causes a process ... involves misusing the word 'cause.' ... Caution: only events or processes can be causally related. Hence it is just a mistake to assert that the brain causes the mind as it is to say that the legs causes the walking."[1] The physical-material is therefore left out as a monocausal trigger. He clarifies accordingly: "there are no causae materiales."[2] This also becomes clear if one considers the smallest units of causes (as the

beschrieben, die Träger unseres Wissens sind, sondern als solche auch unsere Planungen sowie Handlungen steuern.

Das heißt: Werden die Begriffe nicht hinreichend definiert, können Zuhörer*innen/Leser*innen nur darüber spekulieren, was ein*e Redner*in/Autor*in mit einem bestimmten Begriff gemeint haben könnte. In der Folge ziehen sich Diskussionen nicht selten in die Länge. In solchen Fällen sollte man den Diskurs umkrempeln oder wegen fehlender Substanz abbrechen.

Erfahrungsgemäß sind Doktorand*innen nicht selten gehörig irritiert, wenn man sie fragt, was die von ihnen verwendeten Schlüsselbegriffe eigentlich konkret bedeuten.

Fakten

Nicht wenige Doktorand*innen glauben an „wertfreie, harte Fakten". Das ist kaum verwunderlich, schließlich wurden selbst auf dem „March for Science" im April 2017 Plakate mit der Aufschrift „Zu Fakten gibt es keine Alternativen" präsentiert. Viele tun sich deshalb schwer mit der Erkenntnis, dass das mit den Fakten nicht so einfach ist. Seit Langem hat die Wissenschaftstheorie nämlich klargestellt, dass beispielsweise folgender Satz unzutreffend ist: „Man kann unbezweifelbare *harte Fakten*' in der Welt da draußen feststellen." Das Problem auf den Punkt bringt hingegen folgender Satz: „Eine von einer Bewertung unabhängige Feststellung von Sachverhalten (,Fakten') ist nicht möglich."

Anfangs von falschen Vorstellungen getragen, sind Doktorand*innen häufig ratlos, wie sie mit diesem Themenkomplex in ihrer Dissertation umgehen sollen.

Architektonischer beziehungsweise physikalischer Determinismus

Planer*innen gestalten physisch-materielle Räume. Sie tun dies in aller Regel, um günstige Umgebungsbedingungen für Menschen/Lebewesen zu schaffen. Von daher nimmt es nicht wunder, dass unter Planer*innen nicht selten die Idee des sogenannten „architektonischen" beziehungsweise „physikalischen Determinismus" auftaucht, die sich, vereinfacht ausgedrückt, in folgendem Satz widerspiegelt: „Wenn ich den physisch-materiellen Raum so und so gestalte, erziele ich beim Menschen/Nutzenden damit direkt und unmittelbar eine bestimmte von mir gewollte Wirkung, und zwar in Form einer bestimmten Wahrnehmung oder eines bestimmten Verhaltens." Die zugrundeliegende These „Die physisch-materielle Situation X bewirkt bei Menschen die Wahrnehmung / das Verhalten Y" indes ist wenig überzeugend. Sie müsste vielmehr lauten: „Die physisch-materielle Situation X bewirkt bei manchen Menschen hin und wieder die Wahrnehmung / das Verhalten Y, dies aber auch nur in Kombination mit anderen Faktoren wie Vorerfahrungen, Stimmungen etc. der jeweiligen Person, sowie im einem ganz bestimmten Umfeld wie kulturellen oder gesetzlichen Rahmenbedingungen, Zeitbudget, Finanzbudget etc. Zudem gibt es Ereigniskonstellationen, in

instigators of causality), namely "triggering signals," such as a verbal or written prompt to a person, and "energy transfers," as the physical-material—per se—does not send triggering signals nor does it induce energy transfers. A number of discussions at the doctoral college would have run more efficiently if these associations and in particular the resulting consequences had been explained at the outset.

What could be further candidates for a propaedeutic? Some sample topics: What is theory? Is there planning practice at all without theory? What are planning approaches? What are the tools of spatial planning? What is problem-oriented planning? What is strategy? What is space? As well as the subject of methods such as: How does one carry out a case study? How does one execute a survey?—and an array of further topics.

denen die physisch-materielle Situation X durchaus auch Non-Y, also das Gegenteil, bewirken kann."

Folgende Argumente sprechen gegen den „architektonischen" beziehungsweise „physikalischen Determinismus". (i) Es gibt dafür keine belastbaren empirischen Belege. (ii) Auch aus theoretischer Perspektive gibt es Gegenargumente, so erinnert Bunge in Bezug auf das Prinzip von Ursache und Wirkung (Kausalität) an Folgendes: „The causal relation (or nexus) holds exclusively between events. Hence, to say that a thing causes another, or that it causes a process …, involves misusing the word ‚cause'. … Caution: only events or processes can be causally related. Hence it is just a mistake to assert that the brain causes the mind as it is to say that the legs causes the walking."[1] Damit ist das Physisch-Materielle als monokausaler Auslöser außen vor. Entsprechend stellt er klar: „[…] es gibt keine causae materiales."[2] Dies wird auch deutlich, wenn man die kleinsten Einheiten von Ursachen (als Auslöser von Kausalität) betrachtet, nämlich „auslösende Signale", etwa ein mündlicher oder schriftlicher Auftrag an eine Person, und „Energietransfers", schließlich sendet Physisch-Materielles – per se – weder auslösende Signale, noch induziert es Energietransfers.

So manche Diskussion im Doktorandenkolleg wäre effizienter verlaufen, wenn diese Zusammenhänge sowie insbesondere die sich daraus ergebenden Konsequenzen anfangs erläutert worden wären.

Was könnten weitere Kandidaten für ein Propädeutikum sein? Einige Beispielthemen: Was ist Theorie? Gibt es überhaupt Planungspraxis ohne Theorie? Was sind Planungsansätze (planning approaches)? Was sind die Instrumente der räumlichen Planung? Was ist problemorientierte Planung? Was ist Strategie? Was ist Raum? Aber unter anderem auch Methodenthemen wie: Wie macht man eine Fallstudie? Wie macht man eine Befragung?

CROSSING BORDERS: THEMES AND TOPICS

THEMENSPEKTRUM CROSSING BORDERS

BORDER INDEX—
INDEX OF BORDERS

This index is a joint text collection by the doctoral students of the International Doctoral College "Spatial Research Lab" 3 (IDK) beyond borders. But why an index? Index is a widely used term. Here the use of the term is primarily in the sense that a list, a collection, a catalogue is referred to that shows perspectives on borders and crossing them. In relation to the semiotic triangle of Walter Schönwandt, a second level of meaning can be established. Within this construct, an index is a typology that owing to a causal link provides an indication of a specific cause ("Smoke is an index for fire"[1]). This also applies to the following border descriptions: each border indicates specific causes with which they—depending on the perspective—are causally or relationally linked.

Regarding the second notion: border is clearly to be understood here as a construct in the sense of the semiotic triangle. Because all the borders described here, whether transgressed, to be overcome, perceived as blurred, negated, or viewed as necessary, are initially in the "human thinking organ"[2] of the describing person. The respective construct is referred to by means of the written language (that is: language and characters) in these texts. It refers to objects and events that are described in the texts, such as boundary experiences, borderline situations, or limited objects. The constructs may be similar, but they do not necessarily equate. The reason for this can be found both in the different individually gathered experiences and observations as well as in the various learned theoretical knowledge, subject-specific contexts, and terminological understandings of those carrying out the description. This results both in a different language and characters as well as different perspectives. In this sense, bringing the various texts together is an exciting semiotic experiment, because a variety of facets of "border" as a term become clear, a range of propositions are formulated with the term, and quite differing contexts emerge in which borders play a role.

Activating spaces, both in the sense of lastingly improving an unfortunate spatial situation and waking dormant, previously undiscovered spatial usage potential or valorizations, is no doubt the basic motive of all spatial planning disciplines, especially those that have come together at this college. However, addressing this border in planning or research, as well as breaking through, overcoming, or avoiding it, necessitates first of all the acknowledgment of this border. Only then can this border be crossed and only then can further narratives of permeability be developed.

We doctoral students at the college therefore made it our task for this publication to distinctly define acknowledged borders and their possible transgressions in the content considerations of the individual dissertation topic. The gathered border constructs are divided into four categories in the

GRENZINDEX –
INDEX DER GRENZEN

Dieser Index ist eine gemeinsame Textsammlung der Promovierenden des Internationalen Doktorandenkollegs (IDK) „Forschungslabor Raum" 3 über Grenzen. Doch warum Index? Index ist ein sehr vielseitig verwendeter Begriff. Hier erfolgt die Begriffsverwendung in erster Linie in dem Sinne, dass eine Aufzählung, eine Sammlung, ein Katalog bezeichnet wird, der Perspektiven auf Grenzen und ihre Überschreitung aufzeigt.

Es lässt sich bezugnehmend auf das semiotische Dreieck von Walter Schönwandt noch eine zweite Sinnebene feststellen. Innerhalb dieses Konstrukts ist ein Index ein Zeichentypus, der aufgrund einer kausalen Verknüpfung einen Hinweis auf eine bestimmte Ursache gibt („Rauch ist ein Index für Feuer"[1]). Das trifft auch auf die folgenden Grenzbeschreibungen zu: Jede Grenze verweist auf bestimmte Ursachen, mit denen sie – je nach Perspektive – kausal oder relational verknüpft ist.

Zum zweiten Begriff: Grenze ist hier ganz eindeutig als Konstrukt im Sinne des semiotischen Dreiecks zu verstehen. Denn alle der hier beschriebenen Grenzen, ob nun überschrittene, zu überwindende, verschwommen wahrgenommene, negierte oder als notwendig erachtete, befinden sich zunächst einmal im „menschlichen Denkorgan"[2] der beschreibenden Person. Das jeweilige Konstrukt wird mittels geschriebener Sprache (also Sprache und Zeichen) in den hier vorliegenden Texten bezeichnet. Es verweist auf Gegenstände und Ereignisse, die in den Texten beschrieben sind, wie Grenzerfahrungen, Grenzsituationen, begrenzende Objekte. Die Konstrukte mögen sich ähneln, aber sie gleichen sich nicht unbedingt. Die Ursache dafür ist sowohl in den unterschiedlichen selbst gemachten Erfahrungen und Beobachtungen als auch in den verschiedenen erlernten Theoriekenntnissen, fachspezifischen Kontexten und Begriffsverständnissen der Beschreibenden zu finden. Daraus resultieren sowohl eine unterschiedliche Sprache und diverse Zeichen als auch unterschiedliche Perspektiven. So gesehen ist das Zusammenführen der verschiedenen Texte ein spannendes semiotisches Experiment, denn es werden verschiedene Facetten des Begriffs Grenze deutlich, es werden vielfältige Propositionen mit dem Begriff formuliert und ganz unterschiedliche Kontexte erkennbar, in denen Grenzen eine Rolle spielen.

Räume zu aktivieren, sowohl im Sinne eine missliche räumliche Situation nachhaltig zu verbessern als auch schlummernde, bislang unentdeckte räumliche Nutzungsangebote oder In-Wert-Setzungen zu wecken, ist wohl das Grundmotiv aller raumplanerischen Disziplinen, insbesondere jener, die sich in diesem Kolleg begegnet sind. Doch sich mit einer Grenze planerisch oder forschend auseinanderzusetzen, sie zu durchdringen, zu überwinden oder zu vermeiden, setzt zunächst das Erkennen dieser Grenze voraus. Dann erst kann diese Grenze überschritten werden beziehungsweise erst

following index. This index by no means claims to be exhaustive. Even so, this limited selection shows in how many and different ways we approach borders.

The perhaps most important shared insight from these numerous perspectives is that border as a construct always draws a very fine line with an enormous effect between protection and threat, autonomy and dominance, resignation and departure, being closed in or shut out—and that overcoming these borders means changing the status quo.

Changing lifestyles make many spatial border demarcations redundant

A few decades ago, work for the majority of the working population was spatially and temporally bound to the workplace. Today individualized lifestyles and changes in the world of work such as flexible service times, distance work, and mobile work lead to work becoming a part of leisure and the own home. This dissolution of boundaries represents a challenge for the social and spatial organization of work and life.

The boundaries between work and leisure are blurring and changing space
(Lisa Stadtler)

For centuries, the boundary between the city and rural areas was clearly visible. Notions such as *suburbia* or *territories* seek to define and plan the fringes of urban space, in which the boundary between urban and rural areas are increasingly blurred. These spaces are subject to various change dynamics and processes. Digitization, globalization, and extensive logistics infrastructures make planning attention to the urban hinterland more necessary than ever. The seemingly limitless independent logic of the spatial peripheries needs new concepts for placing them in relation to and linking them to the core of the city, in order to be recognized as a living space.

Put the borderlessness of the urban hinterland back into perspective
(Leevke Heeschen)

Within scientific disciplines there are usually special and limited perspectives on research subjects. An interdisciplinary perspective can break through these limitations and fertilize a discipline through new approaches. One example is the cultural dimension of spatial planning, which has been largely neglected for a long time. Especially the influence of organizational, social, and cultural science findings and perspectives could extend the rather inward disciplinary view of planning practice and emphasize planning cultures.

Reintegrate cultural dimensions of planning
(Peter Stroms)

When dealing with landscape(s), we are usually confronted with a subjectivity issue. What we see, and how we see it, is strongly influenced by our cultural background, aesthetic preferences, current state of mind and even viewing aims (or their absence). To overcome these preconditions and thus to adjust to the actual understanding of landscape as a unifying device, or medium, to analyze space, we should strive for a direct but conscious experience of landscape.

Cultivate conscious perception to overcome subjective landscape borders
(Marcello Modica)

dann können weitere Narrative der Durchlässigkeit entwickelt werden. Wir Promovierenden des Kollegs haben es uns deshalb für diese Publikation zur Aufgabe gemacht, in der inhaltlichen Auseinandersetzung mit dem eigenen Dissertationsthema erkannte Grenzen beziehungsweise ihre möglichen Überschreitungen prägnant zu benennen. Die zusammengetragenen Grenzkonstrukte sind im folgenden Index in vier Kategorien gegliedert. Der vorliegende Index erhebt in keiner Weise Anspruch auf Vollständigkeit. Dennoch wird bereits aus dieser überschaubaren Auswahl deutlich, auf wie vielen und unterschiedlichen Wegen wir Grenzen begegnen.

Die wohl wichtigste gemeinsame Erkenntnis aus diesen zahlreichen Perspektiven ist jedoch, dass das Konstrukt Grenze immer einen äußerst schmalen Grat mit enormen Wirkmechanismus markiert zwischen Schutz und Bedrohung, zwischen Autonomie und Herrschaft, zwischen Resignation und Aufbruch, zwischen Eingeschlossen-Sein und Ausgeschlossen-Sein – und dass diese Grenzen zu überwinden, einen Wandel des Bestehenden bedeutet.

Sich verändernde Lebensstile machen viele räumliche Grenzziehungen redundant

Die Grenzen zwischen Arbeit und Freizeit verschwimmen und verändern Raum (Lisa Stadtler)

Vor einigen Jahrzehnten war die Arbeit bei einem Großteil der Erwerbstätigen zeitlich und räumlich an den Betrieb gebunden. Heutzutage führen individualisierte Lebensstile und Veränderungen in der Arbeitswelt wie flexible Dienstzeiten, Telearbeit und mobiles Arbeiten dazu, dass die Erwerbstätigkeit ein Bestandteil der Freizeit und des eigenen Zuhauses wird. Diese Grenzauflösung stellt eine Herausforderung für die gesellschaftliche und räumliche Organisation unserer Arbeits- und Lebenswelt dar.

Grenzenlosigkeiten des urbanen Hinterlandes wieder in Beziehung setzen (Leevke Heeschen)

Über Jahrhunderte war die Grenze zwischen Stadt und Land klar sichtbar. Begriffe wie *Suburbia, Zwischenstadt* oder auch *Territories* versuchen ausfransende urbane Räume, in denen die Grenze zwischen Stadt und Land immer weiter verschwimmt, zu definieren und gleichzeitig planerisch zu fassen. Diese Räume unterliegen diversen Veränderungsdynamiken und -prozessen. Digitalisierung, Globalisierung und raumgreifende Logistikinfrastrukturen machen die planerische Hinwendung zum urbanen Hinterland nötiger denn je. Die scheinbar grenzenlosen Eigenlogiken der räumlichen Versatzstücke brauchen neue Konzepte des In-Bezug-Setzens und der Verknüpfung mit der Kernstadt, um als Lebensraum erkannt zu werden.

Kulturelle Dimensionen von Planung wieder reintegrieren (Peter Stroms)

Innerhalb wissenschaftlicher Disziplinen bestehen meist spezielle und begrenzte Blickwinkel auf Forschungsgegenstände. Ein interdisziplinärer Blick kann diese Begrenztheit durchbrechen und eine Disziplin durch neue Zugänge befruchten. Ein Beispiel stellt die lange weitestgehend vernachlässigte kulturelle Dimension der räumlichen Planung dar. Vor allem der Einfluss organisations-, sozial- und kulturwissenschaftlicher Erkenntnisse und Blickwinkel konnte den eher disziplininternen Blick auf Planungspraxis erweitern und Planungskulturen hervorheben.

"Tricky" problems need a planning culture that overcomes borders

Speed is consciously and subliminally determining current planning: express housing guarantees rapid completion. *Slow urbanism* reacts to small-scale property structures and complex procedures. Delaying tactics, facilitation payments, and building freezes in large projects show that the planning tempo and duration are often underestimated. Interim uses are popular upgrading tools for the economic acceleration of urban spaces. Processes cannot be accelerated and decelerated without consequences: they are ambivalent, move increasingly beyond systemic borders, the exceedance of which must be compensated, synchronized, and balanced.

Flexibilizing the boundaries of planning—learning to oscillate
(Yvonne Siegmund)

Planning influences the ground value—whether it is by building traffic infrastructure, designing open space, or setting usage restrictions through zoning. This raises questions as to a socially just distribution of resulting added and reduced values. The influencing of such distribution mechanisms represents a key task for the planners: countervalues for planning interventions can be demanded by the public that are expected to achieve a benefit for as wide a range of population groups as possible. It is important for planners to sound out and extend the boundaries of these influencing factors.

Sounding out the boundaries of planning to distribute spatial added value fairly
(Roman Streit)

In the Global South, self-building will develop over the next thirty years into the predominant form of urban production, as planning institutions and the real estate market are not capable of covering the demand of wide segments of the population. It is therefore important to anticipate self-building with all its consequences and subsequently to dissolve the boundaries of formal planning tools to adapt them to the requirements and living conditions of those affected.

Dissolving boundaries of formal planning tools to adapt them to informal realities
(Manuel Hauer)

When stakeholders are called to work together, their political and hierarchical mandates create impermeable boundaries, which limit the exchange of ideas and distract them from problem-solving. Even worse, when decision-making is crucial in critical moments, such boundaries limit the potential for holistic approaches to spatial development or cultivate narrow mindsets of those involved in planning. Creating synergies is an answer to bring together stakeholders and the public to discuss and share actions. Even if such a concept often seems impossible, the potential of synergies in the interface of formal and informal responsibility can smooth existing sociopolitical boundaries.

Dissolve limited ways of thinking about planning through synergy processes
(Theodora Papamichail)

Necessary crossings of borders focus not only on urban planning solutions but also on the renewal of framework conditions: structurally, organizationally, and procedurally. The standards of formal urban land-use planning are being increasingly questioned. Knowledge management, organizational learning, and cooperative planning are new challenges for developing in-

Open the framework conditions of borders structurally and organizationally
(Max Haug)

Bewusste Wahr-
nehmung kultivieren,
um subjektive
Landschaftsgrenzen
zu überwinden
(Marcello Modica)

Wenn wir uns mit Landschaft(en) auseinandersetzen, werden wir in der Regel mit einem Subjektivitätsproblem konfrontiert. Was wir sehen und wie wir es sehen, hängt maßgeblich von unserem kulturellen Hintergrund ab, von unseren ästhetischen Präferenzen, unserer gegenwärtigen geistigen Verfassung und unseren (angestrebten oder auch nicht vorhandenen) Zielen. Um diese Voreingenommenheit zugunsten eines Verständnisses von Landschaft als verbindendes Instrument oder Medium zur Analyse von Raum zu überwinden, sollten wir eine direkte, aber bewusste Landschaftserfahrung anstreben.

„Verzwickte" Probleme brauchen eine grenzüberwindende Planungskultur

Grenzen der Planung
flexibilisieren –
Schaukeln lernen
(Yvonne Siegmund)

Bewusst und unterschwellig prägt das Tempo aktuelle Planungen: Expresswohnungen garantieren die zügige Fertigstellung. *Slow urbanism* reagiert auf kleinteilige Eigentumsstrukturen und komplexe Verfahren. Verzögerungstaktiken, Beschleunigungszahlungen und Baustopps in Großprojekten zeigen auf, dass das Planungstempo und die Dauer oft unterschätzt werden. Häufig sind Zwischennutzungen gängige Aufwertungswerkzeuge zur ökonomischen Beschleunigung städtischer Räume. Prozesse sind nicht ohne Abstriche be- und entschleunigbar: Sie sind ambivalent, bewegen sich verstärkt jenseits systemischer Grenzen, deren Überschreitungen kompensiert und synchronisiert, ausgeglichen werden müssen.

Grenzen der Planung
ausloten, um räum-
lichen Mehrwert
gerecht zu verteilen
(Roman Streit)

Planung beeinflusst den Wert des Bodens – sei es durch Schaffung von Verkehrsinfrastruktur, Freiraumgestaltung oder Festlegung von Nutzungsbeschränkungen durch Zonierung. Dies wirft Fragen zu einer gesellschaftlich gerechten Verteilung entstehender Mehr- und Minderwerte auf. Die Einflussnahme auf solche Verteilmechanismen stellt eine Kernaufgabe der Planenden dar: Gegenwerte für Planungseingriffe können durch die öffentliche Hand eingefordert werden, wodurch ein Gewinn für möglichst breite Bevölkerungsgruppen erzielt wird. Grenzen dieser Einflussnahme gilt es, durch Planende auszuloten und zu erweitern.

Grenzen formeller
Planungsinstrumente
auflösen, um sie an
informelle Realitäten
anzupassen
(Manuel Hauer)

Im globalen Süden entwickelt sich Selbstbau in den kommenden 30 Jahren zur vorherrschenden Art der Stadtproduktion, da Planungsinstitutionen und Immobilienmarkt nicht in der Lage sind, die Nachfrage weiter Bevölkerungskreise zu decken. Es gilt daher, den Selbstbau mit all seinen Konsequenzen zu antizipieren und in der Folge die Grenzen formeller Planungsinstrumente aufzulösen, um sie an die Bedürfnisse und Lebensrealitäten der Betroffenen anzupassen.

Begrenzte Denk-
weisen der Planung
durch Synergie-
prozesse auflösen
(Theodora Papamichail)

Wenn Stakeholder zur Zusammenarbeit aufgefordert werden, stellen ihre politischen und hierarchischen Mandate undurchlässige Grenzen dar, welche den Ideenaustausch behindern und Problemlösung verhindern. Schlimmer noch: In kritischen Momenten, in denen eine Entscheidungsfindung maßgeblich von Belang ist, schmälern solche Grenzen das Potenzial für

formal tools that open the borders of the planning procedurally and in the interim.

Leaps in scale can become boundaries in planning. The various disciples may use an interdisciplinary language for working together, but the shared consideration of the different perspectives—due to varying levels of work—should be negotiated anew as part of an overall planning context already in the phase of strategy definition.

Recognizing and focusing on boundaries of strategy finding
(Monika Wächter)

Bottom-up planning as a communal narrative of overcoming borders

While the inward city development of metropolises as a hotbed of economic interests contributes to faceless spatial production, private initiatives succeed in creating narratives in forgotten places, or those not subject to economic utilization pressure, that have a high identification and appropriation potential. What can we learn from these initiatives and apply to the production conditions of the city? How can we overcome the boundaries of an outdated planning culture in order to develop new narratives for urban spaces?

Overcoming boundaries and developing new narratives
(Amelie Rost)

Some borders are existential and should not be shifted. If the existence of free space is fundamentally questioned, an unnegotiable boundary has been reached. Borders are often obstructions in the urban fabric. Their permeability is to be encouraged. Open spaces set out by actor networks contribute to this. They can scarcely be planned. The unplannable should thus be reckoned with—such as the boundary between the sea and land. It exists but is still subject to constant temporary change.

Unplannable spaces can shift boundaries and be supported by (actor) networks
(Andreas Kurths)

In space, we experience and live social reality. Growing boundaries of the commodification and commercialization of urban space not only change spatial practice but also consciousness. Spatial appropriation initiatives therefore go far beyond spatial practice; they rather initiate social processes of consciousness development and emancipation. Spatial disobedience is a political practice. As a democratic process, space appropriations can contribute bottom-up to communally sounding out the question of how we want to live together in future.

Joint space appropriations as a democratic practice
(Lena Flamm)

Old and new infrastructures require spatial negotiation to avoid boundaries

The building of a new stretch of railway and its use by cross-border express trains no doubt link people and promote economic competitiveness. For the transected regions themselves, on the other hand, the track represents a newly drawn border that those affected question critically. The weighing up of the pros and cons is a constant challenge for experts and politicians and perhaps pushes their established procedures to the limits.

Negotiating the double character of large-scale infrastructures as a link and border
(Isabella Schuster und Mathias Niedermaier)

ganzheitliche Ansätze in der Raumentwicklung oder kultivieren Engstirnigkeit aufseiten der in die Planung Involvierten. Das Schaffen von Synergien stellt hier eine Lösung dar: Es veranlasst Stakeholder und Öffentlichkeit zur Diskussion und zu gemeinsamem Handeln. Selbst wenn ein solcher Ansatz oftmals in weiter Ferne erscheint, so vermag das Synergiepotenzial an der Schnittstelle von formellen und informellen Verantwortlichkeiten doch die vorhandenen soziopolitischen Grenzen aufzuweichen.

Die Rahmenbedingungen von Grenzen strukturell und organisatorisch öffnen
(Max Haug)

Benötigte Grenzüberschreitungen fokussieren nicht nur stadtplanerische Lösungen, sondern auch die Erneuerung der Rahmenbedingungen: strukturell, organisatorisch und prozessual. Die Standards der formellen Bauleitplanung werden zunehmend hinterfragt. Wissensmanagement, *organisational learning* und kooperative Planung sind neue Herausforderungen, um informelle Instrumente zu entwickeln, die die Grenzen der Planung prozessual und intermediär öffnen.

Grenzen der Strategiefindung erkennen und fokussieren
(Monika Wächter)

Maßstabssprünge können zu Grenzen in der Planung werden. Die verschiedenen Disziplinen nutzen für die gemeinsame Arbeit zwar eine interdisziplinäre Sprache, der gemeinsame Blick auf die unterschiedlichen Perspektiven – bedingt durch unterschiedliche Bearbeitungsebenen – sollte im Rahmen eines planerischen Gesamtkontextes jedoch bereits in der Phase der Strategiedefinition neu ausgehandelt werden.

Planung von unten als gemeinschaftliches Narrativ der Grenzüberwindung

Grenzen überwinden und neue Narrative entwickeln
(Amelie Rost)

Während die Innenentwicklung von Metropolen als Nährboden ökonomischer Interessen zu identifikationsloser Raumproduktion beiträgt, gelingt es privaten Initiativen, an vergessenen oder dem ökonomischen Verwertungsdruck entzogenen Orten Narrative zu kreieren, die ein hohes Identifikations- und Aneignungspotenzial haben. Was können wir von diesen Initiativen lernen und auf die Produktionsbedingungen von Stadt übertragen? Wie können wir Grenzen einer überkommenen Planungskultur überwinden, um neue Narrative für Stadträume zu entwickeln?

Unplanbare Räume können Grenzen verrücken und durch (Akteurs-)Netzwerke getragen werden
(Andreas Kurths)

Einige Grenzen sind existenziell und sollten nicht verrückt werden. Wenn die Existenz von Freiraum grundlegend infrage gestellt wird, ist eine unverhandelbare Grenze erreicht. Im städtischen Gewebe stören Grenzen oftmals. An deren Durchlässigkeit ist mitzuwirken. Dazu tragen von Akteursnetzwerken veröffentlichte Freiräume bei. Sie lassen sich kaum planen. Umso mehr ist das Unplanbare vorzusehen – so, wie die Grenze zwischen Meer und Land. Sie existiert und ist dabei doch permanent temporärer Veränderung ausgesetzt.

Gemeinsame Raumaneignungen als demokratische Praxis
(Lena Flamm)

Im Raum erfahren und leben wir die gesellschaftliche Realität. Wachsende Grenzen der Kommodifizierung und Kommerzialisierung von Stadtraum verändern nicht nur die räumliche Praxis, sondern auch das Bewusstsein. So gehen Initiativen der Raumaneignung weit über die räumliche Praxis

For convincing spatial planning, measures that dissolve the existing borders of planning and enable fruitful cooperation are absolutely necessary.

More than a century of spatial planning practice proves that the impacts of formal plans cannot be confined to specific administrative boundaries. Rather, the implementation of these plans could be better ensured in combination with transborder cooperation that often leads to enhancement of infrastructure at the borders, e.g., in Basel and Lille. These examples show that borders are not simply bold lines or high walls—instead they can form centers boosting regional growth.

Develop borders as centers
(Mahdokht Soltaniehha)

With the increasing digitization of the city, a range of mutual effects and synergies are being created between virtual and physical space. Digital tools such as 3D models or virtual reality (VR) enable a spatial examination of new urban spaces even before they have been realized. Furthermore, spatial resources in cities become visible and available through digital applications, for example through couch surfing. Mobility rental systems such as e-bikes and e-scooters demand their share of public space and present municipalities with new challenges. Technologies take effect within the district and bring about slow but constant change to the physical urban area.
It makes it all the more important to integrate technologies and digitization processes in space in thinking, planning, and design.

Creating spatially integrative digital-physical border crossings
(Radostina Radulova-Stahmer)

hinaus. Sie initiieren vielmehr gesellschaftliche Prozesse der Bewusstseins-bildung und Emanzipation. Räumlicher Ungehorsam ist politische Praxis. Als demokratischer Prozess können Raumaneignungen von unten dazu beitragen, die Frage, wie wir in Zukunft zusammenleben wollen, gemein-schaftlich auszuloten.

Alte und neue Infrastrukturen bedürfen einer räumlichen Aushandlung zur Grenzvermeidung

Den Doppel-charakter von Großinfrastrukturen als Verbindung und Grenze aushandeln (Isabella Schuster und Mathias Niedermaier)

Der Bau einer neuen Bahnstrecke und ihre Nutzung durch grenzüber-schreitende Schnellzüge verbinden zweifellos Menschen und fördern die wirtschaftliche Wettbewerbsfähigkeit. Für die durchschnittenen Regionen selbst stellt das Trassee dagegen eine neu gezogene Grenze dar, die Betrof-fene kritisch hinterfragen. Dabei fordert die Abwägung zwischen dem Für und Wider Expert*innen und Politiker*innen beständig heraus und bringt sie vielleicht mit ihren gewohnten Verfahren an ihre Grenzen.
Für eine starke Raumplanung sind Maßnahmen, die die bestehenden Gren-zen der Planung auflösen und fruchtbare Zusammenarbeit ermöglichen, zwingend notwendig.

Grenzen als Zentren entwickeln (Mahdokht Soltaniehha)

Mehr als zehn Jahre praktische Planung haben gezeigt, dass die Auswirkun-gen formeller Planung nicht an spezifischen administrativen Grenzen halt machen. Vielmehr könnte die Umsetzung derartiger Planungen wesentlich besser gewährleistet werden im Zuge einer grenzüberschreitenden Zusam-menarbeit, die oftmals mit einer Stärkung der Infrastruktur an den Grenzen einhergeht, etwa in Basel oder Lille. Diese Beispiele zeigen, dass Grenzen nicht einfach nur fette Linien oder hohe Mauern sind – vielmehr können sie Zentren sein, die das regionale Wachstum befördern.

Digital-physische Grenzüberwindungen räumlich integrativ gestalten (Radostina Radulova-Stahmer)

Mit zunehmender Digitalisierung der Stadt entstehen vielfältige Wechsel-wirkungen und Synergien zwischen virtuellem und physischem Raum. Digitale Tools wie 3D-Modelle oder Virtual Reality (VR) ermöglichen eine räumliche Überprüfung von neuen Stadträumen, noch bevor sie entstehen. Auf der anderen Seite werden Raumressourcen in Städten durch digitale Anwendungen sichtbar und verfügbar gemacht, etwa durch Couchsurfing. Mobilitätsleihsysteme wie E-Bikes und E-Scooter fordern ihren Anteil an öffentlichem Raum und stellen Kommunen vor neue Herausforderungen. Technologien werden im Quartier raumwirksam und verändern langsam, aber stetig den physischen Stadtraum. Umso wichtiger wird es, Technolo-gien und Digitalisierungsprozesses im Raum integriert zu denken, zu planen und zu gestalten.

CULTURES OF ASSEMBLAGES
VERKNÜPFUNGS-KULTUREN

CULTURES OF ASSEMBLAGES

UNDINE GISEKE

The garbage mountain is calling

In the north of Munich with its wastewater treatment plant, landfill, and municipal composting plant, there is a concentration of central facilities that organize the metabolism of the city. The technical functional bodies and large forms characterize the area together with the highway, contrasted by the exceptional architectural figure of the football stadium, like a kind of modern city gate. One rarely finds a place with such an assemblage, where the material flows of an urban system manifest spatially in such a distinctive manner.

In July 2017, there was a visit to the Fröttmaning garbage mountain for interested Munich inhabitants. We wanted to explore the area together to gain insights into the urban metabolism of the city of Munich. Many knew the site from driving past, but the material aspects of their city that find their way here were unfamiliar to most. However, the city of Munich does not conceal what happens here. The digestion tanks of the wastewater treatment plant are visible from the highway just like the Allianz Arena. The garbage mountain features a wind turbine. And yet what Sonja Windmüller refers to as concealment through exposure applies to this area as a culmination space for the urban metabolism regarding its handling of rubbish.[1] We appear to have a difficult relationship with the metabolism of the city. We encounter many aspects of not-knowing and making-invisible. In this contribution there is an attempt to reflect on the urban metabolism in relation to our Western concepts of city, countryside, and landscape. This reflection begins with the assumption that our modern Western spatial concepts are founded on notions of separability that are now becoming obsolete as we enter into the geochronological epoch of the Anthropocene.[2]

1 Sites of urban metabolism, Munich-Fröttmaning.
1 *Orte des urbanen Stoffwechsels, München-Fröttmaning.*

The Anthropocene as a challenge

What is the Anthropocene and what consequences do the proclaiming of a new geochronological epoch have for disciplines in spatial planning and spatial design? The Anthropocene supersedes the Holocene. This interglacial period lasting almost 12,000 years with its relatively stable environmental conditions created the preconditions for the development of human

UNDINE GISEKE

Der Müllberg ruft

Im Münchner Norden konzentrieren sich mit dem Klärwerk, den Mülldeponien und der städtischen Kompostierungsanlage zentrale Einrichtungen, die den Stoffwechsel der Stadt organisieren. Die technischen Funktionskörper und Großformen prägen zusammen mit der Autobahn und kontrastiert durch die architektonische Ausnahmefigur des Fußballstadions den Raum wie eine Art modernes Stadttor. Selten findet man einen Ort mit derartiger Ansammlung, an dem sich die Stoffströme eines großstädtischen Systems in so prägnanter Weise räumlich manifestieren.

Im Juli 2017 gab es für interessierte Münchner*innen einen Spaziergang auf den Fröttmaninger Müllberg. Zusammen wollten wir den Raum erkunden und Einblicke in den urbanen Metabolismus der Stadt München bekommen. Viele kannten den Ort vom Vorbeifahren, doch die stofflichen Aspekte ihrer Stadt, die sich hier im Raum niederschlagen, waren den meisten völlig fremd. Dabei verbirgt die Stadt München nicht, was hier passiert. Die Faultürme des Klärwerkes zeigen sich an der Autobahn ebenso wie die Allianz Arena. Der Müllberg ist zeichenhaft mit einem Windrad besetzt. Und doch trifft auf diesen Raum als Kulminationsraum für den städtischen Stoffwechsel zu, was Sonja Windmüller in Bezug auf den Umgang mit Müll als Verbergen durch Exposition bezeichnet.[1] Wir scheinen ein schwieriges Verhältnis zum Stoffwechsel der Stadt zu haben. Aspekte des Nicht-Wissens und des Unsichtbar-Machens begegnen uns in vielfältiger Weise.

In diesem Beitrag wird versucht, den städtischen Stoffwechsel in Bezug zu unseren westlichen Konzepten von Stadt, Land und Landschaft zu reflektieren. Ihm liegt die Annahme zugrunde, dass unsere modernen westlichen Raumkonzepte auf Vorstellungen der Trennbarkeit beruhen, die in der nun eingetreten geochronologischen Epoche des Anthropozäns obsolet werden.[2]

Das Anthropozän als Herausforderung

Was ist das Anthropozän und welche Konsequenzen hat das Ausrufen einer neuen geochronologischen Epoche für die raumplanenden und raumgestaltenden Disziplinen?

Das Anthropozän löst das Holozän ab. Diese fast 12.000 Jahre andauernde Warmzeit schaffte mit ihren relativ stabilen Umweltbedingungen die Voraussetzungen für die Entwicklung der menschlichen Zivilisation. Das Anthropozän kennzeichnet nunmehr die Epoche, in der der Einfluss des Menschen auf das Erdsystem dominant wurde. Während zu Beginn des Anthropozän-Diskurses zunächst das Gewahr-Werden des Einflusses des Menschen im Vordergrund stand, geht es in den aktuellen Diskussionen darum, zukünftige

civilization. The Anthropocene refers to the epoch in which the influence of humankind on the earth system became dominant. Whereas at the beginning of the Anthropocene discourse the focus was initially on becoming aware of the influence of humankind, in current discussions it is about reflecting on future processes of the interaction between humans and the earth and thinking about a changing future.

Dürbeck summarizes: "The Anthropocene therefore appears as a narrative that (a) understands humanity as a geophysical force, (b) casts a planetary perspective on the global environmental crisis, (c) displays a deep time dimension, (d) assumes a close mutual relationship, i.e. non-separability of nature and culture and (e) derives from it the ethical responsibility of humankind for the earth system."[3] She determines further that since the Anthropocene discourse started in 2000 it has brought forth various narratives up until today. These range from the *catastrophe narrative*, to the *(bio)technological narrative*, which places a focus on the technological manageability of the Anthropocene challenges, to what is often called the *interdependence narrative*, which is seeking a critical answer to the abolishment of the nature-culture dichotomy as a basic condition for change. Even if all narratives question established positionings of the humankind-nature relationship from a reflexive point of view, from a strategic point of view they open up different options that guide actions.[4]

The following sets out to cast a brief look, from the perspective of the spatial planning and spatial design disciplines, at these contexts and their connections with the city, landscape, and urban metabolism.

2 *Generating metabolic assemblages between districts, Kigali.*
2 *Metabolische Verknüpfungen zwischen Quartieren generieren, Kigali.*

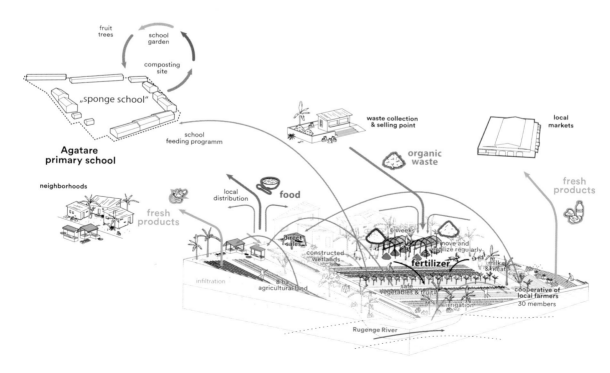

Prozesse der Interaktion zwischen Mensch und Erde zu reflektieren und in eine veränderte Zukunft zu denken.

Dürbeck resümiert: „Das Anthropozän erscheint damit als ein Narrativ, das (a) die Menschheit als geophysikalische Kraft begreift, (b) eine planetarische Perspektive auf die globale Umweltkrise wirft, (c) eine tiefenzeitliche Zeitdimension aufweist, (d) eine enge Wechselbeziehung, d. h., Nicht-Trennbarkeit von Natur und Kultur annimmt und (e) daraus eine ethische Verantwortung des Menschen für das Erdsystem ableitet."[3]

Sie stellt weiter heraus, dass der seit 2000 begonnene Anthropozän-Diskurs bis heute unterschiedliche Narrative hervorgebracht hat. Diese reichen von dem Katastrophen-Narrativ über das (bio-)technologische Narrativ, das die technische Bewältigbarkeit der Anthropozän-Herausforderungen in den Vordergrund stellt, bis hin zum sogenannten Interdependenz-Narrativ, das nach einer kritischen Antwort auf die Aufhebung der Natur-Kultur-Dichotomie als Grundvoraussetzung für eine Veränderung sucht. Wenngleich alle Narrative in reflexiver Hinsicht etablierte Positionierungen des Mensch-Natur-Verhältnisses infrage stellen, so eröffnen sie in strategischer Hinsicht unterschiedliche handlungsleitende Optionen.[4]

Im Folgenden soll aus der Perspektive der raumplanenden und raumgestaltenden Disziplinen ein kurzer Blick auf diese Zusammenhänge und ihre Verknüpfungen mit Stadt, Landschaft und dem urbanen Metabolismus geworfen werden.

Konzepte kategorialer Trennungen: Natur – Kultur, Stadt – Landschaft

Das Konzept der Europäischen Stadt basiert auf einer klaren Unterscheidung von Kultur und Natur, von Stadt und Land. Es zielt auf das Definitive. Die Zivilisierung der Natur, beziehungsweise die Beherrschung von natürlichen Prozessen durch technische Systeme, ist seit dem 19. Jahrhundert zu einer immer wichtigeren Komponente dieses Konzeptes geworden. Wenngleich die Realität beharrlich an diesem Bild nagt, besitzt es nach wie vor starke Verführungskraft. So stellt Siebel in seinen Darlegungen zur Kultur der (Europäischen) Stadt noch einmal deutlich heraus, dass „Stadt [...] als Akt der Befreiung aus den Zwängen der Natur [beginnt]. Städtisches Leben wird erst möglich, wenn die in der Landwirtschaft tätige Bevölkerung mehr produziert, als sie zum Überleben benötigt."[5] In diesem Kontext ist interessant, dass der aus der Landwirtschaft stammende und von *kultivieren* abgeleitete Begriff *Kultur* „in der zweiten Hälfte des 18. Jahrhunderts [...] auf alles ausgedehnt [wird], was der Mensch an Leistungen im Prozess der Emanzipation von der Natur erschafft. [...] Damit wäre Stadt selbst Inbegriff von Kultur."[6] In diesen Ausführungen zeigt sich die enge Verflochtenheit von Stadt und Landwirtschaft – zwei Formen anthropogener Praktiken, die sich parallel überhaupt erst im Holozän herausbildeten. Zugleich geraten die Vorstellungen der Überwindbarkeit des Eingebunden-Seins in die Natur durch Stadt als Lebensform mit dem Gewahr-Werden des Anthropozäns ins Wanken. Es verändert das Mensch-Natur-Verhältnis grundlegend: „Es besteht

Beyond concepts of categoric separations: nature–culture, city–landscape

The concept of the European city is based on a clear distinction between culture and nature, city and countryside. It focuses on the definitive. The civilization of nature and the mastery of natural processes through technical systems have become increasingly important components of this concept since the nineteenth century. Even if reality gnaws at this notion, it is still very enticing. In his considerations about the culture of the (European) city, Siebel emphasizes once again clearly that "the city [starts] as an act of liberation from the constraints of nature. Urban life only becomes possible if the population involved in agriculture produces more than they need for survival."[5] In this context, it is interesting that term *culture* stemming from agriculture and derived from *cultivation* "is extended to everything in the second half of the 18th century … that humankind achieves in the process of emancipation from nature. … That would make the city itself the embodiment of culture."[6] These statements show the close interweaving of city and agriculture, two forms of anthropogenic practices that only emerged in parallel during the Holocene. At the same time, the notion that being integrated into nature can be overcome by the city as a lifeform, with the awareness of the Anthropocene is faltering. It changes the humankind-nature relationship fundamentally: "There is no hope that we might ever return to a 'natural state' of things. People do not act against the background of an immutable nature but are deeply intertwined with its structure and it defines both their immediate and distant future."[7]

Morton calls on us in this context to question our culturally determined forms of perception of landscape and to depart from an image of the landscape that has gradually emerged in the Western world since the late Middle Ages. Petrarch's ascent of Mont Ventoux in the year 1336 is considered a key moment in this process of landscape perception. It is as it were a hinge between the Middle Ages and the modern era, with which a new nature and world awareness starts and central courses are set for developments that lead to what we refer to today as Anthropocene. The aesthetic detachment with which we have since viewed landscape can be overcome—according to Morton—involving giving up a perspective of landscape observation that is based on the separation into the first and third person. We should "embark instead on a search for a zero-person perspective,"[8] which ultimately also enables us to engage in communication with nonhuman actors.

About the making invisible of the urban metabolism and the construction of an outside

Getting back to the landfill in the north of Munich: what does it have to do with these considerations? Here one can refer to the question of how the relationship between city and landscape and the material flow between them were set up in the past—both by means of cultural narratives and by means of concrete physical components such as infrastructure systems. A look at the history of the city shows how in the last three centuries the civ-

keine Hoffnung, dass wir je zu einem ‚natürlichen Stand' der Dinge zurück-kehren könnten. Menschen handeln nicht vor dem Hintergrund einer un-veränderbaren Natur, sondern sind tief mit ihrer Struktur verwoben und prägen sowohl ihre unmittelbare wie ihre ferne Zukunft."[7]

Morton fordert uns in diesem Kontext auf, unsere kulturell geprägten Wahr-nehmungsformen von Landschaft zu hinterfragen und mit einem Land-schaftsbild zu brechen, das sich seit dem späten Mittelalter allmählich in der westlichen Welt herausgebildet hat. Petrarcas Besteigung des Mont Ventoux im Jahr 1336 gilt als ein Schlüsselmoment in diesem Prozess der Landschafts-wahrnehmung. Es ist gleichsam ein Scharnier zwischen Mittelalter und Neu-zeit, mit dem ein neues Natur- und Weltbewusstsein beginnt und zentrale Weichenstellungen für Entwicklungen vorgenommen werden, die zu dem führen, was wir heute als Anthropozän bezeichnen. Die ästhetische Dis-tanziertheit, mit der wir Landschaft seitdem betrachtet haben, ist zu überwinden – so Morton –, und damit ist eine Perspektive der Landschafts-betrachtung aufzugeben, die auf der Trennung in erste und dritte Person basiert. Wir sollten „uns stattdessen auf die Suche nach einer Null-Person-Perspektive machen"[8], die es uns letztendlich auch erlaubt in Kommunika-tion mit nicht menschlichen Akteur*innen zu treten.

Vom Unsichtbar-Machen des urbanen Stoffwechsels und der Konstruktion eines Außen

Zurück zum Müllberg im Münchner Norden: Was hat er mit diesen Über-legungen zu tun? Hier ist eine Brücke zu schlagen zu der Frage, wie in der Vergangenheit das Verhältnis von Stadt und Landschaft und der materielle Fluss zwischen ihnen gestaltet wurde – und zwar sowohl mittels kultureller Erzählungen als auch mittels konkret physischer Komponenten wie Infra-struktursystemen. Ein Blick in die Geschichte der Stadt zeigt, wie in den letzten drei Jahrhunderten die Zivilisierung, Kultivierung und Kontrolle des städtischen Stoffwechsels nicht zuletzt als Antwort auf bürgerliche Werte und Bedürfnisse nach Reinlichkeit, Ordnung und Schönheit immer weiter vorangeschritten ist. Die Leitbilder der hygienischen Stadt und des moder-nen Städtebaus haben zusammen mit den technischen Errungenschaften ein durchgreifendes Unsichtbar-Machen von natürlichen Prozessen und den damit einhergehenden urbanen Stoffströmen bewirkt und dieses zur Norm erhoben. Unter anderem Gandy (2004)[9] und Bernhardt (2005)[10] machen am Beispiel des Wassers deutlich, wie es seit dem 19. Jahrhundert zunehmend aus dem Stadtbild verschwand und unter die Erde verbannt wurde. Hauser (1992)[11] und Frank (2004)[12] verdeutlichen unter anderem am Beispiel der Entwicklung der städtischen Kanalisation, wie in dieser Zeit Abwasser zu einer Kategorie des Abfalls wird. Ähnlich verhält es sich mit anderen mate-riellen Prozessen des städtischen Stoffwechsels. Windmüller zeigt in ihren Untersuchungen die Eigenheiten der räumlichen Verteilung des Mülls auf. Sie stellt heraus, dass die Areale des Mülls eine Tendenz zur Randständig-keit und Verflüchtigung hatten, bis hin zu dem paradoxen Phänomen des Verschwinden-Lassens durch Exponieren, indem der Müll über eine lange

ilization, cultivation, and control of the urban metabolism has increasingly progressed not least in response to civic values and demands for cleanliness, order, and beauty. The models of the hygienic city and international modernism in urbanism and architecture, together with technical accomplishments, have radically made natural processes and the associated urban material flows invisible and made this the norm. Among others, Gandy (2004)[9] and Bernhardt (2005)[10] show based on the example of water how it disappeared increasingly from the cityscape from the nineteenth century and was banished underground. Hauser (1992)[11] and Frank (2004)[12] show, using the example of the development of the municipal sewer system, how wastewater becomes a category of waste at this time. It is similar with other material processes of urban metabolism. Windmüller shows in her studies the particularities of the spatial distribution of garbage. She establishes that the garbage disposal sites have a tendency to marginalization, even the paradoxical phenomenon of disappearance through exposure, in that the garbage is deposited for a long time in the landscape as a mound and becomes invisible through the landscape camouflage of recultivation.[13] Pothukuchi and Kaufman were the first to highlight the blindness of urban planning towards the urban food supply, which relied on the rural areas as a production site and the market as a form of distribution.[14]

The notion of the hygienic city grew from the nineteenth-century parallel to the controlling of the physical facilities and metabolism of the city. The adherence to principles of rationality, common sense, and ethics were supposed to ensure physical integrity, cleanliness, and health, according to Hauser.[15] This went hand in hand with making invisible of these processes and their spatial relocation using industrial technology systems and establishing infrastructure systems.

The invisibility is created structurally and technically and is confined to particular sites, topographies, and spatial systems. The process was accompanied by the establishment of cultural borders—"The systematic cleansing of the city means the establishment of a new city boundary, the boundary between the cultured area of industrial society and what it pushes into an *outside* of its culture in a controlled manner"[16]—into rural areas and the sphere of agriculture.

However, the construction of an outside no longer applies today: "For some time we may have thought that the U-bend in the toilet was a convenient curvature of ontological space that took whatever we flush down it into a totally different dimension called Away, leaving things clean over here. Now we know better: instead of the mythical land Away, we know the waste goes to the Pacific Ocean or the wastewater treatment facility."[17]

It is increasingly part of our everyday experience that "in the Anthropocene more of a patchwork world … has, out of a wide variety of frameworks and links, out of social and technical forms of organization and ecologies, that can scarcely be distinguished anymore from forests and rocks, oceans and atmospheres."[18]

Zeit hinweg in der Landschaft als Berg deponiert und durch die landschaftliche Camouflage der Rekultivierung unsichtbar wurde.[13] Pothukuchi und Kaufman haben als erste die Blindheit der Stadtplanung gegenüber der städtischen Nahrungsversorgung herausgestellt, die sich auf das Land als Ort der Produktion und den Markt als Form der Distribution verlassen hat.[14] Die Vorstellung von der hygienischen Stadt erwuchs ab dem 19. Jahrhundert parallel zur Kontrolle der körperlichen Verrichtungen und des Stoffwechsels der Stadt. Das Einhalten von Prinzipien der Rationalität, Vernunft und Moral sollten körperliche Unversehrtheit, Sauberkeit und Gesundheit gewährleisten, so Hauser.[15] Damit einher gingen ein Unsichtbar-Machen dieser Vorgänge und deren räumliche Verlagerung unter Nutzung industrietechnischer Systeme und der Etablierung von Infrastruktursystemen.

3 *Crossing borders—
end of an outside.*
3 *Grenzüberschreitungen – Ende des Außen.*

Die Nicht-Wahrnehmbarkeit wird baulich und technisch erzeugt und sie ist an besondere Orte, Topografien und Raumsysteme gebunden. Der Prozess war begleitet von dem Erzeugen kultureller Grenzen: „Die systematische Reinigung der Stadt bedeutet die Etablierung einer neuen Stadtgrenze, der Grenze zwischen dem kulturierten Bereich der Industriegesellschaft und dem, was sie kontrolliert in ein Außerhalb ihrer Kultur verlegt"[16] – auf das Land und in den Bereich der Landwirtschaft.
Doch die Konstruktion dieses Außen trägt heute nicht mehr: „For some time we may have thought that the U-bend in the toilet was a convenient curvature of ontological space that took whatever we flush down it into a

New cultures of assemblages and vibrant morphologies

Today with the Anthropocene discourse, the purpose of the separation of technical, cultural, and natural systems is fundamentally being questioned and consequently also the previous knowledge systems that support these separations.[19] The perception of the relationship between the human, nature, and space is changing profoundly.

But what challenges does the Anthropocene then present specifically to disciplines that are concerned with the planning and designing of space? If one follows the Anthropocene discourse strain of the independence narrative—mentioned briefly at the beginning of this contribution—then it means as a first step a critical questioning of categorial allocations and therefore also of boundaries in existing spatial concepts (and the disciplinary allocations in their consideration as city and landscape).[20] As a second step, it means working on cultural narratives for spaces and spatial systems that target an overcoming of traditional dichotomies and developing methodological approaches for such assemblages This is a fundamental process for which neighboring disciplines such as cultural, social, and life sciences can provide important impetus.

A third step is to translate these basic understandings into concrete plans and designs and thus to generate cultures of assemblages. The metabolic processes thematized here appear to be a central reference point for this. This is not only because they make it possible to materially and concretely grasp the previous disregard of links between various spheres, but also because they represent hybrids of technical, social, and natural processes and systems par excellence, through which exchange processes between different spheres, spaces and scales are carried out. The organization, design, and perceptibility of these material exchange process in the sense of the creation of interactive infrastructures and pulsating, linked morphologies represent enormous future tasks. It means shaping the city in terms of its exchange processes.

totally different dimension called Away, leaving things clean over here. Now we know better: instead of the mythical land Away, we know the waste goes to the Pacific Ocean or the wastewater treatment facility."[17] Es dringt immer tiefer in unsere Alltagserfahrung ein, dass „im Anthropozän vielmehr eine Patchwork-Welt [...] entstanden [ist], aus den verschiedensten Gerüsten und Bespannungen, aus sozialen und technischen Organisationsformen und Ökologien, die von Wäldern und Gesteinen, von Ozeanen und Atmosphären kaum mehr zu unterscheiden sind."[18]

Neue Verknüpfungskulturen und pulsierende Morphologien

Heute wird mit dem Anthropozän-Diskurs die Sinnhaftigkeit der Trennung von technischen, kulturellen und natürlichen Systemen grundsätzlich infrage gestellt und das werden damit auch die bisherigen Wissenssysteme, die diese Trennungen stützen.[19] Die Wahrnehmung des Verhältnisses von Mensch, Natur und Raum wandelt sich tief greifend.

Doch vor welche Herausforderungen stellt das Anthropozän damit ganz konkret Disziplinen, die sich mit der Planung und Gestaltung von Räumen befassen? Folgt man dem Anthropozän-Diskursstrang des eingangs kurz erwähnten Interdependenz-Narrativs[20], dann bedeutet es in einem ersten Schritt ein kritisches Hinterfragen von kategorialen Zuordnungen und damit auch von Grenzen in bestehenden Raumkonzepten (und den disziplinären Zuordnungen ihrer Betrachtung als Stadt und Landschaft). In einem zweiten Schritt bedeutet es, an kulturellen Erzählungen für Räume und Raumsysteme zu arbeiten, die auf eine Überwindung der tradierten Dichotomien zielen, und methodische Ansätze für derartige Verknüpfung zu entwickeln. Das ist ein grundlegender Prozess, für den benachbarte Wissenschaften wie die Anthropologie oder die Kultur-, Sozial- und Lebendwissenschaften wichtige Impulse liefern können. Ein dritter Schritt ist es, diese Grundverständnisse in konkrete Planungen und Entwürfe zu übersetzen und somit Verknüpfungskulturen zu generieren. Die hier thematisierten Stoffwechselprozesse scheinen dafür ein zentraler Anknüpfungspunkt zu sein. Und das nicht nur, weil sie das bisherige Ausblenden von Verknüpfungen zwischen verschiedenen Sphären materiell konkret nachvollziehbar machen, sondern auch, weil sie Hybride aus technischen, gesellschaftlichen und natürlichen Prozessen und Systemen par excellence darstellen, über die Austauschprozesse zwischen verschiedenen Räumen und in verschiedenen Skalen vollzogen werden. Die Organisation, Gestaltung und Wahrnehmbarkeit dieser materiellen Austauschprozesse im Sinne der Schaffung interaktiver Infrastrukturen und pulsierender, verknüpfter Morphologien stellen immense Zukunftsaufgaben dar. Es bedeutet, die Stadt von ihren Austauschprozessen her zu gestalten.

In discussion with architect Peter Meyer Berlin, September 2019 – im Gespräch mit Architekt Peter Meyer

NETWORK-SUPPORTED OPEN SPACES— A NEW OPEN SPACE TYPOLOGY OF DIGITAL MODERNITY

ANDREAS KURTHS

The digitization of our everyday experience has already changed the perception of time: time feels like an even scarcer asset. Our digitized everyday life also includes new open spaces in the analog world. More and more "digital modern" people are active in real urban open spaces. Digital tools are used as a matter of course for making arrangements, meeting, reporting, etc. However, these people's demand for participation cannot be served by the offer of a traditional public park. Using a park for the purpose of conventional leisure has absolutely no justification but changes little. Even the offer of being involved in the design of an open space through a participation procedure is not enough, because the negotiation and change of a spatial situation should take place in the here and now and leave its own visible traces at the location. The traditional open space is not programmed for this, and for open space planning impatience and uncertainty can scarcely be applied in conventional planning processes.

Even so, actors within civil society communally succeed in establishing new urban open spaces that not only enable contributions and participation but even demand it. These are often areas that involve uncertain lengthy negotiations and input, due to the persistence of individual actors and the exchanges with other—also nonintentional—actors. The degree of continuity and temporality is worked out by those involved according to quite concrete properties of the space such as accessibility or usability. The boundary between private and public becomes permeable for the duration of use. The resulting openness of the location to the possibility of making a city contributes significantly to its attractiveness.

Up until now, professional open space planning has not dedicated itself adequately through participation to the demands of people in the city for such places of uncertain changeability. Presumably the contradiction between planning security and at the same time open usage represents a boundary that is difficult to overcome. This contradiction is to be tolerated by the planners, as it raises the question about the efficacy of open space planning. This should be prepared to contribute alongside others to acquiring, researching, and preserving open spaces that are stable and at the same time agile. Planning then means not only designing spatial solutions and conveying them between clients and a construction company. It is more about transferring emerging knowledge to comparable processes and continuously accompanying the enabling actor network with the acquired trust, because network-supported open spaces make a contribution in the urban fabric to overcoming boundaries and withstanding contradictions.

NETZWERKGETRAGENE FREIRÄUME – EIN NEUER FREIRAUMTYPUS DER DIGITALMODERNE

ANDREAS KURTHS

Die Digitalisierung unseres täglichen Erlebens hat das Zeitempfinden bereits verändert: Zeit fühlt sich nach einem noch knapperen Gut an. Das Digitalisierte unseres Alltags erschließt aber auch neue Freiräume in der analogen Welt. Immer mehr „digitalmoderne" Menschen sind in realen urbanen Freiräumen aktiv. Dabei werden ganz selbstverständlich digitale Werkzeuge zum Verabreden, Auffinden, Darüber-Berichten usw. verwendet. Doch das Verlangen dieser Menschen nach Mitwirkung kann das Angebot einer klassischen öffentlichen Parkanlage nicht bedienen. Einen Park zum Zweck der konventionellen Erholung zu nutzen, hat absolut seine Berechtigung, ändert aber nur wenig. Selbst das Angebot, sich an der Gestaltung eines Freiraumes über ein Partizipationsverfahren zu beteiligen, genügt nicht. Denn die Aushandlung und die Veränderung einer räumlichen Situation sollen in der Jetzt-Zeit stattfinden und im Raum eigene sichtbare Spuren hinterlassen. Der klassische Freiraum ist dafür nicht programmiert und für die Freiraumplanung lassen sich Ungeduld und Unbestimmtheit kaum in konventionelle Planungsprozesse übertragen.

Dennoch gelingt es Akteur*innen der Zivilgesellschaft, gemeinschaftlich neue urbane Freiräume zu etablieren, die das Mitgestalten und Mitmachen nicht nur ermöglichen, sondern erfordern. Das sind oft Flächen, die durch das Beharren einzelner und die Verknüpfung mit weiteren – auch nicht intentionalen – Akteur*innen zu zeitlich ungewiss lang bestehenden Räumen der Aushandlung und Mitwirkung werden. Das Maß an Kontinuität und Temporalität wird durch die Beteiligten anhand ganz konkreter Eigenschaften des Raumes wie Zugänglichkeit oder Nutzbarkeit ausgehandelt. Die Grenze zwischen privat und öffentlich wird für die Dauer der Nutzung durchlässig. Die daraus resultierende Offenheit des Ortes zum Stadt-machen-Können trägt zur Attraktivität maßgeblich bei.

Bisher hat sich professionelle Freiraumplanung dem Bedarf der Menschen in der Stadt nach solchen Orten unbestimmter Veränderbarkeit durch Mitwirkung nicht ausreichend gewidmet. Vermutlich stellt der Widerspruch zwischen Planungssicherheit bei gleichzeitiger Nutzungsoffenheit eine schwer überwindbare Grenze dar. Dieser Widerspruch ist seitens der Planenden auszuhalten, denn er stellt die Frage nach der Wirkmacht von Freiraumplanung. Diese sollte sich darauf einlassen, als eine unter vielen daran mitzuwirken, stabile und dabei agile Freiräume zu gewinnen, zu erforschen und zu erhalten. Planung heißt dann nicht allein, räumliche Lösungen zu entwerfen und diese zwischen Bauherr*innen und Baufirma zu vermitteln. Vielmehr gilt es, entstehendes Wissen an vergleichbare Prozesse weiterzugeben und mit dem erarbeiteten Vertrauen das ermöglichende Akteursnetzwerk fortlaufend zu begleiten. Denn netzwerkgetragene Freiräume leisten im städtischen Gewebe einen Beitrag dazu, Grenzen zu überwinden und Widersprüche auszuhalten.

METROPOLIS AND AGRICULTURE

LEEVKE HEESCHEN

Since the development of our cities, a fertile hinterland has always been a guarantor of growth and prosperity. Local agriculture as the feeder of the urban organism entered into a close and fruitful interrelationship with the metropolis. During industrialization, this productive interweaving was curtailed. Today, in the twenty-first century, this relationship has undergone a metamorphosis. The metropolis and agriculture are separately optimized systems that are only in a relationship on a larger scale and through various interim stations. This decoupling runs through economic, ecological, cultural, and social levels.

The place where the metropolis and agriculture nevertheless meet spatially is the suburban area or the metropolitan region. Potential synergies of this spatial coexistence are not made use of or only partially. The consequence is that it leads to an increased competition between surface availabilities in these areas due to the assertion of different development and usage claims.

In this regard, the question arises as to a new relationship and new coding of the metropolis and agriculture as a productive *cultivated city landscape*. It is still unclear what synergies or interrelationships would be conceivable between the metropolis and agriculture—respectively how regional cycles can be initiated and strengthened to counter the decoupling of the two spheres. The reconnection could lead to new spatial typologies, but what might these look like?

The initial approaches to these questions and to an integrated development of the metropolis and agriculture are currently being discussed in Hamburg-Oberbillwerder. The ensuing results are to flow into the planning for the realization of Hamburg's 105th district.

At the center of this research are the agriculturists who take on a key role in the suburban area in the creation of a productive cultivated city landscape. They own the targeted areas and facilities and change can be brought about by their actions.

Through exchanges with the agriculturists, a detailed picture of the status quo as well as the starting points for the envisaged recoupling and initiation of local cycles is to be worked out. In support, spatial explorations are carried out in the laboratory area of the Hamburg metropolitan region. The aim is the development of linking modules which are tested by means of small-scale draft designs, evaluated through exchanges with agriculturists and translated into systemic spatial depictions of the productive cultivated city landscape.

The insights contribute to agriculture being understood as part of the metropolitan organism and to the development of resilient and sustainable metropolitan regions through an integrated approach and development, which are able to supply themselves and ensure a resource-efficient economy.

METROPOLE UND LANDWIRTSCHAFT

LEEVKE HEESCHEN

Seit Entstehen unserer Städte war fruchtbares Hinterland stets ein Garant für Wachstum und Wohlstand. Die lokale Landwirtschaft als Ernährerin des städtischen Organismus ging mit der Metropole eine enge und fruchtbare Wechselbeziehung ein. Während der Industrialisierung wurde diese produktive Verflechtung gekappt. Heute, im 21. Jahrhundert, hat sich eine Metamorphose dieser Beziehung vollzogen. Metropole und Landwirtschaft sind voneinander getrennt optimierte Systeme, die nur im größeren Maßstab und über diverse Zwischenstationen miteinander in Beziehung stehen. Diese Entkoppelung durchzieht ökonomische, ökologische, kulturelle und soziale Ebenen.

Der Ort, an dem die Metropole und die Landwirtschaft räumlich dennoch aufeinandertreffen, ist der suburbane Raum beziehungsweise die Metropolregion. Dabei werden mögliche Synergien dieser räumlichen Koexistenz nicht oder nur teilweise genutzt. Die Folge ist, dass es in diesen Räumen durch die Entfaltung unterschiedlicher Entwicklungs- und Nutzungsansprüche zu einer erhöhten Konkurrenz zwischen Flächenverfügbarkeiten kommt.

In diesem Zusammenhang stellt sich die Frage nach einer Neukoppelung und Neukodierung von Metropole und Landwirtschaft als einer produktiven *Stadtkulturlandschaft*. Noch ist unklar, welche Synergien beziehungsweise Verknüpfungen zwischen Metropole und Landwirtschaft denkbar wären – respektive wie regionale Kreisläufe initiiert und gestärkt werden können, um der Entkoppelung der beiden Sphären entgegenzuwirken. Eventuell entstehen durch Neukoppelung neue Raumtypen, doch wie könnten diese aussehen? Erste Ansätze zu diesen Fragen und zu einer intergierten Entwicklung von Metropole und Landwirtschaft werden aktuell in Hamburg-Oberbillwerder diskutiert. Die resultierenden Ergebnisse sollen in die Planung zur Realisierung von Hamburgs 105. Stadtteil einfließen.

Im Zentrum dieser Forschung stehen die Landwirt*innen, die im suburbanen Raum bei der Gestaltung der produktiven Stadtkulturlandschaft eine Schlüsselrolle einnehmen. In ihrem Besitz sind die anvisierten Flächen und Anlagen und von ihrem Tun und Handeln können Veränderungen ausgehen.

Im Austausch mit den Landwirt*innen sollen ein detailliertes Bild des Status quo sowie Ansatzpunkte der angestrebten Neukoppelung und Initiierung lokaler Kreisläufe erarbeitet werden. Unterstützend werden Raumerkundungen im Laborraum der Metropolregion Hamburg vorgenommen. Ziel ist die Entwicklung von Koppelungsmodulen, die durch kleinräumige Testentwürfe überprüft, im Austausch mit Landwirt*innen evaluiert und in systemische Raumbilder der produktiven Stadtkulturlandschaft übersetzt werden.

Die Erkenntnisse tragen dazu bei, dass Landwirtschaft als Teil des metropolitanen Organismus verstanden wird und durch eine integrierte Betrachtung und Entwicklung resiliente und nachhaltige Metropolregionen entstehen, die im Stande sind, sich selbst zu versorgen und ressourcenschonend zu wirtschaften.

POSTCAPITALIST URBAN SPACES

LENA FLAMM

Socioeconomic inequalities and exclusion dynamics are intensifying worldwide. The quality of life in urban societies is being weakened in these processes. Policy-making in this regard focus mainly on social and ecological transformations for a seemingly more sustainable economy. Even if critical urban studies since the 1960s have been revealing progressive dynamics of socioeconomic inequality and their sociospatial effects, politics and planning are missing a critical reflection on the connections between the capitalist profit and growth paradigm and the lifeworld conditions of urban spatial production.

At the same time, a growing number of activists and citizens are pinpointing the economic model of capitalism itself as the cause of increasing disparities. In the context of this criticism, there is growing discussion in academia and civil society about postcapitalist economic concepts oriented towards the common good—such as solidarity economy or postgrowth economy.

The search for space-based solutions to socioeconomic disparities therefore starts in urban niche spaces, in which grassroots initiatives practice experimental models of solidarity economy and new forms of work. The result is a wide range of spatial programs: from cultural projects and coworking spaces, to cooperative cafés, shops and maker spaces. However, in their economic and spatial structure they share a focus on social value and the needs of the people. Organizational models, democratic decision-making processes, work forms, spatial design, and usage are constantly renegotiated. The programmatic opening of spaces for solidarity economy enables civil society to actively participate in cultivating new economies that go beyond monetary profit logic. This involves economic practices such as do-it-yourself, swapping, recycling, collecting, donating, unpaid work, mutual learning, and many others. The spheres of economics, work, leisure, politics, education, and public welfare are intertwined collaboratively in new spatial typologies. This coproduction of urban spaces and solidarity economy is analyzed based on case studies in Berlin and Athens.

The research studies which conditions, constellations, and processes contribute internally and externally to the creation, establishment, or weakening of such postcapitalist urban spaces. The question at stake is what dynamics can emerge from the respective assemblage of space, actors, economies, and practices with regard to upscaling potentials.

A more in-depth understanding of the agencies contributes to exposing the diversity and potentials of postcapitalist urban spaces in order to adress their needs in urban planning and policy-making.

POSTKAPITALISTISCHE STADTRÄUME

LENA FLAMM

Weltweit verschärfen sich sozioökonomische Ungleichheiten und Exklusionsdynamiken. Die Lebensqualität urbaner Gesellschaften wird dadurch geschwächt. Die Politikgestaltung fokussiert in diesem Spannungsfeld hauptsächlich auf soziale und ökologische Transformationen für eine scheinbar nachhaltigere Wirtschaft.

Auch wenn die Critical Urban Studies schon seit den 1960er Jahren sich verschärfende Dynamiken sozioökonomischer Ungleichheit in ihren sozialräumlichen Auswirkungen offenlegen, fehlt in Politik und Planung eine kritische Reflexion der Zusammenhänge zwischen dem kapitalistischen Profit- und Wachstumsparadigma und den lebensweltlichen Bedingungen der urbanen Raumproduktion.

Zeitgleich adressiert eine wachsende Zahl an Aktivist*innen und Bewohner*innen das ökonomische Modell des Kapitalismus selbst als Auslöser zunehmender Disparitäten. Im Kontext dieser Kritik werden in Wissenschaft und Zivilgesellschaft verstärkt postkapitalistische Modelle des Wirtschaftens – etwa die solidarische Ökonomie oder Postwachstum für eine gemeinwohlorientierte gesellschaftliche Transformation – diskutiert.

Die Suche nach gesellschaftlichen Lösungen beginnt daher in urbanen Nischenräumen, in denen Graswurzel-Initiativen solidarische Formen des Wirtschaftens und des Arbeitens praktisch erproben. Mannigfaltige Raumprogrammierungen entstehen: von Kulturprojekten über solidarökonomische Läden bis hin zu Co-Working-Spaces, kooperativen Cafés und Gemeinschaftsgärten. Gemeinsam ist ihnen, dass sie in ihrer ökonomischen und räumlichen Struktur den gesellschaftlichen Mehrwert und die Bedürfnisse der Menschen in den Mittelpunkt stellen. Dazu müssen unternehmerische Organisation, demokratische Entscheidungsprozesse, Arbeitsformen, räumliche Gestaltung und Nutzung neu ausgehandelt werden.

Die programmatische Öffnung von Räumen solidarischen Wirtschaftens ermöglicht es der Stadtgesellschaft, neue Ökonomien fernab von Profit- und Marktlogik aktiv mitzugestalten. Dazu gehören Wirtschaftspraktiken des Selbermachens, des Tauschens, des Recyclings, des Sammelns, des Schenkens, des unbezahlten Arbeitens, des gegenseitigen Lernens und viele mehr. Die Sphären von Ökonomie, Arbeit, Freizeit, Politik, Bildung und Gemeinwohl werden kollaborativ in neuen Raumtypen miteinander verwoben. Diese Koproduktion von Stadträumen und solidarischer Ökonomie wird anhand von Fallstudien aus Berlin und Athen analysiert. Die Forschungsarbeit untersucht, welche Bedingungen, Konstellationen und Prozesse extern und intern zur Schaffung, Etablierung oder Schwächung postkapitalistischer Stadträume beitragen und welche Dynamiken aus der jeweiligen Assemblage aus Raum, Akteur*innen, Ökonomien und Praktiken entstehen können.

Ein tiefer gehendes Verständnis der Wirkmächte trägt dazu bei, die Mannigfaltigkeit und Potenziale postkapitalistischer urbaner Räume für die Gesellschaft sichtbar zu machen und ihre Bedürfnisse politisch und planerisch zu adressieren.

CASABLANCA FLYING VISIT
STIPPVISITE CASABLANCA

CASABLANCA—
AGRICULTURE AS COMPONENT
OF THE EMERGING MEGACITY

UNDINE GISEKE

Casablanca is growing into a new megacity at the gateway to Europe. An increase in economic significance, new city districts, and a rapid population increase go hand in hand. Imposing urban projects along the coast, a new opera house in the center, repurposed railway stations, and a widening tram network give Casablanca the face of a modern city. However, growth also has its flipsides, such as extensive sprawl in the hinterland due to un-controllable land speculation and the emergence of informal settlement structures—even if Casablanca is making significant endeavors to be a city without slums.

In the twentieth century, Casablanca grew from 20,000 to over 4 million inhabitants. In 2004, 3.63 million inhabitants lived on 23,600 hectares of ur-banized area; a decade later it was already 4.27 million. In few years, this is expected to exceed 5 million. Until then—according to the land use plan of 2008—a further 23,000 hectares of the urban area's total of 120,000 hectares are to be built on. The inner-city districts are continuing to transform and densify, while new growth hubs and corridors are emerging that include a patchwork of agricultural areas. However, even if the city continues to grow, the urban region will include several tens of thousands of hectares more of agricultural area in future. What role will agriculture play in future in the urban region?

Even if Casablanca, compared to other megacities, has a differentiated planning system, the same is evident here as in many other places: the de-velopment plans of the city and of agriculture do not correlate; instead each follows its own logic. The result is an incoherent development of the urban region, which does not recognize the value of the agricultural areas for the city. Agriculture, a giant in terms of surface area, remains a dwarf in relation to its function and possible influence on the urban region.

In November 2019, the Spatial Research Lab explored Casablanca as part of a visit. "Crossing borders" was taken quite literally on our part, as we con-sidered matters of spatial relevance outside of Europe.

"Crossing Borders—Activating Spaces" also entailed the concrete question of how the urban and the rural sphere could be linked in the urban sphere and how a range of exchange processes between the spheres can be stimu-lated. This touched on questions that had been addressed first analytically, then conceptually with concrete tests, by the interdisciplinary and trans-disciplinary research project on Urban Agriculture in Casablanca, Morocco (2005–2014) as part of the sponsored program "Future Megacites" of the Fed-eral Ministry of Education and Research (BMBF).[1]

CASABLANCA –
DIE ÖKONOMISCHE
LOKOMOTIVE MAROKKOS

UNDINE GISEKE

Casablanca wächst zu einer neuen Megastadt vor den Toren Europas heran. Wirtschaftlicher Bedeutungszuwachs, neue Stadtquartiere und ein rasanter Anstieg der Bevölkerung gehen Hand in Hand. Imposante urbane Projekte entlang der Küste, ein neues Opernhaus im Zentrum, umgestaltete Bahnhöfe und ein sich ausdehnendes Straßenbahnnetz geben der Stadt das Gesicht einer modernen Großstadt. Aber es gibt auch Kehrseiten des Wachstums, wie weitläufige Zersiedlung des Hinterlandes infolge unkontrollierbarer Bodenspekulation und das Entstehen informeller Siedlungsstrukturen – auch wenn Casablanca gewaltige Anstrengungen unternimmt, eine Stadt ohne Slums zu sein.

Im 20. Jahrhundert wuchs Casablanca von 20.000 auf über 4 Millionen Einwohner*innen an. 2004 lebten auf 23.600 Hektar urbanisierter Fläche 3,63 Millionen Einwohner*innen, ein Jahrzehnt später waren es bereits 4,27 Millionen. In nur wenigen Jahren wird die Überschreitung der 5-Millionen-Grenze erwartet. Bis dahin sollen – nach dem Flächennutzungsplan von 2008 – weitere 23.000 Hektar Fläche der insgesamt 120.000 Hektar umfassenden Stadtregion bebaut werden. Die innerstädtischen Quartiere transformieren und verdichten sich weiter, während sich in der Stadtregion neue Wachstumskerne und Korridore herausbilden, die ein Patchwork landwirtschaftlicher Flächen einschließen. Doch auch wenn die Stadt weiterwächst, die Stadtregion wird auch zukünftig noch mehrere Zehntausend Hektar landwirtschaftliche Fläche einschließen. Welche Rolle wird Landwirtschaft zukünftig in der Stadtregion spielen?

Auch wenn Casablanca im Vergleich zu anderen Megastädten über ein differenziertes Planungssystem verfügt, zeigt sich hier wie vielerorts: Die Entwicklungspläne der Stadt und der Landwirtschaft korrespondieren nicht miteinander, sondern folgen ihren jeweils eigenen Logiken. Das Resultat ist eine inkohärente Entwicklung der Stadtregion, die den Wert der landwirtschaftlichen Flächen für die Stadt nicht erkennt. Der Flächenriese Landwirtschaft bleibt ein Zwerg in Bezug auf seine Funktion und mögliche Strahlkraft für die Stadtregion.

Im November 2019 erkundete das „Forschungslabor Raum" im Rahmen einer Stippvisite Casablanca. „Grenzen überschreiten" wurde unsererseits dabei ganz wörtlich genommen, indem wir uns mit raumrelevanten Fragestellungen außerhalb Europas befassten. „Grenzen überschreiten – Räume aktivieren" bot sich aber auch mit der konkreten Fragestellung an, wie die urbane und die rurale Sphäre in der Stadtregion verknüpft und vielfältige Austauschprozesse zwischen den Sphären stimuliert werden können. Damit

Even years after the conclusion of the project, some of the pilot projects continue. They formed central reference points during our visits. In Dar Bouazza, in the southwestern periphery of Casablanca, there is an education farm for agroecological cultivation, which was built up in cooperation with local farmers and the NGO Terre et Humanisme. It serves among other things as a starting point for the education of small-scale local farmers and the development of a producing-consuming network for the sales of organic food baskets. As part of a workshop, the participants in the doctoral colloquium were able to engage in exchanges with farmers in the region and others involved in the urban production network.

Casablanca has an arid climate. The management of limited water resources is therefore a central challenge for the urban region. The still-developing infrastructure system with a first wastewater treatment plant for wastewater disposal and treatment was a further key point. The central component of the research project was to show with concrete testing, in scenarios as well as pilot projects, how treated water can be used in agriculture for food production. The central observation object for this was the Jardin de Médiouna, a public show garden in the southeast of the urban region, in which urban agriculture is run using water from the neighboring wastewater treatment plant.

For a long time, the food supply to cities was a blind spot in city planning. It is only since recently that the urban food system has become a focus of city and landscape research—and therefore also agriculture, whose role is transforming into a productive green infrastructure. The visits to Casablanca offered the opportunity to explore steps towards a closer connection between the city and agriculture.

knüpften wir an Fragestellungen an, mit denen sich das inter- und trans-disziplinäre Forschungsprojekt zur Urbanen Landwirtschaft in Casablanca, Marokko (2005–2014), im Rahmen des Förderprogramms „Future Megacities" des Bundesministeriums für Bildung und Forschung (BMBF) zunächst analytisch, dann konzeptionell und konkret testend auseinandergesetzt hatte.[1] Auch Jahre nach Abschluss des Projektes besteht ein Teil der Pilotprojekte weiter. Sie bildeten zentrale Anlaufpunkte während unserer Stippvisite. In Dar Bouazza, in der südwestlichen Peripherie Casablancas, befindet sich eine Lehrfarm für agroökologische Anbauweise, die in Zusammenarbeit mit lokalen Farmern und der NGO Terres et Humanism aufgebaut wurde. Sie dient unter anderem als Ausgangspunkt für die Schulung lokaler Kleinstfarmer*innen und dem Aufbau eines Produzierenden-Konsumierenden-Netzwerkes zum Vertrieb von Biokörben. Im Rahmen eines Workshops konnten sich die Teilnehmenden des Doktorandenkolloquiums mit Farmer*innen der Region und weiteren Akteur*innen des urbanen Produktionsnetzwerkes austauschen.

Casablanca weist ein arides Klima auf. Der Umgang mit beschränkten Wasserressourcen ist deshalb eine zentrale Herausforderung für die Stadtregion. Das noch im Aufbau befindliche Infrastruktursystem mit einer ersten Kläranlage zur Wasserentsorgung und -aufbereitung war ein weiterer Anlaufpunkt. Zentrale Komponente des Forschungsprojektes war es, sowohl in Szenarien als auch durch Pilotprojekte konkret testend zu zeigen, wie gereinigtes Wasser in der Landwirtschaft zur Nahrungsmittelproduktion eingesetzt werden kann. Zentrales Anschauungsobjekt dafür war der Jardin de Médiouna, ein öffentlicher Schaugarten im Südosten der Stadtregion, in dem unter Nutzung des Wassers der benachbarten Kläranlage urbane Landwirtschaft betrieben wird.

Lange Zeit war die Nahrungsversorgung der Städte ein blinder Fleck in der Stadtplanung. Erst seit Kurzem rückt das urbane Nahrungssystem in den Fokus der Stadt- und Landschaftsforschung – und damit auch die Landwirtschaft, deren Rolle sich zu einer produktiven grünen Infrastruktur wandelt. Die Stippvisite in Casablanca bot die Möglichkeit, Schritte hin zu einer engeren Verknüpfung von Stadt und Landwirtschaft vor Ort zu erkunden.

Casablanca, November 2018

Casablanca, November 2018

Casablanca, November 2018

Casablanca, November 2018

Casablanca, November 2018

Casablanca, November 2018

Casablanca, November 2018

Casablanca, November 2018

URBAN PERSPECTIVES
URBANE PERSPEKTIVEN

URBAN PERSPECTIVES—BIG PLANS: RENAISSANCE OF THE SPATIALLY ORIENTED URBAN DEVELOPMENT PLANS

MARKUS NEPPL

Preamble

In the final phase of almost all dissertation projects, the question arises of to whom the gained insights should be addressed. There is a challenge behind this that nobody likes to face in this phase: which links with practice are useful and what impulses can really be given by academic works? Such questions are painful at this point in time and are often suppressed—because those working on them supposedly have more important things to do. The chapters "Transferability" and "Further Research Requirements" often remain vague. Some speak of recommendations for action—but for whom? Others suggest manuals—but who reads them? Others state what would still need to be researched—but by whom and when?

In the checking procedures of our domains, these chapters play a subordinate role. Academic achievement is measured according to overall performance and immaculate documentation. It is not only the technologically oriented research disciplines that judge these matters significantly more strictly. The output and the *innovation factor* are international standards and are in some cases demanded exceptionally humorlessly in peer reviews and assessments. At the college in recent years, however, there has been a series of works that formulated very clear demands pertaining to planning practice. Markus Nollert at ETH Zurich established spatial planning design in large-scale processes. Martin Berchthold at KIT worked out methods for making complex data and information usable for planning. And Kristin Barbey from KIT promoted climate adaptation strategies on a regional scale. In many works that dealt with systematic inner development, a link with test planning procedures was always recommended. Anita Grahms from ETH Zurich clearly emphasized this connection of large-scale phenomena with concrete plans in her dissertation *Spielräume der Dichte* (Scopes of density). For Dr. Florian Stadtschreiber from TU Vienna, it was about the adaptation of the binding urban land-use planning to the demands of climate change; while Roman Streit from ETH Zurich clearly positioned the role of nonprofit housing construction in inner development as a demand on politics. These few examples show that research is indeed concerned with fundamental questions and large-scale statements and address them to planning practice. The latter must ask itself, however, how it can implement these findings.

Overburdening through planning routines

In cities and municipalities, usage and development plans are the binding specifications for urban land-use planning. The overarching regional,

URBANE PERSPEKTIVEN – GROßE PLÄNE: RENAISSANCE DER RÄUMLICH ORIENTIERTEN STADTENTWICKLUNGSPLANUNGEN

MARKUS NEPPL

Vorab

In der Endphase fast aller Dissertationsprojekte stellt sich die Frage, an wen die gewonnenen Erkenntnisse adressiert werden sollen. Dahinter verbirgt sich eine Herausforderung, der sich in dieser Phase niemand gerne stellt: Welche Verknüpfungen mit der Praxis sind sinnvoll und welche Impulse können tatsächlich von akademischen Arbeiten ausgehen? Derlei Fragen sind zu diesem Zeitpunkt schmerzhaft und werden gerne verdrängt – die Bearbeitenden haben vermeintlich wichtigere Dinge zu tun. Die Kapitel „Übertragbarkeit" und „Weiterer Forschungsbedarf" bleiben oft wage. Einige sprechen von Handlungsempfehlungen – doch für wen? Andere schlagen Handbücher vor – aber wer liest die? Wieder andere benennen, was noch erforscht werden müsste – doch von wem und wann?

In den Prüfungsprozeduren unserer Domäne spielen diese Kapitel eine untergeordnete Rolle. Die wissenschaftliche Leistung bemisst sich anhand der Gesamtperformance und der tadellosen Dokumentation. Nicht nur die technologisch orientierten Forschungsdisziplinen beurteilen diese Angelegenheiten wesentlich strenger. Der Output und der *innovation factor* sind internationale Standards und werden zum Teil ausgesprochen humorlos in Peer-Reviews und Gutachten eingefordert.

Dabei gab es im Kolleg in den letzten Jahren eine Reihe von Arbeiten, die sehr deutliche Forderungen an die Planungspraxis formulierten. Markus Nollert von der ETH Zürich etablierte das raumplanerische Entwerfen in großmaßstäblichen Prozessen. Martin Berchthold vom KIT erarbeitete Methoden, um komplexe Daten und Informationen für die Planung nutzbar zu machen. Und Kristin Barbey vom KIT forderte Klimaanpassungsstrategien im regionalen Maßstab. In vielen Arbeiten, die sich mit der systematischen Innenentwicklung beschäftigten, wurde stets eine Verknüpfung mit Testplanungsverfahren empfohlen. Anita Grahms von der ETH Zürich arbeitete diesen Zusammenhang von großräumigen Phänomenen mit konkreten Planungen in ihrer Arbeit *Spielräume der Dichte* sehr anschaulich heraus. Dr. Florian Stadtschreiber von der TU Wien ging es schließlich um die Anpassung der verbindlichen Bauleitplanung an die Herausforderungen des Klimawandels; während Roman Streit von der ETH Zürich die Rolle des gemeinnützigen Wohnungsbaus in der Innenentwicklung als eine Forderung an die Politik klar positionierte. Diese wenigen Beispiele zeigen, dass die Forschung sehr wohl grundsätzliche Fragen und großräumig orientierte Aussagen verarbeitet und an die Planungspraxis adressiert. Diese muss sich allerdings fragen, wie sie diese Erkenntnisse umsetzen kann.

transport, and state development plans do have an influence but play a subordinate role in municipal procedures. This often leads to an increased parish-pump state of mind and a fixation on one's own local subdistrict. Intercommunal activities are tiresome and difficult to arrange. The administrations and political decision-makers are veritably trapped in the countless routine procedures and are not capable of processing wider spatial and thematic contexts. Apart from the impermeable sectoral administrative structures, a lack of prioritization on the political agenda is the reason for the overburdening and wasting of municipal planning capacities.

Many communal politicians and especially those responsible for planning are by all means aware of this lack. There are established plans for different topics but they have a short half-life period and are not linked together.

No model?

In the 1990s, Johann Jessen addressed the question of models in planning in a comprehensive publication.[1] The answers at the time appear vague from a present-day point of view. The notion was perceived as too authoritarian and not contemporary enough. Kees Christiaanse wrote at the time: "There is neither a future for harmonious centralism nor for a decentralized laissez-faire."[2] He thus described a differentiated attitude between liberalism and the necessary steering through planning. The authors ultimately agreed, however, that all those involved should concentrate on concrete projects rather than lose themselves in discussions about the wider picture.

No model is not a solution, either

The notion of a model did not play any further role for a long time after. There were regular planning procedures on various scales, but overall urban considerations remained more an exception.

It was more or less by coincidence that the term reappeared on the agenda as part of the spatial model process in Karlsruhe, which the specialist public noted with surprise.[3] Christian Holl said about this: "No model is not a solution, either. Karlsruhe is boldly venturing a big plan. By 2016, a spatial model is to be developed for the city as a whole. ... The procedure is costly, the method is bold, but it opens up the perspective again of viewing the whole city—an approach long neglected by German cities."[4]

Examples of successful model processes, even if they are almost always referred to under another label, are the spatially oriented urban development plans of the cities of Mannheim, Hannover, Rastatt, Hamburg, and Cologne.

Inner-city development concept (EKI) Mannheim, 2006–2010

"Mannheim claims to be a citizens' city. This means: we shape Mannheim together."[5] This quote from Mayor Peter Kurz comes from the year 2009. It was preceded by an almost four-year process that had addressed in many facets the connection between administrative action and the objectives of urban society.

Überbelastung durch Planungsroutinen

In den Städten und Gemeinden sind die Flächennutzungs- und Bebauungspläne die verbindlichen Planwerke für die Bauleitplanung. Die übergeordneten Regional-, Verkehrs- und Landesentwicklungspläne haben zwar einen Einfluss, spielen aber in den gemeindehoheitlichen Prozeduren eine untergeordnete Rolle. Das führt oft zu einem verstärktem Kirchturmdenken und einer Fixierung auf die eigene Gemarkung. Interkommunale Aktivitäten sind langwierig und schwer vermittelbar. In den unzähligen Routineverfahren sind die Verwaltungen und die politischen Entscheidungstragenden regelrecht gefangen und nicht in der Lage, größere räumliche und thematische Zusammenhänge zu bearbeiten. Neben den undurchlässigen sektoralen Verwaltungsstrukturen ist eine mangelnde Priorisierung auf der politischen Agenda der Grund für eine Überlastung und Verschwendung der städtischen Planungskapazitäten.

Dieser Mangel ist vielen kommunalen Politiker*innen und vor allem den Planungsverantwortlichen durchaus bewusst. Zwar gibt es fundierte Planwerke zu verschiedenen Themen, sie haben aber eine kurze Halbwertszeit und sind untereinander nicht verknüpft.

Ohne Leitbild?

In den 1990er Jahren thematisierte Johann Jessen[1] in einer umfangreichen Publikation die Frage nach Leitbildern in der Planung. Die damaligen Antworten erscheinen aus heutiger Sicht diffus. Der Begriff wurde als zu autoritär und wenig zeitgemäß empfunden. Kees Christiaanse schrieb damals: „Es gibt weder eine Zukunft für harmonischen Zentralismus noch für dezentralisiertes laissez-faire."[2] Er beschrieb so eine differenzierte Haltung zwischen Liberalismus und der notwendigen Steuerung durch Planung. Die Autor*innen waren sich aber letztlich einig, dass sich alle Beteiligten eher auf konkrete Projekte konzentrieren sollten, als sich in Diskussionen über das große Ganze zu verlieren.

Kein Leitbild ist auch keine Lösung

Der Leitbildbegriff spielte danach lange keine Rolle mehr. Es gab zwar regelmäßig Planungsverfahren in unterschiedlichen Größenordnungen, aber gesamtstädtische Überlegungen blieben eher die Ausnahme.

Mehr oder weniger zufällig kam der Begriff im Zuge des räumlichen Leitbildprozesses in Karlsruhe[3] wieder auf die Agenda, was die Fachöffentlichkeit verwundert zur Kenntnis nahm. Dazu Christian Holl: „Kein Leitbild ist auch keine Lösung. Karlsruhe wagt sich an den großen Plan. Bis 2016 soll ein räumliches Leitbild für die Gesamtstadt entwickelt werden. [...] Das Verfahren ist aufwendig, die Methode ein Wagnis, aber man öffnet wieder die Perspektive, die ganze Stadt in den Blick zu nehmen – ein von deutschen Städten lange vernachlässigter Anspruch."[4]

Beispielhaft für erfolgreiche Leitbildprozesse sind, auch wenn sie fast immer unter einem anderen Label firmieren, die räumlich orientierten Stadtentwicklungsplanungen der Städte Mannheim, Hannover, Rastatt, Hamburg und Köln.

The impulse for this kind of planning came from several district managers and social space planners who had concerned themselves with problem quarters on the edge of the inner city. The segregation and crowding out processes in the inner city led to the realization that the previously customary sectoral plans were no longer capable of providing the basis for decisions that were necessary.

In the beginning, the massive surface requirements of the retail sector with the necessary infrastructure were seemingly not compatible with the small-scale residential quarters and their need for peace and greenery. The public discussion and planning process finally eased the rigid fronts. It soon became clear that only a mixed and lively inner city could be the common goal. The result was a type of "planning weather chart." Various thematic focuses were defined that set out a necessary division of work for the inner city but without specifying hard boundaries. In particular, they were to be the basis for a dynamic plan that is capable of adapting to the rapidly changing requirements. The subsequent EKI-2 and EKI-3 work phases almost exclusively served the implementation of the results in the administrative structures. Whether Mannheim has become a citizens' city cannot be verified. However, a useful basis was created for the administration that has significantly simplified many decision-making processes. Overall, civic society, politics, and the administration developed a clear sense of community, which had a positive effect especially on the planning culture in the context of carrying out major conversion projects in the subsequent years.

1 Document from the Mannheim model, 2013.
1 Dokumentation Mannheimer Modell, 2013.

Hannover City 2020+, 2007–2011

While many processes are very long-term, the state capital Hannover set out a very brief and precisely defined period of time. Apart from many public accompanying events, the planning procedure concentrated on a two-stage ideas competition that was oriented towards typical procedural patterns.[6] In a first step, the teams were to work on the further development of the entire inner city. The focus was especially on a fundamental demolition of transport areas in favor of new housing areas, as well as on the upgrading of public space. In a second step, the teams were assigned specific partial areas that were then worked on in greater depth. In this way, concrete projects developed very quickly along with a clear agenda for the whole period. Some of the projects have been realized, receiving multiple awards. The intensity was impressive but could only be maintained for a relatively short

Entwicklungskonzept Innenstadt (EKI) Mannheim, 2006–2010

„Mannheim hat den Anspruch, Bürgerstadt zu sein. Das bedeutet: Wir gestalten Mannheim gemeinsam."[5] Dieses Zitat von Oberbürgermeister Dr. Peter Kurz stammt aus dem Jahr 2009. Vorangegangen war ein fast vierjähriger Prozess, der in vielen Facetten den Zusammenhang zwischen Verwaltungshandeln und den Zielvorstellungen der Stadtgesellschaft thematisiert hatte. Der Impuls für diese Art von Planwerk kam von einigen Quartiersmanager*innen und Sozialraumplaner*innen, die sich mit Problemquartieren am Rande der Innenstadt beschäftigt hatten. Die Segregations- und Verdrängungsprozesse in der Innenstadt führten in den unterschiedlichen Resorts zu der Erkenntnis, dass die bisher üblichen sektoralen Planwerke nicht mehr in der Lage waren, die notwendigen Entscheidungen vorzubereiten. Am Anfang standen sich die massiven Flächenansprüche des Einzelhandels mit den dazu notwendigen Infrastrukturen und die kleinräumigen Wohnmilieus mit dem Bedürfnis nach Ruhe und Grün scheinbar unversöhnlich gegenüber. Der öffentliche Diskussions- und Planungsprozess lockerte schließlich die verhärteten Fronten. Es wurde schnell klar, dass nur eine durchmischte und lebendige Innenstadt das gemeinsame Ziel sein konnte. Herausgekommen ist eine Art „planerische Wetterkarte". Es wurden unterschiedliche thematische Schwerpunkte definiert, die eine notwendige Arbeitsteilung für die Innenstadt vorsahen, ohne aber scharfe Grenzen zu definieren. Vor allen Dingen sollten sie Grundlage für ein dynamisches Planwerk sein, das in der Lage ist, sich den schnell ändernden Anforderungen anzupassen. Die anschließenden EKI-2- und EKI-3-Arbeitsphasen dienten fast ausschließlich der Implementierung der Ergebnisse in die Verwaltungsstrukturen. Ob Mannheim deshalb eine Bürgerstadt geworden ist, kann nicht nachgewiesen werden. Für die Verwaltung wurde aber eine brauchbare Basis geschaffen, die viele Entscheidungsprozesse wesentlich vereinfacht hat. Insgesamt entwickelten die Stadtgesellschaft, die Politik und die Verwaltung ein deutliches Wir-Gefühl, was sich insbesondere auf die Planungskultur im Kontext der Durchführung großer Konversionsprojekte in den Folgejahren positiv auswirkte.

HannoverCity 2020+, 2007–2011

Während viele Prozesse sehr langfristig angelegt sind, hat die Landeshauptstadt Hannover sich auf einen sehr kurzen und präzise definierten Zeitraum festgelegt. Neben vielen öffentlichen Begleitveranstaltungen[6] konzentrierte sich das Planungsverfahren auf einen zweistufigen Ideenwettbewerb, der sich an üblichen Verfahrensmustern orientierte. In einem ersten Schritt

2 Redesign of the Klagesmarkt in Hannover.
2 Umgestaltung Klagesmarkt Hannover.

3 Building at the Klagesmarkt in Hannover.
3 Gebäude am Klagesmarkt Hannover.

period. Even so, a stable basis was established in Hannover, as well, upon which, for example, the remarkable Hannover housing construction offensive 2016–2020[7] and the city extension project Kronsrode[8] could be built.

Framework plan Rastatt inner city, 2010–2011

Rastatt's mayor also declared a new era of participation culture—rather unusual for a small town in Baden. In the town of 50,000 inhabitants, this concerned working through, within a very brief time, many urban development problems surrounding the baroque town center with its beautiful facades: a conversion area, a new build area, a new shopping center, an unsightly town square, and two former brewery sites. It was only the presentation of the future projects in a spatial context that showed the opportunities as well as the risks that would emerge for the restructuring of the town center over the following years. This overall perspective was new and unfamiliar for the various administrative offices and the members of the municipal council. The plan was formulated considerably more extensively and principally than conventional project plans, which initially led to the political bodies being overwhelmed.[9] In contrast to larger cities, however, the number of social and political involved parties is more manageable and they are networked better. An intensive and very closely meshed communication with the key actors forged a comprehensive basis of trust and enables significantly more precise plans.

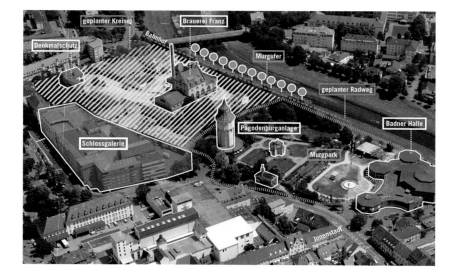

4 Concept for Rastatt inner city.
4 Innenstadtkonzept Rastatt.

Hamburger Building Forum 2019

To draw attention in cities to very abstract plans that are difficult to convey, special formats are required. The Hamburg Building Forums, which have been held at irregular intervals already since the 1980s, have always been major occurrences with an event character.[10] The open workshops by the

sollte von den Teams die Weiterentwicklung der gesamten Innenstadt bearbeitet werden. Im Fokus standen vor allem ein grundsätzlicher Rückbau der Verkehrsflächen zugunsten neuer Wohnbauflächen und die Aufwertung der öffentlichen Räume. In einem zweiten Schritt wurden den Teams konkrete Teilräume zugewiesen, welche dann vertieft ausgearbeitet wurden. Es entstanden auf diese Weise sehr schnell konkrete Projekte und eine klare Agenda für den gesamten Zeitraum. Die Projekte sind zum Teil realisiert und wurden vielfach ausgezeichnet. Die Intensität war beeindruckend, aber auch nur relativ kurz aufrechtzuerhalten. Trotzdem wurde auch in Hannover eine stabile Basis geschaffen, auf der unter anderem die bemerkenswerte Hannover'sche Wohnungsbauoffensive 2016–2020[7] und das Stadterweiterungsprojekt Kronsrode[8] entstehen konnten.

Rahmenplan Innenstadt Rastatt, 2010–2011

Auch Rastatts Oberbürgermeister verkündete eine neue Ära der Beteiligungskultur – für eine Kleinstadt in Baden eher ungewöhnlich. In der 50.000-Einwohner*innen-Stadt galt es rund um die barocke Innenstadt mit ihren schönen Fassaden in sehr kurzer Zeit viele städtebauliche Problemstellungen aufzuarbeiten: eine Konversionsfläche, ein Neubaugebiet, ein neues Einkaufszentrum, ein unansehnlicher Stadtplatz und zwei ehemalige Brauereiareale. Allein die Darstellung der zukünftigen Projekte in einem räumlichen Zusammenhang zeigte die Möglichkeiten und auch Risiken auf, die sich für den Umbau der Innenstadt in den nächsten Jahren ergeben würden. Diese Gesamtperspektive war für die unterschiedlichen Verwaltungsresorts und die Mitglieder des Gemeinderats neu und ungewohnt. Das Planwerk[9] war wesentlich weitgehender und grundsätzlicher als herkömmliche Projektpläne formuliert, was zunächst zu einer Überforderung der politischen Gremien führte. Im Gegensatz zu größeren Städten ist aber die Zahl der gesellschaftlichen und politischen Beteiligten überschaubarer und sie sind besser vernetzt. Eine intensive und sehr kleinteilige Kommunikation mit den Schlüsselakteur*innen erzeugte eine umfassende Vertrauensbasis und ermöglichte wesentlich präzisere Planungen.

Hamburger Bauforum 2019

Um in Großstädten Aufmerksamkeit für sehr abstrakte und schwer vermittelbare Planwerke zu bekommen, bedarf es besonderer Formate. Die Hamburger Bauforen[10], die schon seit den 1980er Jahren in unregelmäßigen Abständen stattfinden, sind seit jeher Großereignisse mit Eventcharakter. Die offenen Werkstätten des jeweiligen Oberbaudirektors mit internationalen Gästen erzeugten für eine Woche eine intensive Arbeits- und Diskussionsatmosphäre. Mit gut gemachten Veröffentlichungen und einem breiten Medienecho

5 *Impressions from Hamburg Building Forum 2019.*
5 *Impressionen vom Hamburger Bauforum 2019.*

6 *Impressions from Hamburg Building Forum 2019.*
6 *Impressionen vom Hamburger Bauforum 2019.*

respective construction director with international guests foster an intensive work and discussion atmosphere for a week. With well-made publications and a wide media echo, they have succeeded in anchoring themes such as the Harbor City or—currently topical—the main streets in public perception. Such a compact form of open workshops only works, however, if it is linked with long-term planning strategies and administrative action—and if one does not expect wonders from these rather spontaneous results.

Cologne perspectives 2030—city strategy 2017–2020

The city of Cologne, on the other hand, seeks to combine and respond to strategic and spatial questions with the process of working out Cologne perspectives.[11] Like almost every major city, Cologne has been confronted in recent years with profound transformation processes. Especially the growth of the city, which places new demands in terms of density, cohabitation, and land use, is a central challenge. It not only requires mobilizing land for construction and creating new living space but also deeply affects all spheres of life.

The project is masterminded by the Urban Development Authority, and with Mayor Henriette Reker it has a strong voice: "The future work requires a targeted, strategic direction and the integrated cooperation of the actors from politics, administration, the economy, and civil society. There are two key questions. How do we want to live in Cologne in the year 2030 and how do we position ourselves in regional and international competition?"[12]

The aim of committing the entire municipal administration of a city to a comprehensive strategy is ambitious and costly. In combination with a structural administrative reform, it will have to be proven to what extent the results can also be measured against the ambitions.

7 Second Future Forum of Cologne perspectives.
7 *2. Zukunftsforum der Kölner Perspektiven.*

8 Design draft of Cologne perspectives, 2019.
8 *Entwurfsfassung der Kölner Perspektiven, 2019.*

Conclusion

All big and small cities in Germany feel a significant dynamic in the areas of population development, workplace securing, mobility offers, climate adaptation, and resource efficiency. Simply waiting, thinking exclusively within one's own local confines, and merely reacting are no longer sufficient for responding to the urgent questions of the future. The plans that set out to meet these challenges must be worked on and communicated publicly. Just these few examples show that every city must seek its own path in line with its planning culture. Whether compact events or drawn-out processes are the right way should be considered thoroughly by those responsible, and the budgets made available accordingly.

In any case, large-scale plans are absolutely ineffective if they are not linked with the available planning levels and synchronized with their content. Of course, conflicts emerge in the process. The strong usage competition surrounding the respective areas only becomes visible in a spatial layering of the sectoral plans. Skeptical and critical voices often blame the failure of this approach on this and generally question the usefulness of large-scale spatial planning.

gelang es, Themen wie die Hafencity oder – gerade aktuell – die Magistralen in der öffentlichen Wahrnehmung zu verankern. Eine derart kompakte Form der offenen Werkstätten funktioniert aber nur, wenn sie mit langfristigen Planungsstrategien und dem Verwaltungshandeln verknüpft ist – und man keine Wunderdinge von den eher spontanen Ergebnissen erwartet.

Kölner Perspektiven 2030 – Stadtstrategie 2017–2020

Die Stadt Köln wiederum versucht mit dem Prozess zur Erarbeitung der Kölner Perspektiven[11] strategische und räumliche Fragestellungen zu kombinieren und zu beantworten. Wie beinahe jede Großstadt wurde Köln in den letzten Jahren mit tief greifenden Transformationsprozessen konfrontiert. Insbesondere das Stadtwachstum, das neue Anforderungen an Dichte, Zusammenleben und Flächennutzungen stellt, ist eine zentrale Herausforderung. Es erfordert nicht nur Baulandmobilisierung und Schaffung von neuem Wohnraum, sondern wirkt weit in alle Lebensbereiche hinein.

Das Projekt wird federführend vom Amt für Stadtentwicklung gesteuert und hat mit der Oberbürgermeisterin Henriette Reker eine starke Stimme: „Die künftige Arbeit bedarf einer zielgerichteten, strategischen Ausrichtung und integrierten Zusammenarbeit der Akteurinnen und Akteure aus Politik, Verwaltung, Wirtschaft und Bürgerschaft. Dabei stehen zwei Fragen im Mittelpunkt. Wie wollen wir in Köln im Jahr 2030 leben und wie positionieren wir uns im regionalen und internationalen Wettbewerb?"[12]

Der Anspruch, die komplette Stadtverwaltung einer Großstadt auf eine umfassende Strategie einzuschwören, ist ambitioniert und aufwendig. In Kombination mit einer strukturellen Verwaltungsreform wird sich erweisen müssen, inwiefern sich die Ergebnisse auch an den Ambitionen messen lassen können.

Fazit

Alle großen und kleinen Städte in Deutschland spüren eine große Dynamik in den Bereichen Bevölkerungsentwicklung, Arbeitsplatzsicherung, Mobilitätsangebot, Klimaanpassung und Ressourceneffizienz. Einfaches Abwarten, ausschließlich auf die eigene Gemarkung gerichtetes Denken und bloßes Reagieren reichen nicht mehr aus, um die drängenden Zukunftsfragen zu beantworten. Die Planwerke, die sich diesen Herausforderungen stellen, müssen öffentlich erarbeitet und kommuniziert werden. Schon die wenigen Beispiele zeigen, dass jede Stadt einen eigenen, auf ihre Planungskultur abgestimmten Weg suchen muss. Ob nun kompakte Events oder langwierige Prozesse der richtige Weg sind, sollten sich die Verantwortlichen reiflich überlegen und auch die Budgets dafür bereitstellen.

The early manifestation of these conflicts also opens up the possibility of seeking a compromise or bringing about a clear decision. The usual "muddling through" of the locality does not accomplish the goal anyway. The frequently demanded measurable success of these urban development plans is an illusion. The effects of these processes are often indirect and only become visible much later. Those responsible should therefore always pay attention to a healthy mix of concrete projects that can be quickly realized and long-term strategic approaches.

The currently observable inflation of procedures shows, on the one hand, the demand for the use of these tools but, on the other hand, can often lead to an oversaturation and false expectations. Perhaps the next generation will not be so patient—and the mindset will be: "We need quick and radical solutions and not long-term strategies!"

In jedem Fall sind großräumige Planwerke absolut wirkungslos, wenn sie nicht mit den vorhandenen Planungsebenen verknüpft und mit deren Inhalten synchronisiert werden. Natürlich treten dabei Konflikte zu Tage. Die starke Konkurrenz der Nutzungen um die jeweiligen Flächen wird erst bei räumlicher Überlagerung der sektoralen Pläne sichtbar. Skeptische und kritische Stimmen machen daran oft das Scheitern dieser Vorgehensweise fest und stellen die Sinnhaftigkeit großmaßstäblicher räumlicher Planung generell infrage.

Das frühzeitige Sichtbarwerden dieser Konflikte eröffnet aber die Möglichkeit, einen Kompromiss zu suchen oder eine klare Entscheidung herbeizuführen. Das übliche „Durchwurschteln" der Resorts führt sowieso nicht zum Ziel. Der oft geforderte messbare Erfolg dieser Stadtentwicklungsplanungen ist eine Illusion. Die Auswirkungen dieser Prozesse sind oft mittelbar und werden erst sehr viel später sichtbar. Deshalb sollten die Verantwortlichen immer auf eine gesunde Mischung aus schnell umsetzbaren konkreten Projekten und langfristigen strategischen Weichenstellungen achten.

Die im Moment beobachtbare Inflation der Verfahren zeigt auf der einen Seite das Bedürfnis nach Anwendung dieser Instrumente, kann aber auf der anderen Seite schnell zu einer Übersättigung und zu falschen Erwartungshaltungen führen. Vielleicht ist die nächste Generation nicht mehr so geduldig – und es heißt dann: „Wir brauchen schnelle und radikale Lösungen und keine langfristigen Strategien!"

Karlsruhe, September 2018

Karlsruhe-Durlach, September 2018

INCREMENTAL CITY—URBAN CODING FOR FUTURE CO-PRODUCED CITIES FOR CONTROLLING DYNAMIC URBAN GROWTH

MANUEL HAUER

According to figures from the United Nations, the worldwide population will grow from around 7.5 billion today to a total of 10 billion by the year 2050. At the same time, the trend towards urbanization continues. Virtually the whole population increase will take place in cities and consequently the urban population will increase from 3.6 to over 6 billion by the year 2050. However, this growth will not be spread evenly but concentrated primarily in emerging and developing nations. It is estimated, due to local economic conditions, that the majority of this growth will be absorbed by informal settlements. Prognoses by the UN assume that by the year 2050 the number of inhabitants of informal settlements will increase significantly from one billion today and as a consequence around two thirds of the future urban development will occur in the informal sector.

In light of these developments, various experts are demanding that we accept the informal sector as the predominant form of future urban space production, anticipate the development of self-built settlements, and incorporate them into formal planning processes. This dissertation takes up this approach and develops it further into a hybrid urban development model that brings together aspects of top-down planning and bottom-up self-organization as well as giving ample space for informal self-building. A key concept of this model is shaped by adaptable infrastructure frameworks that are intended to guide future developments into coordinated trajectories of development. The spaces in between the resulting framework will be filled primarily with various self-built housing typologies and supplemented by public services.

Such an urban development model equates to a paradigm change in urban planning, as informal growth must be anticipated and formal planning methods adapted for handling self-built settlements. Affected authorities or municipalities are concerned that current extra-legal forms of city production could be permissible in future within their territories. This work illustrates which fundamental rules and obligations the authorities, as well as the future inhabitants of self-built neighborhoods, must follow to enable the successful coproduction of future urban extensions.

The *urban coding* of the resulting urban development model is based on two pillars: the urban plan, a structural concept and the associated figures for city planning, as well as the urban code, the fundamental rules and obligations for inhabitants and responsible authorities. Through the combination of spatial urban structures and application-oriented regulations, an alternative urban development model will be created that may serve as a tool in various planning processes in the context of future coproduced cities.

INCREMENTAL CITY – URBAN CODING FÜR ZUKÜNFTIGE KOPRODUZIERTE STÄDTE ZUR STEUERUNG DYNAMISCHEN STADTWACHSTUMS

MANUEL HAUER

Gemäß Zahlen der Vereinten Nationen (United Nations) wird die weltweite Bevölkerung bis ins Jahr 2050 von heute circa 7,5 auf insgesamt 10 Milliarden wachsen. Gleichzeitig schreitet der Trend zur Urbanisierung weiter voran. In Summe wird nahezu der gesamte Bevölkerungszuwachs in Städten stattfinden und demnach die Stadtbevölkerung bis ins Jahr 2050 von 3,6 auf über 6 Milliarden ansteigen. Dieses Wachstum verteilt sich jedoch nicht gleichförmig, sondern konzentriert sich vornehmlich auf Schwellen- und Entwicklungsländer. Es ist aufgrund der dortigen ökonomischen Rahmenbedingungen anzunehmen, dass ein Großteil dieses Wachstums von informellen Siedlungen aufgefangen werden muss. Prognosen der UN gehen davon aus, dass sich die Zahl der Einwohner*innen informeller Siedlungen von heute einer Milliarde bis ins Jahr 2050 deutlich erhöht und damit etwa zwei Drittel der zukünftigen städtischen Entwicklung im informellen Sektor stattfinden wird.

Vor dem Hintergrund dieser Entwicklungen rufen verschiedene Expert*innen dazu auf, den informellen Sektor als zukünftig vorherrschende Form der Stadtproduktion zu akzeptieren und das Entstehen von Selbstbausiedlungen zu antizipieren und in formelle Planungsprozesse einzubeziehen. Die Arbeit greift diesen Ansatz auf und entwickelt ihn zu einem hybriden Stadtentwicklungsmodell weiter, welches sowohl Aspekte von Top-down-Planungen als auch Freiräume für informellen Selbstbau und Bottom-up-Selbstorganisation in sich vereint. Ein Schlüsselkonzept dieses Modells bilden adaptierbare Infrastrukturgerüste, welche zukünftige Entwicklungen in geordnete Bahnen lenken sollen. Die Zwischenräume des somit entstehenden Gerüsts werden vornehmlich im Selbstbau mit verschiedenen Wohntypologien gefüllt und durch dienende Nutzungen ergänzt. Ein solches Stadtentwicklungsmodell gleicht einem Paradigmenwechsel in der Stadtplanung, da informelles Wachstum antizipiert und formelle Planungsmethoden für den Umgang mit Selbstbausiedlungen adaptiert werden müssen. Betroffene Behörden oder Kommunen befürchten, dass derzeit extralegale Formen der Stadtproduktion zukünftig innerhalb ihrer Territorien zulässig sein könnten. Sowohl die Behörden als auch die zukünftige Bewohnerschaft selbstgebauter Nachbarschaften müssen dabei grundlegenden Regeln und Pflichten folgen, um eine erfolgreiche Koproduktion zukünftiger Stadterweiterungen zu ermöglichen.

Das *Urban Coding* des resultierenden Stadtentwicklungsmodells basiert auf zwei Säulen: dem *Urban Plan*, einem räumlichen Strukturkonzept und den zugehörigen Kennzahlen für die Stadtplanung, sowie dem *Urban Code*, den grundlegenden Regeln und Pflichten für Siedler*innen und zuständige Behörden. Durch die Kombination räumlicher Stadtstrukturen mit einem anwendungsorientierten Regelwerk entsteht ein alternatives Stadtentwicklungsmodell, welches im Kontext zukünftiger koproduzierter Städte in verschiedenen Planungsprozessen als Werkzeug dienen kann.

INNOVATION AND AGILITY IN URBAN DEVELOPMENT

MAX HAUG

The current challenges presented by urban development in Germany are complex and multifaceted: digitization and the energy transition, structural change and immigration, housing shortages and demographic change, to name but a few.

The municipal administrations play a key role in overcoming these challenges. However, too many authorities serve as mere administrative bodies, rarely able to initiate innovations independently or venture to counter these challenges. This therefore raises the question of how the framework conditions in administration can be stimulated in terms of innovation and agility.

Based on four fundamental observations, there is an evident pressure to take action. First of all, one can observe a gap between theory and practice and a clear discrepancy between declared political intentions and everyday reality in the cities. In addition, while the authorities set the formal agendas, the implementation must take place in the communities. A further aspect is that the situation will become more acute in the medium term alongside the current challenges of urban development: it is scarcely conceivable how cities are supposed to handle, for example, a true mobility revolution or a larger wave of migrants.

This basic constellation gives rise to the question of how action options can be developed for cities in order to handle urban development planning with agility and innovation. This leads to the necessity of scientific studies about, with, and through public representation. If cities and municipalities are truly interested in improving their urban development management, then new impulses must be set by the political decision-makers, in order for municipalities to be equipped for the tasks they face. Links with science and research, cooperation between cities, networks with the economy, exchanges with the inhabitants, as well as internal communication and knowledge transfer—these are the decisive factors. Stagnant and outdated structures should therefore be broken down and cities should be prepared for this change, in order to think outside the box with innovative and agile impulses and continuously drive urban development forwards.

There are numerous studies of individual challenges in urban development, but references are lacking to the neighboring disciplines of politics, economics, and administration. It is therefore important to fill the interdisciplinary gap and to develop a method that can continuously and lastingly improve the innovation and agility capability in the context of urban development. Accordingly, the focus must not be on the planning solution of the problems themselves but directed towards the renewal of the framework conditions of urban development management: structurally, organizationally, and in terms of procedure.

INNOVATION UND AGILITÄT IN DER STADTENTWICKLUNG

MAX HAUG

Die aktuellen Herausforderungen der Stadtentwicklung in Deutschland sind komplex und vielseitig: Digitalisierung und Energiewende, Strukturwandel und Zuwanderung, Wohnraumknappheit und demografischer Wandel, um nur einige zu nennen.

Die kommunalen Verwaltungen haben eine Schlüsselfunktion bei der Bewältigung dieser Herausforderungen. Zu viele Behörden dienen jedoch als reine Abwicklungsapparate und können selten eigenständig Innovationen anstoßen oder größere Wagnisse zur Bewältigung der Herausforderungen eingehen. Es stellt sich daher die Frage, wie die Rahmenbedingungen in den Verwaltungen hinsichtlich Innovation und Agilität stimuliert werden können.

Ausgehend von vier grundsätzlichen Beobachtungen wird der Handlungsdruck ersichtlich: Zunächst sind eine Kluft zwischen Theorie und Praxis und eine deutliche Diskrepanz zwischen politischer Willensbekundung und Alltagsrealität in den Städten zu beobachten. Des Weiteren ist der Bund durch Verabschiedung von Agenden formaler Taktgeber, die Umsetzung jedoch ist in den Kommunen angesiedelt. Ein weiterer Aspekt ist, dass sich die Lage neben den aktuellen Herausforderungen der Stadtentwicklung mittelfristig verschärfen wird: Es ist kaum vorstellbar, wie Städte beispielsweise eine wirkliche Mobilitätsrevolution oder eine größere Flüchtlingswelle stemmen sollen.

Aus dieser Grundkonstellation heraus stellt sich die Frage, wie für Städte Handlungsoptionen entwickelt werden können, um die Stadtentwicklungsplanung agil und innovativ zu bewältigen. Hieraus resultiert die Notwendigkeit von wissenschaftlichen Arbeiten mit, durch und über öffentliche Vertretungen. Wenn Städte und Gemeinden an der Verbesserung ihres Stadtentwicklungsmanagements wirklich aufrichtig interessiert sind, dann sind neue Impulse durch die politischen Entscheidungsträger*innen zu setzen, um für die anstehenden Aufgaben gewappnet zu sein.

Verknüpfungen mit Wissenschaft und Forschung, Kooperationen zwischen Städten, Netzwerke mit der Wirtschaft, Austausch mit der Bevölkerung sowie interne Kommunikation und Wissenstransfer – das sind die entscheidenden Faktoren. Festgefahrene und veraltete Strukturen sind daher aufzubrechen und Städte auf diesen Wandel vorzubereiten, um mit innovativen und agilen Impulsen querzudenken und die Stadtentwicklung kontinuierlich voranzutreiben.

Zu einzelnen Herausforderungen der Stadtentwicklung liegt eine Vielzahl an Forschungsarbeiten vor, jedoch fehlen Anknüpfungspunkte zu den Nachbardisziplinen der Politik, der Wirtschaft und der Verwaltung. Es gilt also, die interdisziplinäre Lücke zu schließen und eine Methode zu entwickeln, welche die Innovations- und Agilitätsfähigkeit im Kontext der Stadtentwicklung nachhaltig und kontinuierlich verbessern kann. Demzufolge darf der Fokus nicht auf der planerischen Lösung der Probleme selbst liegen, sondern muss auf die Erneuerung der Rahmenbedingungen von Stadtentwicklungsmanagement gelenkt werden: strukturell, organisatorisch und prozessual.

SMART URBAN SPACES

RADOSTINA RADULOVA-STAHMER

The need for new, modern city districts is increasing. A great deal is demanded of them: that they be resource-efficient, energy-efficient, socially tolerant, affordable, resilient, and generally raise the quality of life of their inhabitants. Cities worldwide use information and communication technologies, for example, in the face of current urban challenges such as global warming, environmental pollution, and resource scarcity. However, it is only global pilot projects such as "Songdo" or "Masdar City" that show that the one-sided orientation towards technological solutions may improve the efficiency of the city but not its spatial qualities and therefore the quality of life of the inhabitants. In this context, what is still missing is spatial consideration of urban digitization processes and the necessity of a smart-spatial nexus becomes clear, meaning a direct connection between technologies and urban space quality. The technological leap in the last twenty years has brought about spatial changes on a district level. Smart city concepts have an increasing impact on the urban area. The interfaces and mutual effects between physical urban space and digital technologies must be examined to avoid the technocratic use of urban technologies. The aim is therefore to examine the spatial effectiveness of urban technologies on a district level, to find out how the discipline can make use of the technological progress to qualify the urban spaces of the future, and thus to create the best conditions for a high quality of life. The theory pursued is that smart city districts, with regard to mobility and the environment, even with optimal technical conditions, can only achieve the declared objective of raising the quality of life if they have an integrated spatial planning design.

Technological measures are first studied in terms of content and design for their spatial effectiveness and principles for smart spaces are derived from this effectiveness. For this study, three district pairs on different scales in the German-speaking area serve as a comparison, of which one bears the smart city label. The quality of the district areas thus becomes visible in connection with the label. Spatial factors and criteria are developed for the city districts, and these are checked in test designs and finally discussed and evaluated in an expert workshop. The results contribute to establishing spatial smartness as an additional third dimension of the understanding of a smart city, in order to enable spatial planning design strategies to physically materialize the concept of the smart city in the urban area, as well as to raise the quality of life—because the greatest potential for a sustainable, robust, integrative, and livable district with a high quality of life lies especially in the smartness of its spaces and less in its technologies.

SMARTE URBANE RÄUME

RADOSTINA RADULOVA-STAHMER

Der Bedarf an neuen, modernen Stadtquartieren steigt. Sie sollen vieles können: ressourcenschonend, energieeffizient, sozialverträglich, kostengünstig, belastbar sein und allgemein die Lebensqualität der Bürger*innen erhöhen. So werden weltweit in Städten unter anderem Informations- und Kommunikationstechnologien eingesetzt, um den aktuellen urbanen Herausforderungen wie globale Erwärmung, Umweltverschmutzung und Ressourcenknappheit zu begegnen. Doch erste globale Pilotprojekte wie „Songdo" oder „Masdar City" zeigen, dass die einseitige Ausrichtung auf technologische Lösungen zwar die Effizienz der Stadt verbessern kann, jedoch nicht die räumlichen Qualitäten der Stadt und damit die Lebensqualität der Bürger*innen. In diesem Kontext fehlt es an einer räumlichen Auseinandersetzung mit dem urbanen Digitalisierungsprozess und es wird die Notwendigkeit eines Smart-Spatial-Nexus deutlich, also einer direkten Verbindung zwischen Technologien und Stadtraumqualität.

Der Technologiesprung der letzten 20 Jahre hat räumliche Veränderungen auf der Quartiersebene bewirkt. Smart-City-Konzepte wirken zunehmend auf den urbanen Raum. Die Schnittstellen und Wechselwirkungen zwischen dem physischen Stadtraum und den digitalen Technologien müssen untersucht werden, um den technokratischen Einsatz urbaner Technologien zu vermeiden. Ziel ist es daher, die Raumwirksamkeit urbaner Technologien auf der Quartiersebene räumlich zu untersuchen, um herauszufinden, wie die Disziplin den technologischen Fortschritt nutzen kann, um die Stadträume der Zukunft zu qualifizieren und somit die beste Voraussetzung für eine hohe Lebensqualität zu schaffen. Dabei wird der These nachgegangen, dass Smart-City-Quartiere in Hinblick auf Mobilität und Umwelt, auch bei optimalen technischen Voraussetzungen, nur dann das erklärte Ziel der Erhöhung der Lebensqualität erreichen können, wenn sie räumlich integriert gestaltet sind.

Dazu werden technologische Maßnahmen inhaltlich und zeichnerisch zunächst auf ihre Raumwirksamkeit hin untersucht und daraus werden Prinzipien für smarte Räume abgeleitet. Zum Vergleich dienen drei Quartierspaare mit unterschiedlichen Maßstäben im deutschsprachigen Raum, von denen jeweils eines das Smart-City-Label trägt. Dadurch wird die Qualität der Quartiersräume im Zusammenhang mit dem Label sichtbar. Räumliche Faktoren und Kriterien werden für Stadtquartiere entwickelt und diese in Testentwürfen überprüft und schließlich in einem Expertenworkshop diskutiert und evaluiert.

Die Ergebnisse tragen dazu bei, die räumliche Smartness als zusätzliche dritte Dimension des Smart-City-Verständnisses zu etablieren, um Raumgestaltungsstrategien zu ermöglichen, das Konzept der Smart City im Stadtraum physisch zu materialisieren und die Lebensqualität zu erhöhen. Denn das größte Potenzial für ein nachhaltiges, robustes, integratives und lebenswertes Quartier mit hoher Lebensqualität liegt vor allem in der Smartness seiner Räume und weniger in seinen Technologien.

DISTRICT DEVELOPMENTS ARE OSCILLATING PROCESSES

YVONNE SIEGMUND

Dynamics across a variety of scales and different or diverging interests are constantly and increasingly driving urban development processes. Urban planning authorities are therefore looking for an appropriate handling of change and acceleration, amid ambiguity and contradictions.

In development processes that are geared towards requirements and are not linear, the time dimension becomes a significant process-defining factor. Whether it is Rapid Planning, Cittàslow or Slow Urbanism—urban development processes are either accelerated and target-oriented or decelerated and process-oriented.

However, rapid processes cannot be endlessly accelerated without consequences. Slowness and openness also have their limits, namely, where transitions, conclusions, and purposefulness are lost. A research-guided thesis advances the claim that ambivalences are more pronounced in nonlinear developments. Accelerated and decelerated processes therefore tend to move more frequently beyond systemic boundaries, associated with spatial, processual, or social compensation measures.

The study tested this thesis on district developments that describe their characteristics as "express," "turbo," "slow," "decelerated," or "open to process," examining spatial and programmatic characteristics, processual features, and social practices for the first time with greater temporal differentiation. Apart from speeds, the focus was on the influences of further time aspects (events, rhythms, time periods and sequences) as well as instances (actors, spaces, control mechanisms).

Typical features, particularities, and contradictions were established from different perspectives with the help of triangulation. Through the abduction, associations of meaning were deciphered and interpreted. Regular field research was associated with the controlled procedure of grounded theory in order to establish changes in the process, space, and viewpoints of the parties involved.

The research path led from acknowledged phenomena to a new theoretical understanding culminated in its core hypothesis (compensating—synchronizing—fluctuating). Driving forces outside of the area of influence of planning institutions directed district developments in the long term. In response, development planning procedures were turned around, building lifecycles were extended, and the boundaries of permit rights were crossed. The studied districts compensate as "pressure valves" or "deceleration oases" for their immediate surroundings. Communicative and coordinating interfaces helped to synchronize objectives and actions.

The core hypothesis—that "district developments are oscillating processes"—advocates seeing, in unpredictability, an opportunity to develop the city in a more context-related, situational, and visionary manner and to negotiate and juggle in live processes, as well as to create stability, permit uncertainty, and synchronize and withstand contradictions.

QUARTIERSENTWICKLUNGEN SIND SCHAUKELPROZESSE

YVONNE SIEGMUND

Maßstabsübergreifende Dynamiken und unterschiedliche, mitunter divergierende Interessen treiben Stadtentwicklungsprozesse fortwährend und zunehmend an. Stadtplanende Instanzen suchen daher nach einem angemessenen Umgang mit Wandel und Beschleunigung, mit Mehrdeutigkeiten und Widersprüchlichem. In bedarfsgerechten und nicht linearen Entwicklungsprozessen wird die zeitliche Dimension zu einem wesentlichen prozessgestaltenden Faktor. Ob *Rapid Planning* oder Beschleunigungsgesetzgebung, ob *Cittàslow* oder *Slow Urbanism* – urbane Entwicklungsprozesse sind entweder beschleunigt und zielorientiert oder entschleunigt und prozessorientiert gestaltet.

Jedoch sind schnelle Prozesse nicht ohne Abstriche unendlich beschleunigbar. Auch Langsamkeit und Offenheit haben ihre Grenzen, und zwar dort, wo Übergänge, Abschlüsse und Sinnhaftigkeit verloren gehen. Mit der forschungsleitenden These wird behauptet, dass in nicht linearen Entwicklungen Ambivalenzen stärker ausgeprägt sind. Daher bewegen sich be- und entschleunigte Prozesse tendenziell häufiger jenseits systemischer Grenzen, mit deren Überschreiten räumliche, prozessuale oder soziale Kompensationsmaßnahmen verbunden sind.

Geprüft wurde die These an Quartiersentwicklungen, die ihre Merkmale als „express", „im Turbo", „slow", „entschleunigt" oder „prozessoffen" umschreiben. Räumlich-programmatische Charakteristika, prozessuale Merkmale und soziale Praktiken wurden erstmals zeitlich differenzierter erforscht. Neben Geschwindigkeiten standen die Einflüsse weiterer Zeitaspekte (Ereignisse, Rhythmen, Zeiträume und Reihenfolgen) sowie von Eigenzeiten (Akteur*innen, Räume, Steuerungsinstrumente) im Fokus.

Mithilfe der Triangulation wurde Typisches, wurden Besonderheiten und Gegensätzlichkeiten aus unterschiedlichen Perspektiven herausgearbeitet. Durch die Abduktion wurden Sinnzusammenhänge dechiffriert und interpretiert. Mit dem kontrollierten Verfahren der Grounded Theory waren regelmäßige Feldforschungen verbunden, um Veränderungen im Prozess, im Raum und in den Sichtweisen handelnder Akteur*innen festzustellen.

Der Erkenntnisweg führte von erkannten Phänomenen zur These und verdichtete sich hin zur Kernhypothese (Kompensieren – Synchronisieren – Schaukeln). Treibende Kräfte, außerhalb des Einflussbereichs planender Institutionen, lenken Quartiersentwicklungen nachhaltig. Darauf reagierend wurden Bebauungsplanverfahren umgedreht, Gebäudelebenszyklen verlängert und genehmigungsrechtliche Grenzen überschritten. Die untersuchten Quartiere kompensieren als „Druckventile" oder „Entschleunigungsoasen" ihre nähere Umgebung. Kommunikative und koordinierende Schnittstellen halfen, Ziele und Handlungen zu synchronisieren.

Die Kernhypothese „Quartiersentwicklungen sind Schaukelprozesse" plädiert dafür, in der Unberechenbarkeit eine Chance zu sehen, Stadt kontextbezogener, situativer und visionärer zu entwickeln und in lebendigen Prozessen zu verhandeln und zu jonglieren, Stabilität zu schaffen und Unsicherheit zuzulassen, zu synchronisieren und Widersprüche auszuhalten.

STRASBOURG FLYING VISIT
STIPPVISITE STRASSBURG

IN THE MIDST, BUT NOT (YET) PART OF IT!

MARKUS NEPPL

If one looks at the aerial picture of the Upper Rhine region, it is dominated at first glance by the big cities of Karlsruhe, Strasbourg, Freiburg, and Basel. Upon second glance, however, one discovers a dense network of medium-sized and small towns that form the background with almost consistent sizes and distances from each other. From a geographical point of view, between the Black Forest in the east and the Vosges in the west, lies the Rhine valley, wide along this stretch before narrowing again in Switzerland. But if one superimposes the national borders, the three-country situation between Germany, France, and Switzerland becomes visible, which has a great influence on the regional relationships and spatial development between the big cities.

The Karlsruhe professor Martin Einsele researched the region intensely in the 1980s and propagated a perspective on regional development that was new at the time with his exhibition contribution *The Upper Rhine— A Different Metropolis*, as part of the XVII Triennale di Milano 1988.[1] According to the architect and landscape planner, "settlement areas with a decentralized structure" such as the Upper Rhine are a counter model to the traditional metropolises and the "global urbanization."

The region in the Upper Rhine was developing a role as a "central link in a European city landscape from London to Rome" and as "a region in the midst of Europe without borders."[2]

These research works were the basis for the foundation of the Upper Rhine Tripartie Metropolitan Region in the year 2010 (TMO; Région métropolitaine trinationale du Rhin supérieur).[3] This region comprises the Alsace in France, southern and central Baden, and the southern Palatinate in Germany, along with the Swiss cantons of Basel-City, Basel-Country, Jura, Solothurn, and Aargau with around 6 million inhabitants on 21,500 square kilometers.[4] Almost ten years later, the TMO has never really gotten beyond vague declarations of intent. In the invitation to the conference about the cross-border metropolitan area Strasbourg-Karlsruhe, there is still talk of great opportunities in the current cross-border context: "The moment is particularly opportune for the Euro metropolis and the city of Strasbourg, the city of Karlsruhe and their Euro districts to dedicate themselves together to consolidating their metropolitan cooperation and to set a signal for a stronger European integration."[5]

The main problem remains the national border between Germany and France. The city of Strasbourg with 280,000 inhabitants and the agglomeration with 785,000 inhabitants on the French side have surprisingly little influence on the opposite German side with the cities of Kehl and Offenburg. The linking of the infrastructure still has astounding gaps and the cities'

MITTENDRIN, ABER (NOCH) NICHT DABEI!

MARKUS NEPPL

Wenn man das Luftbild der Region Oberrhein betrachtet, dominieren die großen Städte Karlsruhe, Straßburg, Freiburg und Basel auf den ersten Blick. Beim zweiten Hinsehen entdeckt man aber ein dichtes Netzwerk mittlerer und kleiner Städte, die in fast gleichbleibenden Größenordnungen und Abständen den Hintergrund bilden.

Geografisch gesehen liegt zwischen dem Schwarzwald im Osten und den Vogesen im Westen das an dieser Stelle breite Rheintal, bevor es sich in der Schweiz wieder verengt. Blendet man allerdings die Staatsgrenzen ein, wird die Dreiländerlage zwischen Deutschland, Frankreich und der Schweiz sichtbar, welche großen Einfluss auf die regionalen Bezüge und die Raumentwicklung zwischen den großen Städten hat.

Der Karlsruher Professor Martin Einsele hat die Region in der 1980er Jahren intensiv erforscht und mit seinem Ausstellungsbeitrag *Der Oberrhein – eine andere Metropole* im Rahmen der XVII. Triennale di Milano 1988[1] eine damals neue Sichtweise auf die Regionalentwicklung propagiert. Ein Gegenmodell zu den klassischen Metropolen und der „globalen Verstädterung" sind nach Aussage des Architekten und Landschaftsplaners „dezentral gegliederte Siedlungsräume" wie der Oberrhein. Der Region am Oberrhein wachse eine Rolle als „zentrales Glied einer europäischen Städtelandschaft von London bis Rom" und als „Region in der Mitte eines Europas ohne Grenzen" zu.[2]

Diese Forschungsarbeiten waren die Grundlage für die Gründung der Trinationalen Metropolregion Oberrhein im Jahr 2010 (TMO; Région métropolitaine trinationale du Rhin supérieur)[3]. Sie umfasst das Elsass in Frankreich, Süd- und Mittelbaden sowie die südliche Pfalz in Deutschland und des Weiteren die Schweizer Kantone Basel-Stadt, Basel-Landschaft, Jura, Solothurn und Aargau mit rund 6 Millionen Einwohner*innen auf 21.500 Quadratkilometern.[4] Fast zehn Jahre später ist die TMO aber über vage Absichtserklärungen nicht wirklich hinausgekommen. In der Einladung zur Konferenz über den grenzüberschreitenden Metropolraum Straßburg-Karlsruhe wird immer noch von großen Chancen im aktuellen grenzüberschreitenden Kontext gesprochen: „Der Moment ist besonders günstig für die Eurometropole und die Stadt Straßburg, die Stadt Karlsruhe und ihre Eurodistrikte, sich gemeinsam zu engagieren, um ihre metropolitane Zusammenarbeit zu festigen und ein Signal für eine stärkere europäische Integration zu setzen."[5]

Das Hauptproblem bleibt die nationale Grenze zwischen Deutschland und Frankreich. Die Stadt Straßburg mit 280.000 Einwohner*innen und die Agglomeration mit 785.000 Einwohner*innen auf der französischen Seite haben erstaunlich wenig Einfluss auf die gegenüberliegende deutsche Seite mit den Städten Kehl und Offenburg. Die Verknüpfung der Infrastruktur

view of themselves is also more nationally defined. Although significant sums have been invested in recent years in the city of Kehl in spectacular bridges and new embankments, as well as in the further development of local economic relationships, there has not yet been a "major European effect." The same is true of Strasbourg, even though it is experienced today as a pulsating and very attractive metropolis. All around the historical old town, compact districts have developed that represent an urban way of life with a French character. In addition, the city of Strasbourg is the seat of numerous European institutions, including the Council of Europe, the European Parliament, the European Court of Justice for Human Rights, the European Ombudsman, and Eurokorps. For this reason, Strasbourg views itself as the "Capital of Europe."

With the project "Development region deux Rives," the city has enormous area reserves with a quality and centrality that scarcely another European city has. The master plan of the French landscape architecture firm agence ter addresses dense urban quarters, and no-longer-needed harbor areas, on the one hand, and links the cities of Kehl and Strasbourg, on the other hand, with a dense infrastructural, green area, and waterway network.

Martin Einsele propagated the Upper Rhine region at the time as a countermodel to the traditional metropolises because the "exceptional economic, political and cultural functions at a tightly limited area also always mean an accelerating and densifying growth with the consequence of traffic problems, social tension and the destruction of valuable building substance."[6]

As the metropolitan region has not experienced resounding success and national borders continue to be real barriers, one should rather speak of a fruitful trinational coexistence of the four metropolises Basel, Freiburg, Strasbourg, and Karlsruhe. The intensive city network of the Upper Rhine does not have to be a countermodel but is rather a highly developed regional "connective tissue," without which metropolises can only function poorly in future.

The key question, however, remains an effective integration of the "European capital" Strasbourg. It remains a true European acid test for the forthcoming generations.

hat nach wie vor erstaunliche Lücken und auch das Selbstverständnis der Städte ist eher national geprägt. Obwohl in den letzten Jahren in der Stadt Kehl erhebliche Mittel in spektakuläre Brücken und neue Ufergestaltungen investiert wurden und auch die lokalen Wirtschaftsbeziehungen weiter ausgebaut werden, bleibt der „große europäische Effekt" aus. Dabei erlebt man Straßburg heute als pulsierende und sehr attraktive Metropole. Rund um die historische Altstadt haben sich kompakte Stadtteile entwickelt, die für ein französisch geprägtes urbanes Lebensgefühl stehen. Zudem ist die Stadt Straßburg Sitz zahlreicher europäischer Einrichtungen, unter anderem Europarat, Europaparlament, Europäischer Gerichtshof für Menschenrechte, Europäische*r Bürgerbeauftragte*r und Eurokorps. Aufgrund dessen versteht sich Straßburg als „Hauptstadt Europas".

Mit dem Projekt „Entwicklungsgebiet deux Rives" besitzt die Stadt enorme Flächenreserven, die kaum eine europäische Stadt in dieser Qualität und Zentralität vorweisen kann. Der Masterplan des französischen Landschaftsarchitekturbüros agence ter thematisiert auf der eine Seite dichte urbane Quartiere auf den nicht mehr benötigten Hafenarealen und verknüpft auf der anderen Seite die Städte Kehl und Straßburg mit einem dichten Infrastruktur-, Grünraum- und Wassernetzwerk.

Martin Einsele hat damals die Region Oberrhein als Gegenmodell zu den klassischen Metropolen propagiert, weil die „herausragende wirtschaftliche, politische und kulturelle Funktionen an einem eng begrenzten Ort immer auch ein sich beschleunigendes und verdichtendes Wachstum bedeuten mit der Folge von Verkehrsproblemen, sozialen Spannungen und der Zerstörung wertvoller Bausubstanz."[6] Da der durchschlagende Erfolg der Metropolregion ausgeblieben ist, und nach wie vor die Bundesgrenzen wirkliche Barrieren sind, sollte man eher von einer fruchtbaren trinationalen Koexistenz der vier Metropolen Basel, Freiburg, Straßburg und Karlsruhe sprechen. Das intensive Städtenetzwerk des Oberrheins muss kein Gegenmodell sein, sondern ist vielmehr ein hochentwickeltes regionales „Bindegewebe", ohne das Metropolen in Zukunft nur schlecht funktionieren können. Die Schlüsselfrage aber bleibt eine wirkungsvolle Integration der „europäischen Hauptstadt" Straßburg. Es bleibt eine echte europäische Nagelprobe für die nächsten Generationen.

Strasbourg, May 2019
Straßburg, Mai 2019

Strasbourg, May 2019
Straßburg, Mai 2019

Strasbourg, May 2019
Straßburg, Mai 2019

SPATIAL SIMULATION
RAUMBEZOGENE SIMULATION

SPATIAL SIMULATION

ANDREAS VOIGT

The concrete addressing of real spaces as research laboratories is essential for practice and for spatial planning and planning studies. These considerations comprise the exploration of the problems and the associated perspectives on the problems determined socially and in relation to planning culture, as well as the related academic questions. Building on this are, in turn, necessary hypotheses (assumptions) and theses (propositions) about the methodological processing and gradual solution of existing problems or the avoidance of future problems. The Spatial Research Lab is the programmatic short version of this approach to space, time, and planning.

Parallel to this, digitally supported methods are increasingly offering extensive help in order to gain an *overview* in relation to space, time, actors, and problems; to obtain an *insight* into all scales and thematic levels (multiscalar); to gain a perspectival *outlook* on possible futures and concrete measures; and to conceive concrete measures or interventions that are tendentially suitable for solving problems or even avoiding them in the first place. In the context of a doctoral college, the focus of attention is especially on complex or novel, unsolved or only partially solved problems.

To adequately understand and work through social and regional administrative problems, it is necessary to formulate them precisely and model them within a reference framework. Spatial modeling can be understood as both the permissible and necessary reduction of spatial complexity.[1] This is linked to the fact that we inevitably "simplify, leave out, abstract"[2]—and therefore that the result cannot be completely objectivized.[3] Models are abstractions of an original, presenting its essential and important characteristics "representatively, reliably and true to structure."[4]

(Real) *objects* and *occurrences* can be viewed as originals, in the sense of the semiotic triangle, that are named through language (words) and characters and are, in turn, semiotically interpreted through notions, concepts, and constructs.[5] The basic classes of constructs range from "concept" ("units with which one constructs propositions"[6]) and "proposition" ("what is referred to with a sentence"[7]) to the respective spatial or thematic "context" and to the "theory" ("a closed context with regard to the logical interpretations"[8]). The precise working out of the concepts (terminology) and a shared basic understanding in the sense of a work definition are of fundamental and essential importance in both academic work and in a simplified form in everyday planning, as well, in order to enable a mutual understanding and a subsequent dialogue.

The language of planners is also characterized by many specialist concepts that are even defined and interpreted differently within a language region. The semiotic triangle can therefore be viewed as a "conceptual tool during planning."[9]

RAUMBEZOGENE SIMULATION

ANDREAS VOIGT

Die konkrete Auseinandersetzung mit realen Räumen als Forschungslabore ist für praxisnahe raumbezogene Planung und Planungswissenschaft unverzichtbar. Diese Auseinandersetzung umfasst die Erkundung der Problemstellungen, der damit verbundenen planungskulturell und gesellschaftlich geprägten Problemsichten, der verknüpften wissenschaftlichen Fragestellungen. Darauf wiederum aufbauend sind Hypothesen (Vermutungen) und Thesen (Behauptungen) zur methodischen Bearbeitung und schrittweisen Lösung vorhandener oder zur Vermeidung zukünftiger Probleme notwendig. Das „Forschungslabor Raum" ist die programmatische Kurzfassung dieses Zuganges zu Raum, Zeit und Planung.

Parallel dazu bieten zunehmend digital gestützte Methoden weitreichende Hilfestellungen, um mit Raum-, Zeit-, Akteurs- und Problembezug *Überblick* zu gewinnen; über die Maßstabsebenen und thematischen Ebenen (multiskalar) *Einblick* zu erhalten; und perspektivisch *Ausblick* in mögliche Zukünfte zu erlangen und konkrete Maßnahmen beziehungsweise Eingriffe zu konzipieren, die geeignet sind, Probleme tendenziell zu lösen oder gar zu vermeiden. Im Kontext eines Doktorandenkollegs stehen vor allem komplexe oder neuartige, ebenfalls ungelöste oder nur ansatzweise gelöste Problemstellungen im Zentrum der Betrachtung.

Um gesellschaftlich und gebietskörperschaftlich relevante Problemstellungen sachgerecht zu verstehen und zu bearbeiten, ist deren präzise Formulierung und Modellierung samt Bezugsrahmen erforderlich. Raumbezogene Modellbildung kann als gleichermaßen zulässige wie erforderliche Reduzierung der räumlichen Komplexität verstanden werden.[1] Dies ist damit verbunden, dass wir zwangsläufig „vereinfachen, zusammenfassen, weglassen, abstrahieren"[2] – und damit ist das Ergebnis auch nicht vollständig objektivierbar.[3] Modelle sind gleichsam Abstraktionen eines Originals, dessen wesentliche und wichtige Merkmale sie „stellvertretend, zuverlässig und strukturtreu"[4] wiedergeben.

Als Originale können im Sinne des semiotischen Dreiecks[5] (reale) *Gegenstände* (Objekte) und *Ereignisse* betrachtet werden, die mittels Sprache (Worte) und Zeichen benannt werden, die wiederum durch Begriffe, Konzepte beziehungsweise Konstrukte semiotisch interpretiert werden. Die Grundklassen der Konzepte umfassen die Bandbreite von *Begriff* („Einheiten, mit denen man Propositionen konstruiert"[6]) und *Proposition* („das, was mit einem Satz bezeichnet wird"[7]) über den jeweiligen räumlichen beziehungsweise thematischen *Kontext* bis hin zur *Theorie* („ein hinsichtlich der logischen Operationen geschlossener Kontext"[8]). Die präzise Bearbeitung der Konzepte (Begriffe) und ein gemeinsames Grundverständnis im Sinne einer Arbeitsdefinition sind sowohl im wissenschaftlichen Arbeiten als auch in

As defined by system theory, originals can also be understood as *systems*. "Perceiving the world as a network of phenomena that are fundamentally linked and are mutually dependent is a significant realization of our time."[10] A system is an "object composed of system elements that are linked in a characteristic system structure. It can therefore fulfil certain system functions in a given system environment that can be interpreted as a system purpose. The system border is permeable to influence from and influence on the system environment. The identity and autonomy of the system are also defined through the system limit."[11]

This general definition of a system allows a differentiated and presumably enlightened perspective on complex, multifaceted entities in a spatiotemporal context: as examples, apart from buildings, districts, cities, municipalities, regions, states, and the world, conscious living beings—such as humans—can be regarded as systems. Despite their variety, systems always have two completely different types of structures: "a form-determining physical structure and a function-determining system structure."[12] The latter cannot be directly *seen*, it "must be concluded from the elements of the system and its connections."[13]

This means that both questions about the possibilities and limits of spatial perception (e.g., eidetically, with all the physiological senses) and questions about the grasping of information and knowledge (e.g., logic), as well as fundamental philosophical questions of ontology and epistemology, become a focus of the considerations of planning disciplines and planning studies.

With regard to current research fields, namely spatial energy planning and recycling (modeling of material and energy flows) or urban and regional metabolisms, this twofold perception of systems (form-determining physical structure and function-determining system structure—two sides of the same coin) is significant. The structures are linked.

The key to the suitable model development essential for planning theory and methodology, to the reduction of complexity through abstraction and concentration on the essentials, lies in the purpose of the model (what, what for?), which is to be linked to the formulation and understanding of the problem and therefore also the various perspectives on the problem. All planning methodology aspects are therefore also relevant in relation to the processing and solution of complex problems.[14]

The striving for similarity of a model applies to those properties, characteristics, and criteria to be modeled in accordance with the purpose of the model. According to Gosztonyi, one can distinguish between the philosophical complex (spatial analyses of sensory psychology and phenomenology), the geometric complex, and the mathematical-physical complex.[15] The degree of detail of a model is also connected to the purpose of the model. The selection and representation of the properties, characteristics, and criteria of an original, the respective degree of resolution, and the scaling are to be carried out in accordance with the problem.[16]

Models can be differentiated according to the carrier medium (material, physical-analog or immaterial, virtual-digital), scale (1:1, true to size, scale

vereinfachter Form im Planungsalltag von grundlegender und unverzichtbarer Bedeutung, wenn ein wechselseitiges Verstehen und darauf aufbauend ein Dialog gelingen sollen. Auch die Sprache der Planenden ist durch zahlreiche Fachbegriffe geprägt, die selbst innerhalb eines Sprachraumes unterschiedlich definiert und interpretiert werden. Das semiotische Dreieck kann daher als „gedankliches Werkzeug beim Planen"[9] aufgefasst werden.

Im Sinne der Systemtheorie können Originale auch als *Systeme* verstanden werden. „Die Welt als Netz von Phänomenen zu erkennen, die grundsätzlich miteinander verbunden und wechselseitig voneinander abhängig sind, ist eine wesentliche Erkenntnis unserer Zeit."[10] Ein System ist ein „Objekt, das aus Systemelementen zusammengesetzt ist, die in einer charakteristischen Systemstruktur verbunden sind. Dadurch kann es in einer gegebenen Systemumwelt bestimmte Systemfunktionen erfüllen, die sich als Systemzweck interpretieren lassen. Die Systemgrenze ist durchlässig für Einwirkungen aus der und Auswirkungen auf die Systemumwelt. Über die Systemgrenze definieren sich auch die Identität und Autonomie des Systems."[11]

Diese allgemeine Definition eines Systems ermöglicht einen differenzierten und vermutlich erhellenden Blick auf durchaus komplexe, vielgestaltige Gebilde im raum-zeitlichen Kontext: Beispielhaft können neben Gebäuden über Stadtquartier und Stadt, Gemeinde, Region und Staat bis Welt auch Lebewesen mit Bewusstsein – sprich Menschen – als Systeme betrachtet werden. Systeme haben, trotz aller Verschiedenheit, immer zwei völlig verschiedene Arten von Strukturen: „eine gestaltbestimmende physische Struktur und eine funktionsbestimmende Systemstruktur"[12]. Zweitere kann nicht direkt *gesehen* werden, sie „muß aus den Elementen des Systems und ihren Verkopplungen geschlossen werden"[13].

Damit gelangen sowohl Fragen der Möglichkeiten und Grenzen der Raumwahrnehmung (z. B. bildhaft, mit allen physiologischen Sinnen) als auch Fragen des Erschließens von Informationen und Erkenntnis (z. B. Logik) bis hin zu philosophischen Grundfragen der Ontologie und Epistemologie in den Mittelpunkt der Betrachtungen der Planungsdisziplinen und Planungswissenschaft. Im Hinblick auf aktuelle Forschungsfelder, namentlich Energie-Raumplanung und Recycling (Modellierung von Stoff- und Energieströmen) oder urbane und regionale Metabolismen, ist diese zweifache Betrachtung der Systeme (gestaltbestimmende physische Struktur und funktionsbestimmende Systemstruktur – gleichsam zwei Seiten derselben Medaille) von Bedeutung. Die Strukturen sind verbunden und verkoppelt.

Der Schlüssel zur planungstheoretisch und -methodisch unverzichtbaren, sachgerechten Modellbildung, der Komplexitätsreduzierung durch Abstraktion und Konzentration auf das Wesentliche, liegt im Modellzweck (was? wozu?), der wiederum mit der Problemformulierung, dem Problemverständnis und damit auch den verschiedenartigen Sichtweisen auf Probleme zu verbinden ist. Somit sind auch sämtliche planungsmethodischen Aspekte im Zusammenhang mit dem Bearbeiten und Lösen komplexer Probleme relevant.[14]

model 1:n, or scalable) and dimension (2D, 3D and, with the incorporation of the time dimension, 4D).[17]

Carrier media comprise the whole traditional palette of materials (paper, cardboard, wood, synthetics, etc.) and range to techniques of 3D printing on the basis of digital models, available at an increasingly low price. The progressive digitization of many spheres of life promotes the creation of digital spatiotemporal models, such as models relating to buildings and lifecycles (building information modeling), digital city models that are provided free of charge (e. g., the digital model of the city of Vienna), or spatial data sets for the territory of the European Union (ESPON). The digital modeling of reality enables the development of virtual realities (VR) and their extension in the digital world.

The incorporation of the time dimension allows a differentiation according to point in time and time continuum and therefore spatial models relating to a point in time that represent a concrete system condition—currently, in the future or even in the past—or models relating to a time period that convey changes over a period of time, either at intervals or continuously.

Models form the condition and basis for simulations. The concepts are closely linked and overlap. The concept simulation, also especially characterized by disciplines, comprises a wide range of aspects. Models and simulations are "tools for handling reality."[18] Simulations serve the purpose of approximation, showing similarities, reflecting and affecting current, future or historical system circumstances, the presentation of the system behavior under specific or changed conditions, or of the expected or anticipated system behavior with regard to changes over time at intervals or as a time continuum—as a plausible projection or anticipation of possible future system conditions. Simulations should always contribute to gaining knowledge, preparing and supporting decisions and communicating the gained knowledge.[19]

The simulation types can be classified according to their degree of abstraction (high to low) into analytical and symbolic simulations, homomorphic laboratory simulations, or isomorphic and identical simulations.[20]

Tendentially, increased processing capacities enable computer simulations in real time and therefore provide the reply to "what if" questions within work sessions, workshops, or team discussions, leading to a dialogue-oriented, interactive and iterative way of working with efficient use of time resources.

In relation to planning disciplines, apart from numerical simulations, eidetic and expressive simulations, which also incorporate the additional human senses and perceptions, are of great and growing importance. The concept "pictorial" comprises graphic and visual (material images, visual objects), as well as *mental* and *linguistic* images (referring to mental processes).[21] A new category that has emerged through digitization are *digital* images, which are therefore an interesting research subject.[22]

Target groups for simulations are both actors in the planning world, along with specialist colleagues, as well as in the life world, i.e., citizens. The

Die angestrebte Ähnlichkeit eines Modells bezieht sich auf jene Eigenschaften, Merkmale und Kriterien, die es gemäß Modellzweck zu modellieren gilt. Mit Gosztonyi[15] kann zwischen dem philosophischen Komplex (Raumanalysen der Sinnespsychologie und Phänomenologie) und dem geometrischen sowie dem mathematisch-physikalischen Komplex differenziert werden. Auch der Detaillierungsgrad eines Modells ist mit dem Modellzweck verknüpft. Die Auswahl und Abbildung der Eigenschaften, Merkmale und Kriterien eines Originals, der jeweilige Auflösungsgrad beziehungsweise die Rasterung sind problemgerecht vorzunehmen.[16]

Modelle können nach Trägermedium (materiell, physisch analog beziehungsweise immateriell, virtuell-digital), Maßstab (1:1, in wahrer Größer, Maßstabsmodell 1:n beziehungsweise maßstabslos skalierbar) und Dimension (2D, 3D und, unter Einbeziehung der Dimension Zeit, 4D) differenziert werden.[17] Gegenständliche Trägermedien umschließen die gesamte traditionelle Palette an Materialien (Papier, Karton, Holz, Kunststoffe etc.) bis hin zu den zunehmend kostengünstig verfügbaren Techniken des 3D-Druckes auf der Grundlage digitaler Modelle. Die fortschreitende Digitalisierung vieler Lebensbereiche befördert die Erstellung digitaler raum- und zeitbezogener Modelle, zum Beispiel gebäude- und lebenszyklusbezogene Modelle (Building Information Modeling), digitale Stadtmodelle, die kostenlos zur Verfügung gestellt werden (z.B. digitales Stadtmodell der Stadt Wien) oder raumbezogene Datensätze für das Territorium der Europäischen Union (ESPON). Die digitale Modellierung der Realität ermöglicht den Aufbau virtueller Realitäten (VR) und deren Erweiterung in der digitalen Welt.

Die Einbindung der Dimension Zeit erlaubt eine Differenzierung nach Zeitpunkt und Zeitkontinuum, und somit zeitpunktbezogene räumliche Modelle, die einen konkreten Systemzustand repräsentieren – gegenwärtig, in der Zukunft oder auch in der Vergangenheit –, oder zeitraumbezogene Modelle, welche Veränderungen über einen Zeitraum vermitteln, und zwar in Intervallen zeitdiskret oder kontinuierlich.

Modelle bilden die Voraussetzung und Grundlage für Simulationen. Die Begriffe liegen nahe beieinander beziehungsweise überlappen einander geradezu. Der Begriff Simulation umfasst, vor allem auch disziplinär geprägt, durchaus vielfältige Aspekte. Modelle und Simulationen sind „Hilfsmittel zum Umgang mit der Realität"[18]. Simulationen dienen sowohl der Annäherung, dem Ähnlich-Machen, dem Vorspiegeln und Vortäuschen von gegenwärtigen, zukünftigen oder auch historischen Systemzuständen, der Darlegung des Systemverhaltens unter gewissen beziehungsweise veränderten Rahmenbedingungen oder des zu erwartenden oder vermutenden Systemverhaltens im Hinblick auf Veränderungen über die Zeit in zeitdiskreten Schritten oder im Zeitkontinuum – gleichsam als plausible Hochrechnung beziehungsweise Antizipation möglicher künftiger Systemzustände. Stets sollen Simulationen zum Erkenntnisgewinn, zur Entscheidungsvorbereitung und -unterstützung und zur Kommunikation der gewonnenen Erkenntnisse beitragen.[19]

briefly outlined simulation functions make methods and techniques of space- and time-related simulations, based on validated models and problem formulations, indispensable for all planning disciplines—in relation to all stages of thought in planning processes.[23]

The current challenges facing society and planning disciplines provide a wide range of fields for suitable and innovative methods and techniques of spatiotemporal model formation and simulation, namely:

– Climate change as well as handling of growing natural hazards
– Handling demographic change (aging, migration, or individualization)
– Questions pertaining to food and energy supply
– Integrated infrastructure and settlement development, preferably *inward* and not *outward* (avoidance of further sprawl and appropriation of land for construction purposes)
– Securing and structuring of sustainable mobility
– A conception of resilient spaces and infrastructures, and much more

Progressive digitization, both in spatial usage processes and in planning processes, presents itself as an additional challenge—both its integration into planning processes in spatial research labs and the purposeful linking of proven *analog* and innovative *digital* techniques.

Regarding the scope of research at TU Wien (Vienna University of Technology), the following research foci are cited in connection with sustainable and resilient spatial development and digital techniques and technologies: energy and environment; urban and regional transformation (additional fields of research); computational science and engineering (modeling and simulation).[24] The Faculty for Architecture and Planning currently cites the following research foci in this regard: eco-efficient development and structuring of the built environment, and digital technologies in architecture and spatial planning.

Digitally supported laboratories can support work in real laboratories or *living labs*, new forms of dialogue, and cooperation between academia and civil society, undoubtedly supplementing and enriching all of these collaborations. The spatial simulation laboratory at TU Wien (Simlab) is based on the following principles:[25]

– Clarity and applications in practice
– Support through teamwork and dialogue using digital spatial models and simulations, especially also in *early*, informal phases of thinking and planning processes (gaining an overview and insight, enabling an outlook, and generating variety regarding the spectrum of solutions)
– Effective combination of analog and innovative digital techniques (e.g., VR) and software tools (e.g., GIS, CAD, databases, Paintbox)
– Cross-domain model building and simulation (interdisciplinary and transdisciplinary)

Die Simulationsarten können nach ihrem Abstraktionsgrad (hoch bis gering) in analytische und symbolische Simulationen über homomorphe Laborsimulationen und isomorphe beziehungsweise identische Simulationen gegliedert werden.[20] Tendenziell ermöglichen gestiegene Rechenleistungen der Computer Simulationen in Echtzeit und damit die Beantwortung von Was-wäre-wenn-Fragen innerhalb von Arbeitssitzungen, Workshops oder Teambesprechungen und damit eine dialogorientierte, interaktive und iterative Arbeitsweise mit großer Zeiteffizienz.

Neben numerischen Simulationen haben mit Bezug zu Planungsdisziplinen vor allem auch bildhafte, anschauliche Simulationen, die gegebenenfalls auch die weiteren menschlichen Sinne und Wahrnehmungsmöglichkeiten einbeziehen, eine große und wachsende Bedeutung. Der Bildbegriff umfasst sowohl *grafische* beziehungsweise *optische* (materielle Bilder, Sehobjekte) und *geistige* Bilder als auch *sprachliche* Bilder (betreffend mentale Prozesse).[21] Eine durch Digitalisierung neu entstandene Kategorie sind *digitale* Bilder, und daher ein interessanter Forschungsgegenstand.[22]

Zielgruppen von Simulationen sind sowohl Akteur*innen der Planungswelt, gleichsam Fachkolleg*innen, als auch der Alltagswelt, also Bürger*innen. Die kurz skizzierten Simulationsfunktionen machen Methoden und Techniken raum- und zeitbezogener Simulationen, die auf validierten Modellen und Problemformulierungen gründen, unverzichtbar für sämtliche Planungsdisziplinen – und dies bezogen auf sämtliche Denkschritte in Planungsprozessen.[23]

Die aktuellen Herausforderungen für Gesellschaft und Planungsdisziplinen bieten reiche Betätigungsfelder für geeignete und innovative Methoden und Techniken raum- und zeitbezogener Modellbildung und Simulation, namentlich:

- Klimawandel und -anpassung sowie Umgang mit wachsenden Naturgefahren;
- Umgang mit dem demografischen Wandel (ob Alterung, Wanderung oder Individualisierung);
- Fragen der Nahrungsmittel- und Energieversorgung;
- integrierte Infrastruktur- und Siedlungsentwicklung, vorzugsweise nach innen und nicht nach *außen* (Vermeidung weiterer Zersiedelung und Inanspruchnahme des Bodens für bauliche Zwecke);
- Sicherung und Gestaltung einer nachhaltigen Mobilität;
- Konzeption resilienter Raum- und Infrastrukturen und vieles mehr.

Die fortschreitende Digitalisierung, sowohl in Prozessen der Raumnutzung als auch in Planungsprozessen, stellt sich als zusätzliche Herausforderung; ebenso deren Integration in Planungsprozesse in realen Laborräumen und die zweckmäßige Verknüpfung bewährter *analoger* mit innovativen *digitalen* Techniken.

Im Forschungsfeld[24] der Technischen Universität Wien werden im Zusammenhang mit nachhaltiger und resilienter Raumentwicklung und digitalen

- Multiscalar processing (including at the level of regional administrative bodies)
- Experimental exploration of possible spatial developments and solutions to problems (supported by the question "What if?")

On the basis of the spatial simulation laboratory (Simlab) at TU Wien, a series of research projects were and are being worked on that currently involve the following research and subject areas, among others: inward development of the settlement system—automation-supported exploration of the potential on a regional and local scale (2D, 3D, and 4D); integrated infrastructure, settlement, and spatial development along sustainable rail infrastructure corridors (in metropolitan regions, in an overall European context); spatial energy planning (in the context of inward development and integrated spatial development).

For the research field of spatial simulation, digitization opens up a wide array of possibilities that should be carefully integrated and cultivated in connection with "living labs" and real planning processes.

Techniken beziehungsweise Technologien folgende Forschungsschwerpunkte benannt: Energy and Environment; Urban and Regional Transformation (Additional Fields of Research); Computational Science and Engineering (Modeling and Simulation). Die Fakultät für Architektur und Raumplanung benennt in diesem Zusammenhang aktuell folgende Forschungsschwerpunkte: öko-effiziente Entwicklung und Gestaltung der gebauten Umwelt; digitale Technologien in Architektur und Raumplanung.

Digital gestützte Labore können die Arbeit in Reallaboren beziehungsweise *living labs*, die neue Formen des Dialogs und der Kooperation zwischen Wissenschaft und Zivilgesellschaft unterstützen, vermutlich zweckmäßig ergänzen und bereichern. Das Raumsimulationslabor TU Wien (Simlab, spatial simulation lab[25]) gründet beispielhaft auf folgenden einfachen Grundprinzipien:

– Anschaulichkeit und Praxisnähe;
– Unterstützung von Teamwork und Dialog anhand digitaler raumbezogener Modelle und Simulationen, vor allem auch in *frühen*, informellen Phasen der Denk- und Planungsprozesse (Überblick und Einblick gewinnen, Ausblick ermöglichen und Varietätserzeugung hinsichtlich des Lösungsspektrums);
– zweckmäßige Kombination analoger und innovativer digitaler Techniken (z. B. VR) und Softwarewerkzeuge (z. B. GIS, CAD, Datenbanken, Paintbox);
– domänenübergreifende Modellbildung und Simulation (inter- und transdisziplinär);
– multiskalare Bearbeitung (einschließlich der gebietskörperschaftlichen Maßstabsebenen);
– experimentelle Erkundung möglicher Entwicklungen im Raum und Lösungen für Probleme (Unterstützung der Frage „Was wäre, wenn?").

Auf Grundlage des Raumsimulationslabors Simlab der TU Wien wurde und wird eine Reihe an Forschungsprojekten bearbeitet, die derzeit unter anderem folgende Forschungs- und Themenfelder betreffen: Innenentwicklung des Siedlungssystems – automationsgestützte Erkundung der Potenziale im regionalen und lokalen Maßstab (2D, 3D und 4D); integrierte Infrastruktur-, Siedlungs- und Raumentwicklung entlang nachhaltiger Bahninfrastrukturkorridore (in Metropolregionen, im gesamteuropäischen Kontext); Energie-Raumplanung (im Kontext Innenentwicklung und integrierter Raumentwicklung).

Für das Forschungsfeld raumbezogene Simulation eröffnen sich durch Digitalisierung weitreichende Möglichkeiten, die es im Zusammenhang mit realen Forschungslaborräumen und realen Planungsprozessen behutsam zu integrieren und zu kultivieren gilt.

Vienna, September 2019
Wien, September 2019

Vienna, September 2019
Wien, September 2019

189

Vienna, September 2019
Wien, September 2019

Vienna, September 2019
Wien, September 2019

HIGH-QUALITY TRAIN INFRASTRUCTURE AS A DRIVER OF STRATEGIC SPATIAL DEVELOPMENT

ISABELLA SCHUSTER

The European Union strives for the establishment of a homogenous and gapless trans-European transport network. A high-quality, multimodal transport infrastructure network for the member states seems to be important both for economy and European cohesion policy. However, the planned measures comprise not only opportunities but also risks for affected areas.

Examined sample cases along the Austrian south axis display a variety of characteristics. Through new improved connections to the urban areas of major agglomerations, some regions are facing the challenge of strategic growth. Other areas, far away from these new main routes, have to expect more negative trends and therefore also create appropriate future perspectives. By means of an early definition of strategies for a targeted and deliberately effected development, the arisen potentials can be optimally exploited. In the reality of spatial planning practice or political decisions, there is a lack of an interlinking of complex planning problems and specialised planning disciplines. Future-oriented planning, with sustaining desired impacts, can only be successful if significant spatial aspects are integrated into the planning process across all planning disciplines. Spatial and infrastructural development should not run in sequence but in parallel, as part of a masterplan for regions. The metamorphosis of the interpretation of spatial planning from a centrally administered regulation to strategic spatial development means, that not only different sectors of planning are coordinated within themselves on various, hierarchic levels. There is instead the need of a coordination of all spatial measures along different involved disciplines, stakeholders, authorities and periods.

For the spatial development along promoted corridors, the implemented projects mean changes that were not actively forced, but emerged as a result. The framing conditions for regional development will change; new opportunities as well as risks and foci for further action will arise. This leads to the question of to what extent the expectable changes of the bases of spatial planning are already being considered in the regions and which measures or processes may promote a proactive spatial development for the planned transport infrastructure extension on all administrative levels.

The Baltic-Adriatic core network corridor enables a real-time analysis of expansion projects that serve as a basic framework for the future development of the regions. This analysis will examine currently ongoing developments and impacts of previous projects, which are already evident, in order to demonstrate concepts, measures, and procedures for strategic and integrated development.

HOCHLEISTUNGSINFRASTRUKTUR ALS TREIBERIN STRATEGISCHER RAUMENTWICKLUNG

ISABELLA SCHUSTER

Seitens der Europäischen Union gibt es Bestrebungen, ein möglichst homogenes und lückenloses transeuropäisches Verkehrsnetz zu etablieren. Die Bedeutung eines hochleistungsfähigen multimodalen Verkehrsinfrastrukturnetzes für die Mitgliedstaaten scheint sowohl wirtschaftlich als auch in Hinblick auf ein spürbares Zusammenrücken innerhalb der EU maßgeblich. Die geplanten Maßnahmen bergen jedoch für die betroffenen Räume nicht nur Möglichkeiten, sondern auch Gefahren. Untersuchte Fallbeispiele entlang der österreichischen Südachse weisen verschiedene Charakteristika auf. Durch neue, verbesserte Verbindungen zu den Agglomerationsräumen stehen manche Regionen der Herausforderung strategischen Wachstums gegenüber. Andere Räume fernab dieser neuen Haupttrassen müssen negativere Trends erwarten und daher auch entsprechende Zukunftsperspektiven kreieren. Mithilfe frühzeitiger Bildung von Strategien für eine gezielte und bewusst forcierte Entwicklung können Potenziale bestmöglich ausgeschöpft werden.

In die praktische Raumplanungsrealität oder in die Realität der politischen Entscheidungen findet eine Verzahnung der komplexen Planungsproblemkreise und Fachplanungen nur unzureichend Eingang. Eine auf die Zukunft gerichtete Planung, mit nachhaltig anhaltenden gewünschten Effekten, kann nur dort funktionieren, wo disziplinenübergreifend alle raumbedeutsamen Aspekte in den Planungsprozess integriert werden. Raum- und Infrastrukturentwicklung sollen keine aufeinanderfolgenden, sondern möglichst parallel verlaufende Bereiche einer gesamtheitlichen Planung für Regionen sein. Die Metamorphose des Raumplanungsverständnisses von hoheitlicher Ordnung hin zu strategischer Raumentwicklung bedeutet, dass Fachplanungen nicht nur in sich selbst auf verschiedenen Hierarchieebenen abgestimmt werden. Vielmehr erfolgt eine Abstimmung aller im räumlichen Zusammenhang stehenden geplanten Maßnahmen über Planungsdisziplinen, -akteur*innen, -zeiträume und -instanzen hinweg.

Für die Raumentwicklung entlang geförderter Korridore bedeuten die umgesetzten Projekte Veränderungen, die nicht aktiv hervorgerufen wurden, sondern als Resultat dieser entstehen. Die Rahmenbedingungen für die Regionalentwicklung werden sich wandeln, neue Chancen aber auch Risiken und Handlungsschwerpunkte werden entstehen. Dabei stellt sich die Frage, inwiefern auf zu erwartende Veränderungen der Planungsgrundlagen in den Regionen bereits eingegangen wird und welche Maßnahmen oder Prozesse eine für den geplanten Verkehrsinfrastrukturausbau proaktive Raumentwicklung auf allen administrativen Maßstabsebenen begünstigen.

Der Baltisch-Adriatische Kernnetzkorridor ermöglicht eine Echtzeitanalyse von Ausbauprojekten, welche als Grundgerüst der zukünftigen Entwicklung der Regionen dienen. Anhand aktuell laufender Entwicklungen, aber auch bereits spürbarer Auswirkungen vergangener Projekte werden Konzepte, Maßnahmen und Verfahren für eine strategische und integrierende Raumentwicklung aufgezeigt.

INTEGRATED SPATIAL AND RAILWAY DEVELOPMENT

MATHIAS NIEDERMAIER

Railway tracks are a spatially defining infrastructure that has a long-term effect on the development of entire regions. Rail tracks connect and bisect; they are a burden through emissions. In order to operate the railway system efficiently and reorient it, numerous extension and new construction projects are being realized in Europe. For each project, conflicts with existing land usages must be duly identified in order to develop suitable solutions. If this process is not successful, conflicts that remain without an adequate solution will lead to long periods of delay.

The example of the Karlsruhe-Basel extension, part of the Trans-European Transport Network (TEN-T), provides an illuminating study in this regard. For instance: preliminary planning for a four-track extension of the Karlsruhe-Offenburg section was initiated as early as 1975, but forty-five years later only about two-thirds of this extension has been completed. Completion for the adjacent Offenburg-Basel segment is planned for 2041—in other words, fifty-five years after the start of planning in 1986. One of the delaying circumstances was the reunification of Germany, as subsequently extensive investments were directed towards "German unity transport projects." Even so, this case raises the question of why an infrastructure project that was considered necessary was implemented with such delays. One reason is evidently the planning approach of the Federal Republic of Germany as the owner of the national rail company Deutsche Bahn AG (DB AG). Since the railway reform in 1994, DB AG has pursued purely economic objectives and optimizes the development of the infrastructure accordingly. Consequently, DB AG refuses to take responsibility for planning for the common good. The sponsors of public interests did not succeed in countering this in formal permit procedures that would have directed planning towards the common good. A further reason is that permit procedures do not sufficiently take social and technical developments into account. For example, findings about the harmfulness of railway track noise were not integrated into the planning. With references to specifications in previous procedures, substantiated objections were rejected. It was only after protests in the region and the founding of a legally unprecedented project council that consensual solutions could be found.

If delays are caused by an inadequate coordination of spatial and railway development, the solution must lie in a further development of the corresponding procedures. Based on the insights gained from the case example, a procedure for the integration of the spatial and railway development is being drafted for a further section of the TEN-T. New approaches to finding solutions are urgently needed, as numerous infrastructure projects need to be realized in order to complete the TEN-T in Germany and Europe.

INTEGRIERTE RAUM- UND EISENBAHNENTWICKLUNG

MATHIAS NIEDERMAIER

Bahnlinien sind eine raumprägende Infrastruktur, die langfristig auf die Entwicklung ganzer Regionen wirkt. Bahnlinien verbinden, sie zerschneiden, belasten durch Emissionen. Um das System Eisenbahn leistungsfähig zu betreiben und neu auszurichten, werden in Europa zahlreiche Aus- und Neubauprojekte realisiert. Für jedes Projekt sind Konflikte mit bestehenden Landnutzungen rechtzeitig zu erkennen und angepasste Lösungen zu entwickeln. Gelingt dieser Prozess nicht, dann führen die unzureichend geklärten Konflikte zu langen Verzugszeiten.

Diese Überlegungen werden am Beispiel der Ausbaustrecke Karlsruhe–Basel, Teil der Transeuropäischen Verkehrsnetze (TEN-T), anschaulich untersucht: Nachdem im Abschnitt Karlsruhe–Offenburg die Vorplanung für einen viergleisigen Ausbau bereits 1975 aufgenommen wurde, sind auf diesem Abschnitt 45 Jahre später nur zwei Drittel des Ausbaus abgeschlossen. Im folgenden Abschnitt Offenburg–Basel ist die Fertigstellung für 2041 geplant, also 55 Jahre nach Planungsbeginn 1986. Ein verzögernder Umstand war dabei die Wiedervereinigung Deutschlands, in deren Folge umfangreiche Investitionen in die „Verkehrsprojekte Deutsche Einheit" gelenkt

wurden. Dennoch stellt sich die Frage, weshalb ein als notwendig angesehenes Infrastrukturprojekt nur mit derartigen Verzögerungen umgesetzt wurde.

Eine Ursache ist offenbar der Planungsansatz der Bundesrepublik Deutschland als Eigentümerin der Deutschen Bahn AG (DB AG). Seit der Bahnreform 1994 ist die DB AG rein wirtschaftlichen Zielen verpflichtet und optimiert den Ausbau der Infrastruktur entsprechend. Konsequenterweise weist die DB AG eine Verantwortung für gemeinwohlorientierte Planung von sich. Den Trägerschaften öffentlicher Belange gelang es in den formellen Genehmigungsverfahren nicht, diesen Mangel zu beheben und die Planung auf das Gemeinwohl auszurichten. Eine weitere Ursache ist, dass gesellschaftliche und technische Entwicklungen in den Genehmigungsverfahren nicht ausreichend berücksichtigt wurden. Beispielsweise wurden Erkenntnisse zur Schädlichkeit von Schienenlärm nicht in die Planung integriert. Mit Verweis auf Festlegungen in vorherigen Verfahrensschritten wurden begründete Einwände dazu abgelehnt. Erst nach Protesten in der Region und der Gründung eines gesetzlich nicht vorgesehenen Projektbeirates konnten einvernehmliche Lösungen gefunden werden.

Werden Verzögerungen durch eine unzureichende Abstimmung der Raum- und Eisenbahnentwicklung verursacht, muss die Lösung in einer Weiterentwicklung der entsprechenden Verfahren liegen. Anhand der aus dem Fallbeispiel gewonnenen Erkenntnisse wird für einen weiteren Abschnitt der TEN-T ein Verfahren zur Integration der Raum- und Eisenbahnentwicklung entworfen. Neue Lösungsansätze werden dringend benötigt, sind doch zur Vollendung der TEN-T in Deutschland und Europa zahlreiche Infrastrukturprojekte zu realisieren.

STRATEGIES FOR AREA DEVELOPMENTS ALONG REGIONAL RELIEF CORRIDORS AND DEVELOPMENT AXES

MONIKA WÄCHTER

Settlement pressure on metropolises and their surrounding regions is increasing. Many transformation areas in the municipalities of metropolitan regions, however, offer a decentral relief area and opportunities for a high-quality inward settlement development.

Reserves are available along well-connected corridors that have the potential to grow as *relief corridors* for metropolises and *development axes* between cities. The reserves consist of partly not-yet-repurposed areas as well as unexploited area reserves of already built-up plots in small and medium-sized municipalities. A systematic large-scale presentation will show the potential corridors in Switzerland and attempt to characterize this special independent spatial typology. The potential of these relief corridors lies in their proximity and very good connection to metropolises and their surrounding landscape areas, which careful strategies can further strengthen *for* future development. In a selected laboratory space, future action potential for inward development will be shown as part of cross-border communal planning: in the Zurich-Zug-Lucerne area, the interfaces between structure plans, regional models, and urban design for transformation areas are the primary object of research.

An interdisciplinary and multiscale approach links information from spatial planning, urban development, and open space planning, as well as area development. The overall view allows analyses from different perspectives. The aim is to work out the characteristic potential of inward development, as well as action recommendations in the development axis of spatial typology. Building on this, scenarios will be derived for future integrated settlement and infrastructure measures—beyond municipality and canton borders—and suitable procedures for future transformation areas in these special spaces will be formulated.

Current examples of repurposed areas in these corridors show structural developments that do not correspond in terms of design either to the respective location or to an overall spatial idea of the region: uniform large structures reflect investor interests; poorly usable public spaces testify to little assertion or planning power by the responsible parties. Area developments in the context of regional concepts are always accompanied by various challenges: in relation to the process setup, especially the actor constellations are often very complex. Through sample case analyses, the relevant elements of the process design will be established and action options for all phases of the transformation in these spaces will be shown. The derived strategies for area developments in the context of regional planning supplement the action schemes for the interior development in the newly defined relief areas with a wealth of opportunity.

STRATEGIEN FÜR AREALENTWICKLUNGEN ENTLANG VON REGIONALEN ENTLASTUNGSKORRIDOREN UND ENTWICKLUNGSACHSEN

MONIKA WÄCHTER

Der Siedlungsdruck auf die Metropolen und die sie umgebenden Regionen steigt. Zahlreiche Transformationsareale in den Gemeinden der Metropolregionen bieten jedoch dezentralen Entlastungsraum und Chancen für eine qualitätsvolle Siedlungsentwicklung nach innen.

Entlang gut erschlossener Korridore sind Reserven vorhanden, welche das Potenzial haben als *Entlastungskorridore* für die Metropolen und *Entwicklungsachsen* zwischen den Städten zu wachsen. Die Reserven bestehen aus teils noch nicht umgenutzten Arealen sowie nicht ausgenutzten Flächenreserven bereits bebauter Parzellen in kleinen und mittelgroßen Gemeinden. Eine systematische großräumige Erfassung zeigt die potenziellen Korridore in der Schweiz auf und versucht, diesen besonderen eigenständigen Raumtypus zu charakterisieren.

Potenziale dieser Entlastungskorridore sind die Nähe *zu den* und sehr gute Anbindung *an die* Metropolen und ihre umgebenden Landschaftsräume, welche mittels sorgfältiger Strategien weiter gestärkt werden können für die künftige Entwicklung. In einem ausgewählten Laborraum werden künftige Handlungsspielräume der Innenentwicklung im Rahmen grenzüberschreitender kommunaler Planung aufgezeigt: Im Raum Zürich-Zug-Luzern sind die Schnittstellen zwischen Richtplänen, regionalen Leitbildern und städtebaulichem Entwurf für Transformationsareale prioritärer Untersuchungsgegenstand.

In einem interdisziplinären und multiskalaren Ansatz werden Informationen aus Raumplanung, Städtebau und Freiraumplanung sowie Arealentwicklung miteinander verknüpft. Die ganzheitliche Sicht erlaubt Analysen aus verschiedenen Perspektiven. Ziel ist die Erarbeitung charakteristischer Potenziale der Innenentwicklung sowie von Handlungsempfehlungen im Raumtypus Entwicklungsachse. Darauf aufbauend werden Szenarien für künftige integrierte Siedlungs- und Infrastrukturmaßnahmen – über Gemeinde- und Kantonsgrenzen hinaus – abgeleitet und geeignete Verfahren für künftige Transformationsareale in diesen besonderen Räumen formuliert.

Aktuelle Beispiele von umgenutzten Arealen in diesen Korridoren zeigen bauliche Entwicklungen, welche gestalterisch weder dem jeweiligen Ort noch einer räumlichen Gesamtidee der Region entsprechen: Uniforme Großstrukturen spiegeln Investoreninteressen; schlecht nutzbare öffentliche Räume zeugen von geringer Durchsetzungs- oder Gestaltungskraft der verantwortlichen Akteur*innen. Arealentwicklungen im Kontext von Regionalkonzepten werden immer von verschiedenen Herausforderungen begleitet: In Bezug auf die Prozessgestaltung sind besonders die Akteurskonstellationen oftmals sehr komplex. Durch Fallbeispielanalysen werden die relevanten Elemente des Prozessdesigns ausgearbeitet und Handlungsoptionen für alle Phasen der Transformation in diesen Räumen aufgezeigt. Die daraus abgeleiteten Strategien für Arealentwicklungen im Kontext von Regionalplanungen ergänzen die Handlungsmuster für die Innenentwicklung in den neu definierten chancenreichen Entlastungsräumen.

BELGRADE FLYING VISIT
STIPPVISITE BELGRAD

ACTIVATING SPACES— RENAISSANCE OF THE SILK ROAD

ANDREAS VOIGT

Belgrade, the capital of Serbia, lies in a geostrategic location in the European, Eurasian, and global context and is therefore subject to a wide field of interests. The history of the city has been checkered, including in recent times. The fall of the Iron Curtain in 1989 led to significant social and associated spatial changes, especially in the countries of the former east and southeast of Europe. The internal collapse of Yugoslavia brought military conflicts, and the 1999 bombardment by NATO left marks that are still visible in some places in the city of Belgrade. Since 2012, Serbia has had the status of an accession candidate to the European Union, with negotiations being held since 2014. Corresponding reforms for integration into EU structures have been agreed.

At the same time, the city of Belgrade and the state of Serbia lie in the strategic field of interest of Russia, China, Turkey, and the United Arab Emirates. The interests of these states manifest themselves in a variety of ways, most visibly in major infrastructure projects and big urban development projects that are financed or co-financed by these states.

One Belt, One Road

The "One Belt, One Road" initiative of the People's Republic of China (PRC) is leading, in the form of new "Silk Roads" on a wide range of railway routes on land as well as maritime routes between China and Europe, to investments and structural changes in port and rail infrastructure—including in Europe. Through the shipping company COSCO, state-owned by the PRC, the important Greek port of Piraeus has been leased and modernized. The port is of great and growing European and international significance, not only for passenger transport in the Mediterranean region but also for container transport following the involvement of the PRC. The goods discharged at the port are to be transported efficiently by land into the European inland area, which in turn is leading to further investment in the rail infrastructure, such as the new construction of the Budapest-Belgrade rail segment with the help of investments by the PRC and furthermore by Russia. This rail link is a connection between Central and Southeast Europe that has historically been important and continues to be so today.

Belgrade waterfront

The site of the former Belgrade main railway station—a key station that provided relatively central access to the historical city center—and the adjoining logistics areas are currently being radically repurposed as a

RÄUME AKTIVIEREN – RENAISSANCE DER SEIDENSTRASSE

ANDREAS VOIGT

Belgrad, die Hauptstadt Serbiens, liegt sowohl im europäischen als auch im eurasiatischen und globalen Kontext in geostrategischer Lage und daher in einem vielfältigen Interessensfeld. Die Geschichte der Stadt war auch in jüngster Zeit wechselhaft. Der Fall des sogenannten Eisernen Vorhanges 1989 führte vor allem in den Ländern des ehemaligen Ostens und Südostens Europas zu großen gesellschaftlichen und damit verbundenen räumlichen Veränderungen. Der innere Zerfall Jugoslawiens war mit kriegerischen Auseinandersetzungen verbunden, das Bombardement 1999 durch die NATO hat Spuren hinterlassen, die auch in der Stadt Belgrad noch immer an einigen Orten sichtbar sind. Seit 2012 hat Serbien den Status eines Beitrittslandes zur Europäischen Union, die Verhandlungen werden seit 2014 geführt, entsprechende Anpassungen zur Integration in EU-Strukturen wurden vereinbart.

Gleichzeitig liegen die Stadt Belgrad und der Staat Serbien im strategischen Interessensfeld Russlands, Chinas, der Türkei und der Vereinigten Arabischen Emirate. Die Interessen dieser Staaten manifestieren sich in vielfältiger Weise, am sichtbarsten in großen Infrastrukturprojekten und in großen städtebaulichen Projekten, die durch diese Staaten finanziert oder kofinanziert werden.

One Belt, One Road

Die Initiative „One Belt, One Road" der Volksrepublik (VR) China führt im Zuge neuer „Seidenstraßen" auf vielfältigen schienengebundenen Landwegen und Seewegen zwischen China und Europa zu Investitionen und baulichen Veränderungen in der Hafen- und Schieneninfrastruktur – und zwar auch in Europa. Über die im Staatseigentum der VR China befindliche Reederei COSCO wurde der bedeutsame griechische Hafen Piräus gepachtet und modernisiert. Er ist nicht nur für den Personenverkehr im Mittelmeerraum, sondern im Zuge des Engagements der VR China zunehmend auch für den Containerverkehr von großer und wachsender europäischer und internationaler Bedeutung. Die im Hafen gelöschten Güter sollen auf dem Landweg auch wirkungsvoll ins europäische Hinterland transportiert werden, was konsequent zu weiteren Investitionen in die Schieneninfrastruktur führt. So erfolgt der Neubau der Bahnstrecke Budapest–Belgrad, eine nicht nur historisch besonders wichtige Verbindung zwischen Mittel- und Südosteuropa, mithilfe von Investitionen durch die VR China und des Weiteren durch Russland.

high-density, high-rise development with investments from the United Arab Emirates, under the name "Belgrade Waterfront." Belgrade's urban structure and cityscape—previously characterized by the historical city center situated on the right bank of the Sava and Danube on a hill topped by the Kalemegdan fortification, and the New Belgrade district situated on the left bank of the Sava near Danube confluence—as well as the government district of this former capital of Yugoslavia are being significantly changed by the new development.

From an overall European perspective and from the point of view of the EU, the city of Belgrade and its metropolitan region, as well as Serbia as a nation, should be viewed as a significant key region not only for the Balkans but also for Europe as a whole. This estimation is supported by the location of the city of Belgrade and Serbia as a country on an important European spatial corridor, the Danube region. This is the catchment area for an important European spatial corridor: the TEN corridor Oriental/East-Med (OEM, formerly Hamburg-Athens), which is of particular importance for the connection to Southeast Europe and the Mediterranean region. TEN corridors could and should be viewed to a greater extent not only as transport corridors but also as corridors for European spatial development and cohesion. The main route of the OEM corridor leads, in accordance with EU agreements, from Vienna and Budapest to Thessaloniki, crossing mountain ranges three times, as well as the Danube, before continuing to Athens and Piraeus.[1] The historically significant main route to Southeast Europe leads primarily across river basins and valley areas from Budapest via Novi Sad, Belgrade, Niš, and Skopje to Thessaloniki. This route should be viewed as a significant branch of the OEM corridor.

Belgrade is facing further enormous challenges regarding its urban and spatial development in an overall social context and has therefore, as a "spatial research lab," already twice been the subject of a doctoral symposium (Curriculum 2) and a visit[2] (Curriculum 3) as part of the International Doctoral College with its associated methodical procedures.

Belgrade Waterfront

Das Gelände des ehemaligen Belgrader Hauptbahnhofes – mit diesem Kopfbahnhof wurde der historische Stadtkern relativ zentral erschlossen – und anschließende Logistikflächen werden aktuell mit Investitionen aus den Vereinigten Arabischen Emiraten unter dem Namen „Belgrade Waterfront" als *High-density-* und *High-rise*-Bebauung radikal umgestaltet. Belgrads Stadtstruktur, Stadtgestalt und Stadtbild – bislang geprägt durch den rechtsufrig an Save und Donau auf einem Stadthügel gelegenen historischen Stadtkern samt Festung Kalemegdan und den Stadtteil Neu-Belgrad, der linksufrig an der Save im Mündungsbereich zur Donau liegt – sowie das Regierungsviertel dieser ehemaligen Hauptstadt Jugoslawiens werden erheblich verändert. Aus gesamteuropäischer Perspektive und aus Sicht der EU sollten die Stadt Belgrad und der Metropolregionsraum sowie das Land Serbien als ein wesentlicher Schlüsselraum nicht nur für den Balkan, sondern für Europa als Ganzes betrachtet werden. Diese Einschätzung wird gestützt durch die Lage der Stadt Belgrad und des Landes Serbien an einem wesentlichen europäischen Raumkorridor, dem Donauraum. Dabei handelt es sich um den Einzugsbereich eines für Europa bedeutsamen Raumkorridors: Der TEN-Korridor Oriental/East-Med (OEM, vormals Hamburg–Athen) ist für die Verbindung nach Südosteuropa und zum Mittelmeerraum von besonderer Bedeutung. TEN-Korridore könnten und sollten verstärkt nicht nur als Verkehrskorridore, sondern als Korridore europäischer Raumentwicklung und Kohäsion betrachtet werden. Die Hauptroute des sogenannten OEM-Korridors führt gemäß EU-Vereinbarungen von Wien und Budapest mit dreifacher Querung von Gebirgszügen und Querung der Donau nach Thessaloniki und sodann weiter nach Athen und Piräus.[1] Die historisch bedeutsame Hauptroute nach Südosteuropa führt im Wesentlichen über Beckenlandschaften und Talräume von Budapest über Novi Sad, Belgrad, Niš und Skopje nach Thessaloniki. Diese Route sollte als wesentlicher Zweig des OEM-Korridors betrachtet werden.

Belgrad steht vor weiteren enormen Herausforderungen in Hinblick auf die Stadt- und Raumentwicklung im gesamtgesellschaftlichen Kontext und war daher im Rahmen des Internationalen Doktorandenkollegs bereits zweimal als Forschungslaborraum Gegenstand einer Doktorandenwoche (Curriculum 2) beziehungsweise einer Stippvisite[2] (Curriculum 3) und damit verbundener methodischer Bearbeitungen.

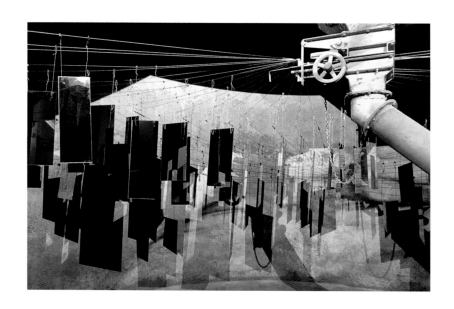

Belgrade, May 2017
Belgrad, Mai 2017

Belgrade, May 2017
Belgrad, Mai 2017

URBAN RESEARCH
STADTFORSCHUNG

URBAN RESEARCH IN TIMES OF UNBOUNDED URBANIZATION AND MAJOR SOCIAL CHALLENGES

STEFAN SIEDENTOP

Urban research is not an independent discipline: it is an academic field of work with a strong interdisciplinary character that brings together sociology, geography, planning studies, economics, ecology, history, and political science. The subject-related perspectives pursued in these disciplines with regard to the city differ in some cases significantly in their thematic interests, their theoretical bases, and the methods they use.

Urban research crosses disciplinary borders

Perhaps it is precisely this specific positioning in a mélange of established disciplines that makes urban research appear so inconstant or—to formulate it more positively—so dynamic. Due to its interdisciplinary disposition, urban research does not follow any clear methodological paradigm, as is characteristic of many traditional scientific disciplines. It has repeatedly adapted its theoretical and methodological orientations as a reaction to self-attested epistemological crises and changes in social requirements. One gets the impression that debates about theory and method are held with particular vehemence here, and that compared to established academic fields there are more frequent and more radical reorientations—both in relation to the research objects that are considered as significant and regarding theoretical orientations and methodologies.

In the third curriculum of the International Doctoral College "Spatial Research Lab" (IDK), urban research was once again accorded an important role, as many dissertations explicitly addressed academic issues in the context of urban development. Critical discussions about the field's conception of itself, normative approaches, and methodological cultures undoubtly enriched and contributed to defining the college. This contribution attempts to provide a brief outline of these debates. It partly refers to thoughts that were already set out in Jessen und Siedentop[1] as well as in ILS.[2]

Object: the city as a spatially tangible object or theoretical category?

It is part of the routines of self-assurance of urban research to emphasize the relevance of one's own actions through references to a dynamically progressing global urbanization. Dozens of books and articles start with the supposedly undisputed statement that worldwide already more than 50 percent of the population live in cities and that this will increase

STADTFORSCHUNG IN ZEITEN ENTGRENZTER URBANISIERUNG UND GROẞER GESELLSCHAFTLICHER HERAUSFORDERUNGEN

STEFAN SIEDENTOP

Die Stadtforschung ist keine eigenständige Disziplin, sie ist ein stark inter-disziplinär geprägtes wissenschaftliches Arbeitsgebiet im Spannungsfeld von Soziologie, Geografie, Planungswissenschaften, Ökonomie, Ökologie, Geschichtswissenschaften und Politologie. Die in diesen Disziplinen verfolgten fachlichen Perspektiven auf den Erkenntnisgegenstand Stadt unterscheiden sich in ihren thematischen Interessen, ihrer theoretischen Fundierung und den eingesetzten Methoden zum Teil gravierend.

Stadtforschung ist eine disziplinäre Grenzgängerin

Vielleicht ist es gerade diese spezifische Lokalität in der Gemengelage etablierter Disziplinen, welche die Stadtforschung so unstetig oder – positiver formuliert – so dynamisch erscheinen lässt. Durch ihre interdisziplinäre Veranlagung folgt die Stadtforschung keinem klaren methodologischen Paradigma, wie dies für viele klassische Wissenschaftsdisziplinen charakteristisch ist. Immer wieder hat sie ihre theoretischen und methodischen Orientierungen als Reaktion auf selbst attestierte epistemologische Krisen und veränderte gesellschaftliche Anforderungen neu justiert. Es entsteht der Eindruck, dass Theorie- und Methodendebatten hier mit besonderer Leidenschaft geführt werden und dass es im Vergleich zu etablierteren Wissenschaftsgebieten zu häufigeren und radikaleren Neuorientierungen kommt – sowohl in Bezug auf die als maßgeblich angesehenen Forschungsgegenstände als auch mit Blick auf theoretische Orientierungen und Methodologien.

Im dritten Curriculum des Internationalen Doktorandenkollegs (IDK) „Forschungslabor Raum" kam der Stadtforschung erneut eine maßgebliche Rolle zu, da zahlreiche Dissertationen explizit wissenschaftliche Fragen im Kontext der Stadtentwicklung adressierten. Die kritischen Diskussionen über das Selbstverständnis, normative Zugänge und Methodenkulturen bereicherten und prägten das Kolleg ohne Zweifel mit. In diesem Beitrag wird versucht, einzelne dieser Debatten kursorisch nachzuzeichnen. Der Beitrag greift dabei teilweise auf Gedanken zurück, die bereits in Jessen und Siedentop[1] sowie in ILS[2] niedergelegt wurden.

Gegenstand: Stadt als räumlich fassbares Objekt oder theoretische Kategorie?

Es gehört zu den Routinen der Selbstvergewisserung der Stadtforschung, die Relevanz des eigenen Tuns mit Verweisen auf eine dynamisch

continuously over the forthcoming decades. This is not wrong but can lead to a distorted notion of the spatial effect of urbanization.

In a much-noticed paper, Neil Brenner and Christian Schmid frontally attacked the widespread understanding of urbanization as a spatially delineated process that manifests in the development and growth of cities.[3] Urbanization should rather be viewed, they argue, as a multiscalar, global process of a continuous functional, sociospatial, and morphological transformation within flexible boundaries. According to this understanding, urbanization expresses itself in unbounded—i.e., no longer spatially delineated according to specific locations and territories—networks and exchange relationships between people, capital, resources, and information. According to Brenner and Schmid, "the urban" is less an empirical object and more a theoretical category.

Contrary to this, there are voices that still consider the city as a spatially tangible category. Storper und Scott understand cities as gravitationally generated agglomerations of people, their economic activities and social interactions, and the elements of the built environment created by them.[4] Storper and Scott therefore argue against a deterritorialized understanding of the urban as advocated by Brenner and Schmid.

But they also see urban areas as hubs in transregional, global networks of migration and mobility, trade with goods and services, and resource transfer, as well as innovation and information exchanges. For practical urban research, this especially has an effect on the choice of spatial references in empirical work. Instead of viewing cities as spatially enclosed "containers," flexible and relational spatial reference systems are to be preferred, which address specific places with their manifold interactions and links with other places. Cities and regions with an urban character are understood in this sense as network hubs whose transformation is inherently linked to the restructuring and repositioning of their regional and global "hinterland."

Relevance of the urban: cities as a stage or power factor?

A second much-discussed question of urban research is whether the city merely represents a "stage" for economic and social developments or whether it is to be viewed as a subject, as an independent factor of social, economic, or environmentally related development. Especially Marxist urban research has vehemently denied that the city and its defining morphological-functional and sociospatial structures could be more than an external expression of economic conditions and developments. According to this notion, there are no genuine urban problems, only problems of a social nature that become visible in urban settlement areas.[5] For urban research, this position requires us to consider the economic, social, or political phenomena encountered in cities in their constitutive social contexts. Over recent years, contrary to this, an understanding has increasingly established itself according to which the properties of cities can by all means be viewed as independent causal factors of the explanation of individual behavior and—as an aggregate of individual actions—sociospatial and

voranschreitende globale Urbanisierung zu unterstreichen. Dutzende von Büchern und Fachartikeln beginnen mit der vermeintlich unbestreitbaren Feststellung, dass weltweit bereits mehr als 50 Prozent der Bevölkerung in Städten leben und es in den kommenden Jahrzehnten immer mehr sein werden. Dies ist nicht falsch, kann aber zu einer verzerrten Vorstellung der räumlichen Wirksamkeit der Urbanisierung führen.

In einem viel beachteten Aufsatz haben Neil Brenner und Christian Schmid[3] das verbreitete Verständnis von Urbanisierung als räumlich gefasstem Prozess, der sich in der Entstehung und im Wachsen von Städten manifestiert, frontal angegriffen. Urbanisierung müsse eher als multiskalarer, globaler Prozess einer kontinuierlichen funktionalen, sozialräumlichen und morphologischen Transformation in flexiblen Grenzen angesehen werden. Nach diesem Verständnis äußert sich Urbanisierung in weltumspannend entgrenzten – räumlich nicht mehr auf bestimmte Orte und Territorien eingrenzbaren – Netzwerken und Austauschbeziehungen von Menschen, Kapital, Ressourcen und Informationen. Das Urbane ist nach Brenner und Schmid weniger ein empirisches Objekt, sondern eher eine theoretische Kategorie.

Demgegenüber stehen Stimmen, die an der Stadt als räumlich fassbarer Kategorie festhalten. So verstehen Storper und Scott[4] Städte als gravitativ erzeugte Agglomerationen aus Menschen, ihren ökonomischen Aktivitäten und sozialen Interaktionen sowie aus den von ihnen geschaffenen Elementen der gebauten Umwelt. Storper und Scott wenden sich damit gegen ein deterritorialisiertes Verständnis des Urbanen, wie es Brenner und Schmid proklamieren. Aber auch sie sehen städtische Räume als Knoten in überregionalen, globalen Netzwerken der Migration und Mobilität, des Handels mit Gütern und Dienstleistungen, des Ressourcentransfers sowie des Innovations- und Informationsaustausches.

Für die praktische Stadtforschung hat dies vor allem für die Wahl von räumlichen Bezügen in der empirischen Arbeit Auswirkungen. Anstatt einer Betrachtung von Städten als räumlich abgeschlossene „Container" sind flexible, relationale Raumbezugssysteme zu präferieren, welche bestimmte Orte in ihren vielfältigen Interaktionen und Verflechtungen mit anderen Orten thematisieren. Städte und städtisch geprägte Regionen werden in diesem Sinne als Netzwerkknoten verstanden, deren Wandel mit der Restrukturierung und Repositionierung ihres regionalen und globalen „Hinterlandes" inhärent verbunden ist.

Relevanz des Urbanen: Stadt als Bühne oder Wirkfaktor?

Eine zweite viel diskutierte Fragestellung der Stadtforschung ist, ob Stadt lediglich eine „Bühne" für ökonomische und gesellschaftliche Entwicklungen darstellt oder ob sie als Subjekt, als eigenständiger Faktor gesellschaftlicher, wirtschaftlicher oder umweltbezogener Entwicklung zu betrachten ist. Insbesondere die marxistische Stadtforschung hat vehement abgestritten, dass Stadt und die sie kennzeichnenden morphologisch-funktionalen und sozialräumlichen Strukturen mehr als ein äußerer Ausdruck ökonomischer

constructional-physical developments.[6] In this respect, the city is not just a materialization of society, not just a "social fact" that has "formed spatially."[7] Instead the city affects urban life as a specific factor. We refer here to the intensive discussion about what are known as neighborhood and context effects in urban sociology.[8] This means certain properties of cities or districts that obstruct, prevent, facilitate, or prompt human behavior. For example, life in districts with a concentration of disadvantaged segments of the population and inadequate infrastructure can have a negative effect on educational success and professional integration. The transport infrastructure has a significant influence on people's choice of means of transport. Cities and their respective functional, morphological, and sociospatial patterns can thus be understood as an "opportunity structure"[9] that either widens or narrows people's ability to act on different levels.

Socially constructivist research approaches take quite a different perspective, viewing the city as socially produced or discursively constructed. According to this notion, urban spaces are artifacts of social construction processes that are constituted by language and everyday actions and are constantly being reproduced. This theoretical approach to the city emphasizes the significance of a subjectivist, interpretative perspective on the phenomena to be researched. Special importance is accorded to linguistic constructions, because the power of interpretation is exerted through the formulation of communicative rules that can also change material processes.

Normativity: knowledge-oriented or transformative urban research?

Traditional urban research acts in a knowledge-oriented manner. It aims to gain a better understanding of the processes of urban change. In this sense, it does not follow any normative agenda, is not subject to social concerns, but acts with a view to the research desiderata forming discursively in the scientific sphere. Contrary to this, more recent urban research movements call for a greater participation in social problem-solving in the interests of sustainable development. This is part of wider considerations of the role of research in times of global challenges such as climate change, resource scarcity, increasing economic inequality, or forced migration. References can be made to debates about "responsible research" or "third mission."

In Germany, the discussion about transformative science has drawn significant attention. According to Schneidewind, this refers to a science "that not only observes social transformation processes and describes them from the outside but also initiates and catalyzes these change processes itself and thus learns about these changes as an actor in transformation processes."[10] For researchers, such an understanding of research has fundamental consequences, because the role of actor in transformation processes requires different forms of action and competences. It is necessary to step out of the protective academic sphere and into social and political disputes. New concepts of transdisciplinary research in which practitioners are involved

Zustände und Entwicklungen sein können. Nach dieser Vorstellung gibt es keine genuin städtischen Probleme, sondern nur Probleme gesellschaftlicher Art, die in städtischen Siedlungsräumen sichtbar werden.[5] Für die Stadtforschung wurde daraus die Forderung abgeleitet, die in der Stadt anzutreffenden ökonomischen, sozialen oder politischen Phänomene in den sie konstituierenden gesellschaftlichen Zusammenhängen zu thematisieren.

In den vergangenen Jahren hat sich im Gegensatz dazu mehr und mehr ein Verständnis durchgesetzt, nach dem Eigenschaften von Städten durchaus als eigenständige kausale Faktoren der Erklärung individuellen Verhaltens und – als Aggregat von Einzelhandlungen – sozialräumlicher und baulichphysischer Entwicklungen anzusehen sind.[6] Stadt ist insofern nicht nur ein Abbild von Gesellschaft, nicht nur eine „soziale Tatsache", die sich „räumlich geformt" hat.[7] Die Stadt wirkt vielmehr als spezifischer Faktor auf das städtische Leben zurück. Verwiesen sei hier auf die intensive Diskussion über sogenannte Nachbarschafts- und Kontexteffekte in der Stadtsoziologie.[8] Gemeint sind bestimmte Eigenschaften von Städten oder Quartieren, die menschliches Verhalten erschweren, verhindern, erleichtern oder nahelegen. Beispielsweise kann das Leben in Quartieren mit einer Konzentration benachteiligter Bevölkerungsgruppen und unzureichender Infrastruktur negativ auf den Bildungserfolg und die berufliche Integration wirken. Die Verkehrsinfrastruktur übt maßgeblichen Einfluss auf die Verkehrsmittelwahl der Bevölkerung aus. Städte und ihre jeweiligen funktionalen, morphologischen und sozialräumlichen Muster lassen sich insofern als „Opportunitätsstruktur"[9] verstehen, die Handlungsmöglichkeiten von Menschen in unterschiedlichen Dimensionen eröffnet oder auch einengt.

Eine gänzlich andere Perspektive nehmen sozialkonstruktivistische Forschungsansätze ein, die Stadt als gesellschaftlich produziert beziehungsweise diskursiv konstruiert ansehen. Nach dieser Vorstellung sind städtische Räume Artefakte gesellschaftlicher Konstruktionsprozesse, die sich durch Sprache und alltägliches Handeln konstituieren und stetig reproduzieren. Dieser theoretische Zugang zu Stadt betont die Bedeutung einer subjektivistischen, interpretativen Perspektive auf die zu erforschenden Phänomene. Besondere Bedeutung kommt dabei sprachlichen Konstruktionen zu, denn über die Herausbildung kommunikativer Regeln werde Deutungsmacht ausgeübt, die auch materielle Prozesse verändern könne.

Normativität: erkenntnisorientierte oder transformative Stadtforschung?

Klassische Stadtforschung agiert erkenntnisorientiert. Sie zielt darauf ab, Prozesse urbanen Wandels besser zu verstehen. In diesem Sinne folgt sie keiner normativen Agenda, sie ist keinen gesellschaftlichen Anliegen unterstellt, sondern agiert mit Blick auf die sich im Wissenschaftssystem diskursiv herausbildenden Forschungsdesiderate. Dagegen mahnen neuere Strömungen der Stadtforschung eine stärkere Beteiligung an gesellschaftlichen Problemlösungen im Sinne einer nachhaltigen Entwicklung

in the formulation of research requirements and research questions have experienced great popularity in recent years. The same applies to novel methods of intervening and experimental research such as real laboratories. Scientific and academic communication must also develop further, because the demand for social effectiveness of research requires that scientists and academics communicate in a generally comprehensible manner and can also explain more complex relationships. It remains to be seen how the (inter)disciplinary understanding and the methods of urban research will change on account of this. One should also mention at this point that the postulate of transformative science has experienced criticism as well as agreement. Peter Strohschneider pointed out possible dangers if science is no longer only subject to the principles of the search for truth and novelty but is also assessed according to its usefulness with regard to normative objectives.[11] Another criticism by Strohschneider refers to a possible dissolution of boundaries of science and politics, which could express itself both in a weakening of politics and in a loss of autonomy of the sciences.[12]

Methodology: studies of individual cases or comparative research?

In recent years there has been increasing criticism of the fact that the theoretical foundations of urban research exclusively reflect Western experiences. In view of this, the postcolonial school demands a radical reorientation that includes urban developments in the Global South. Comparative research has a key importance in this. "Think the urban through the diversity of urban experiences"—with this sentence, Jennifer Robinson expressed the demand for a new generation of theories of the urban.[13] What is essential is an open, reflexive culture of theoretical and empirical considerations that is open to being reviewed. Uncovering similarities and diversity in urban developments in various world regions with the greatest possible sensitivity towards the respective effective context conditions can be understood as both a task and an ethos of cosmopolitan comparative research.

International comparisons of cities as well as urban phenomena make it possible to assess the validity of theories beyond regional and national borders. They thus draw the attention of research to what is generalizable and special, to the context-related aspects of urban development. In this respect, the value of comparative design lies in addressing the question of the extent to which social and built-physical phenomena emerge through the effect of universal-systemic factors, on the one hand, and specific location, time, and culture-dependent factors, on the other.

From a methodological point of view, comparative research includes approaches that are based on universally valid theories of the urban and that seek to identify and explain differences and similarities through systematic comparisons. At the same time, there are approaches that work largely without generalizing presuppositions and that understand and explain processes in their specific context.

an. Dies ordnet sich ein in breitere Auseinandersetzungen über die Rolle der Forschung in Zeiten globaler Herausforderungen wie Klimawandel, Ressourcenverknappung, zunehmender ökonomischer Ungleichheit oder Fluchtmigration. Verwiesen sei auf Debatten über *responsible research* oder *third mission*.

In Deutschland hat die Diskussion über die transformative Wissenschaft große Aufmerksamkeit erfahren. Nach Schneidewind wird damit eine Wissenschaft bezeichnet, „die gesellschaftliche Transformationsprozesse nicht nur beobachtet und von außen beschreibt, sondern diese Veränderungsprozesse selber mit anstößt und katalysiert und damit als Akteur von Transformationsprozessen über diese Veränderungen lernt."[10] Für die Forschenden hat ein solches Forschungsverständnis fundamentale Konsequenzen, denn die Rolle als Akteur*in in Transformationsprozessen erfordert andersartige Handlungsweisen und Kompetenzen. Erforderlich ist ein Heraustreten aus dem geschützten Wissenschaftsraum, hinein in gesellschaftliche und politische Auseinandersetzungen. Neue Konzepte einer transdisziplinären Forschung, in der Praxisakteur*innen an der Formulierung von Forschungsbedarfen und Forschungsfragen beteiligt sind, haben in den vergangenen Jahren starken Zuspruch erfahren. Gleiches gilt für neuartige Methoden intervenierender und experimenteller Forschung wie Reallabore. Auch muss sich die Wissenschaftskommunikation weiterentwickeln, denn gesellschaftliche Wirksamkeit von Forschung setzt voraus, dass Wissenschaftler*innen Erkenntnisse allgemeinverständlich kommunizieren und auch komplexere Zusammenhänge erklären können.

Es bleibt abzuwarten, wie sich das Selbstverständnis und die Arbeitsweise der Stadtforschung hierdurch verändern. Nicht unerwähnt bleiben soll an dieser Stelle, dass das Postulat transformativer Wissenschaft neben Zustimmung auch Kritik erfahren hat. So hat Peter Strohschneider[11] auf mögliche Gefahren hingewiesen, wenn Wissenschaft nicht mehr allein den Prinzipien von Wahrheitssuche und Neuheit unterworfen ist, sondern auch nach ihrer Nützlichkeit im Hinblick auf normative Ziele bewertet wird. Ein weiterer Vorwurf Strohschneiders bezieht sich auf eine mögliche Entgrenzung von Wissenschaft und Politik, die sich sowohl in einer Schwächung des Politischen als auch einem Autonomieverlust der Wissenschaften äußern könnte.[12]

Methodologie: Erforschung des Einzelfalls oder vergleichende Forschung?

In den vergangenen Jahren wurde zunehmend kritisiert, dass sich die theoretischen Fundamente der Stadtforschung im Wesentlichen aus westlichen Erfahrungen speisen. Die post-koloniale Schule fordert vor diesem Hintergrund eine radikale Neuorientierung unter Einbeziehung urbaner Entwicklungen im globalen Süden. Dabei kommt der vergleichenden Forschung eine Schlüsselbedeutung zu. „Think the urban through the diversity of urban experiences"[13] – mit diesem Satz hat Jennifer Robinson den Anspruch an eine neue Generation von Theorien des Urbanen zum Ausdruck

Epilog

The subject-related standpoints on various matters outlined in this contribution are deliberately not intended to be evaluated here. They indicate a lively discourse within which researchers must position themselves with their specific research interest. This is a particular challenge for up-and-coming academics. The IDK "Spatial Research Lab" pursued the aim of supporting the doctoral students by offering a platform for exchanges, differences of opinion, and reflection. The differences in theoretical approaches, normative foundations, or methodological preferences of the doctoral theses that became apparent are the expression of a plural urban research whose quality is evident especially in its scope and diversity.

gebracht. Essenziell sei, dass eine offene, reflexive und revisionsbereite Kultur theoretischer und empirischer Auseinandersetzung räumliche Öffnung voraussetzt. Das Aufzeigen von Gemeinsamkeiten und Diversität in urbanen Entwicklungen in verschiedenen Weltregionen unter größtmöglicher Sensibilität gegenüber den jeweilig wirksamen Kontextbedingungen kann als Auftrag wie Ethos einer kosmopolitisch agierenden vergleichenden Forschung verstanden werden.

Internationale Vergleiche von Städten beziehungsweise städtischen Phänomenen ermöglichen es, die Gültigkeit von Theorien über Regions- und Ländergrenzen hinaus zu bewerten. Sie schärfen damit den Blick der Forschung für das Verallgemeinerbare und das Besondere, das Kontextgebundene der Stadtentwicklung. In diesem Sinne liegt der Wert vergleichender Forschung in der Auseinandersetzung mit der Frage, in welchem Umfang sich soziale und baulich-physische Phänomene durch das Wirken universellsystemischer Faktoren auf der einen Seite und spezifischer orts-, zeit- und kulturabhängiger Faktoren auf der anderen Seite herausbilden.

In methodologischer Hinsicht finden sich in der vergleichenden Forschung einerseits Ansätze, die von universal geltenden Theorien des Städtischen ausgehen und durch systematisches Vergleichen Unterschiede und Ähnlichkeiten erkennen und erklären wollen. Dem gegenüber stehen Ansätze, die weitgehend ohne generalisierende Vorannahmen arbeiten und Prozesse in ihrem spezifischen Kontext verstehen und erklären.

Epilog

Die in diesem Beitrag zu unterschiedlichen Fragestellungen skizzierten fachlichen Standpunkte sollen bewusst nicht bewertet werden. Sie markieren einen lebendigen Diskurs, innerhalb dessen sich Forschende mit ihrem spezifischen Forschungsinteresse positionieren müssen. *Insbesondere für Nachwuchswissenschaftler*innen ist dies herausfordernd. Das IDK „Forschungslabor Raum" hat das Ziel verfolgt, die Promovierenden dabei zu unterstützen, indem es eine Bühne für Austausch, Meinungsstreit und Reflexion geboten hat. Die dabei deutlich gewordenen Unterschiede in den theoretischen Zugängen, den normativen Grundierungen oder methodischen Präferenzen der Promotionsvorhaben sind Ausdruck einer pluralen Stadtforschung, deren Qualität gerade in der Breite und Vielfalt zu sehen ist.

Dortmund-Hörde, March 2019
Dortmund-Hörde, März 2019

Dortmund, March 2019
Dortmund, März 2019

Dortmund-Hörde, March 2019
Dortmund-Hörde, März 2019

Emscher Canal, March 2019
Emscherkanal, März 2019

Dortmund-Hörde, March 2019
Dortmund-Hörde, März 2019

Dortmund-Hörde, March 2019
Dortmund-Hörde, März 2019

JOB HERE, HOME THERE—WORK-RELATED MULTILOCAL LIVING

LISA STADTLER

In Germany and other Western industrial nations, job-related mobility is constantly increasing against the background of deregulated and flexibilized labor markets. More and more people are commuting long distances between their places of residence and work or move several times in their life for professional reasons. At the same time, the number of people with multiple residences is increasing, which is called multilocal living. This applies in particular to knowledge-based professional groups who often change their job due to project-based work and short-term contracts. The rising high-qualified employment of women had also led to a rise in multilocal living, as it is increasingly rare for couples to find work in the same town or region. If they then decide to keep two separate households at a distance, this arrangement is referred to as "living apart together." Another form of multilocal living is weekly commuters who have a second home at the work location. These living arrangements are especially common in large cities with many knowledge-based workplaces in international companies, research institutions, and universities, as well as a good connection to long-distance transport. Living in more than one place has an effect not only on the everyday life of the households and their social relationships but also on the district, city, and regional development of the respective areas.

In this context, the question arises as to what influences decisions regarding mobility and place of residence made by persons living multilocal and what attachments these individuals develop to specific localities and companies. In addition, the study asks what influences the time-space-structure of these living-arrangements.

In contrast to previous studies, the focus of the research is on the influence of employers, as these play a special role due to the increasing flexibility and mobility requirements in the current working world.

It is evident that until now companies have not been concerned, or have been too little concerned, with living in multiple places. Owing to the increasing lack of skilled personnel in knowledge-based sectors, it is however essential for employers to consider to a greater extent where and how their employees live and how they can support them in everyday life. By offering suitable support and fostering a high degree of attachment to the company, companies can also attract and retain those workforces who do not want to relocate their main residence to the vicinity of the company. This allows them to keep their job as well as their job-related second residence or long-distance relationship.

Until now it has become clear that especially flexible working hours and workplace regulations in companies improve the work-life balance of employees and can therefore also facilitate living in several places.

JOB HIER, ZUHAUSE DORT – BERUFSBEDINGTES MULTILOKALES WOHNEN

LISA STADTLER

In Deutschland und anderen westlichen Industrieländern steigt die berufsbedingte Mobilität vor dem Hintergrund deregulierter und flexibilisierter Arbeitsmärkte zunehmend. Immer mehr Menschen pendeln weite Strecken zwischen Wohn- und Arbeitsorten oder ziehen aus beruflichen Gründen mehrmals in ihrem Leben um. Gleichzeitig wächst die Zahl an Menschen mit mehreren Wohnsitzen, was als multilokales Wohnen bezeichnet wird. Dies betrifft insbesondere wissensbasierte Berufsgruppen, die häufig ihren Arbeitsplatz aufgrund von projektbasiertem Arbeiten und befristeten Verträgen wechseln.

Auch die steigende qualifizierte Frauenerwerbstätigkeit führt zur Zunahme des multilokalen Wohnens, da Paare immer seltener in derselben Stadt oder Region eine Arbeitsstelle finden. Entscheiden sie sich dann, zwei getrennte Haushalte auf Distanz zu führen, wird dieses Arrangement als „Living apart together" bezeichnet. Eine weitere Form sind Wochenpendler*innen, die einen Zweitwohnsitz am Arbeitsort haben. Vor allem in Großstädten mit einer Vielzahl an wissensbasierten Arbeitsplätzen in international tätigen Unternehmen, Forschungseinrichtungen und Universitäten sowie einer guten Anbindung an den Fernverkehr sind diese Wohnarrangements vorzufinden. Das Wohnen an mehreren Orten

wirkt sich nicht nur auf den Alltag der Haushalte und ihre sozialen Beziehungen, sondern auch auf die Quartiers-, Stadt- und Regionalentwicklung der betroffenen Räume aus.

In diesem Zusammenhang stellt sich die Frage, wodurch die Mobilitäts- und Wohnstandortentscheidungen der multilokal wohnenden Personen beeinflusst werden und welche Orts- und Unternehmensbindungen sie entwickeln. Zusätzlich wird der Frage nachgegangen, wodurch ihre Raum-Zeit-Gestaltung beeinflusst wird. Anders als in bisherigen Untersuchungen, steht dabei der Einfluss von Arbeitgebenden im Fokus der Forschung. Denn ihnen kommt aufgrund der steigenden Flexibilitäts- und Mobilitätsanforderungen in der heutigen Arbeitswelt eine besondere Rolle zu.

Es zeigt sich, dass sich Unternehmen bisher nicht oder zu wenig mit dem Wohnen an mehreren Orten beschäftigen. Aufgrund des voranschreitenden Fachkräftemangels in wissensbasierten Branchen ist es jedoch unabdingbar, dass sich Arbeitgebende vermehrt damit befassen, wo und wie ihre Beschäftigten wohnen und wie sie diese im Alltag unterstützen können. Durch geeignete Unterstützung und hohe Unternehmensbindung können Unternehmen auch diejenigen Erwerbstätigen anziehen und halten, die nicht ihren Lebensmittelpunkt in die Nähe des Unternehmens verlagern möchten. So können Erwerbstätige ihren Arbeitsplatz und auch ihren berufsbedingten Zweitwohnsitz oder ihre Fernbeziehung beibehalten.

Bisher wird deutlich, dass vor allem flexible Arbeitszeit- und Arbeitsortregelungen in Unternehmen die Work-Life-Balance der Beschäftigten verbessern und damit auch das Wohnen an mehreren Orten erleichtern können.

OPEN SPACE DEVELOPMENT AS AN EXPRESSION OF LOCAL PLANNING CULTURES

PETER STROMS

Open spaces are under significant pressure especially in growing German cities. There is strong usage competition within the scarce open space. Under shrinkage conditions, the situation is quite different: in many shrinking cities, open spaces are even quantitively increasing due to areas falling into disuse and being demolished. Open space development, in this context, is often understood as an opportunity for urban development—as a soft location factor, an interim usage option, or the possibility of climate adjustment. But even so, shrinkage processes also present open space planning with problems: the municipal finance budget must suffice for a larger number and range of open spaces with fewer users and increasing usage claims. It can be assumed that the handling of urban open spaces differs greatly, despite similar problems and embedding in the same national planning system, and that local open space planning develops quite individual solutions. The framework of formal action possibilities, such as laws or tools, is concretely supplemented by specific local values and traditions, as well as patterns of perception and interpretation. A central role is played by the constellations of involved parties and negotiation processes, as administration, politics, civil society, associations, or the economy have an influence on the shaping of open space development. In sum, this complex results in a unique local planning culture.

These local cultural particularities have been largely sidelined for a long time in planning disciplines. The planning culture research that is increasingly becoming the focus of planning disciplines addresses this fact and understands planning cultures not as fixed configurations but as changeable and adaptable. The transition from growth to shrinkage-oriented planning gives rise to the expectation of a change in planning culture in which the framework conditions are to be redetermined and new ways of thinking and approaches are required of those involved.

For relatively recent planning culture research, one must point out a lack of empirical work, specialist sectoral perspectives, and matters of transformations of planning cultures.

For the case study cities Gelsenkirchen, Saarbrücken, Halle (Saale), and Chemnitz, empirical proof of local planning cultures in open space development will be provided and their adaptability since the year 1990 will be analyzed. Initial results indicate that specific traditions and constellations of key actors, as well as patterns of perception and interpretation are evident in open space development that are a central expression of the locally and regionally anchored planning cultures. Change through shrinkage processes presents itself locally as highly varied.

FREIRAUMENTWICKLUNG ALS AUSDRUCK LOKALER PLANUNGSKULTUREN

PETER STROMS

Freiräume stehen vor allem in wachsenden deutschen Großstädten unter erheblichem Druck. Es bestehen starke Nutzungskonkurrenzen um den knappen Freiraum. Unter Schrumpfungsbedingungen stellt sich die Situation anders dar: In vielen schrumpfenden Städten nehmen Freiräume durch Brachfallen von Nutzflächen und deren Rückbau sogar quantitativ zu. Freiraumentwicklung wird in diesem Kontext zwar oftmals als Chance für die Stadtentwicklung – als weicher Standortfaktor, Zwischennutzungsoption oder Möglichkeit zur Klimaanpassung – verstanden; dennoch konfrontieren Schrumpfungsprozesse die Freiraumplanung auch mit Problemen: Das Budget im kommunalen Finanzhaushalt muss für eine größere Zahl und Vielfalt an Freiräumen bei weniger Nutzenden mit zunehmenden Nutzungsansprüchen reichen.

Es ist anzunehmen, dass sich der Umgang mit urbanen Freiräumen trotz ähnlicher Problemlagen sowie Einbettung in das gleiche nationale Planungssystem stark unterscheidet und die lokale Freiraumplanung ganz individuelle Lösungen entwickelt. Der Rahmen der formalen Handlungsmöglichkeiten, beispielsweise Gesetze oder Instrumente, wird konkret durch lokalspezifische Werte, Traditionen sowie Wahrnehmungs- und Deutungsmuster ausgestaltet und umgesetzt. Dabei spielen Akteurskonstellationen und Aushandlungsprozesse eine zentrale Rolle, da Verwaltung, Politik, Zivilgesellschaft, Verbände oder Wirtschaft Einfluss auf die Ausgestaltung der Freiraumentwicklung nehmen. In summa ergibt dieser Komplex eine einzigartige lokale Planungskultur.

Diese lokalen kulturellen Besonderheiten wurden lange Zeit in den Planungswissenschaften weitestgehend ausgeblendet. Die aktuell stärker in den planungswissenschaftlichen Fokus gerückte Planungskulturforschung greift dies auf und versteht Planungskulturen dabei nicht als fixe Konfigurationen, sondern als wandelbar und adaptionsfähig. Der Übergang von einer wachstums- zu einer schrumpfungsorientierten Planung lässt einen planungskulturellen Wandel erwarten, bei dem die Rahmenbedingungen neu zu bestimmen sind und neue Denk- und Herangehensweisen der Akteur*innen verlangt werden.

Für die relativ junge Planungskulturforschung ist ein Mangel an empirischen Arbeiten, fachsektoralen Perspektiven sowie Fragestellungen nach Transformationen von Planungskulturen hervorzuheben. Für die Fallstudienstädte Gelsenkirchen, Saarbrücken, Halle (Saale) und Chemnitz soll demnach der empirische Nachweis von lokalen Planungskulturen in der Freiraumentwicklung erbracht und deren Wandlungsfähigkeit seit dem Jahr 1990 analysiert werden. Erste Ergebnisse deuten darauf hin, dass sich spezifische Traditionen, Konstellationen von Schlüsselakteur*innen sowie Wahrnehmungs- und Deutungsmuster in der Freiraumentwicklung ausbilden, die zentraler Ausdruck der lokal und regional verankerten Planungskulturen sind. Der Wandel durch Schrumpfungsprozesse stellt sich dabei lokal sehr unterschiedlich dar.

COPENHAGEN/ MALMÖ FLYING VISIT

STIPPVISITE KOPENHAGEN/ MALMÖ

COPENHAGEN AND MALMÖ—
THE PATH TOWARDS A TRANSNATIONAL
METROPOLITAN REGION

STEFAN SIEDENTOP, LISA STADTLER, PETER STROMS

For those interested in urban and regional development, there are many reasons to travel to Copenhagen and Malmö. Both cities—especially Copenhagen—are known worldwide for their cycle transport policy. What is pioneering is not only the achieved standard of the material infrastructure but also the strategic approach by which it has been developed further over the years. Both cities are striving to become climate-neutral over the course of the next decade. Transport policy plays a central role in this aim.

The Öresund region is a worthwhile excursion destination, also with a view to experiences in handling industrial structural change. For a long time, Copenhagen and Malmö were considered to be shrinking cities. Malmö was severely hit by the decline of shipbuilding industries and was forced to face high employment and increasing poverty. The change in this trend starting at the beginning of the 1990s was also due to structural policy measures. In Malmö, the founding of the university at the end of the 1990s had a positive impact, especially in form of the influx of younger people. Knowledge-based and creative industries played a significant role in the economic upturn. Copenhagen has even grown over the last two decades to such an extent that it has triggered controversial debates about the dangers of an exclusive, green gentrification and the possibilities of a more socially inclusive development.

A central issue of the Copenhagen/Malmö visits was the supportive role of regional infrastructure in urban and regional development. With the opening of the Öresund bridge in the year 2000, the framework conditions for regional development had changed radically. The short travel time between the centers of both cities since that time has led to a leap in regional connections. The economy and population growth in Malmö also stems from the spillover effects of Copenhagen—alongside the already mentioned effects of a state-promoted structural change. It is foreseeable that both cities will grow together increasingly into a transnational metropolitan region that can raise its international attractiveness also through magnitude and scale effects.

One can also identify signs of a spatial work division with specific economic focuses in both cities. In addition, Malmö's housing market is increasingly important for the Copenhagen population, which is burdened by high living costs. Living in Malmö and working in Copenhagen, which is practiced by increasing numbers of people, shows the creation of an integrated metropolitan region even in the minds of people. Whether this will bring new conflicts in future in relation to the gentrification debate spilling over into Malmö remains to be seen.

KOPENHAGEN UND MALMÖ – WEG ZU EINER TRANSNATIONALEN METROPOLREGION

STEFAN SIEDENTOP, LISA STADTLER, PETER STROMS

Für Interessierte der Stadt- und Regionalentwicklung gibt es zahlreiche Gründe nach Kopenhagen und Malmö zu reisen. Beide Städte – insbesondere aber Kopenhagen – sind weltweit bekannt für ihre Radverkehrspolitik. Richtungsweisend ist dabei nicht allein der erreichte Standard der materiellen Infrastruktur, sondern auch der strategische Ansatz, mit dem diese in den vergangenen Jahren weiterentwickelt wurde. Beide Städte streben an, bereits im Laufe des nächsten Jahrzehnts klimaneutral zu werden. Die Verkehrspolitik spielt dabei eine zentrale Rolle.

Ein lohnenswertes Exkursionsziel ist die Öresundregion auch mit Blick auf die Erfahrungen im Umgang mit dem industriellen Strukturwandel. Kopenhagen und Malmö galten lange Zeit als schrumpfende Städte. Malmö wurde durch den Niedergang der Schiffsbauindustrie schwer getroffen und musste mit hoher Arbeitslosigkeit und verfestigter Armut umgehen. Die Anfang der 1990er Jahre einsetzende Trendwende geht auch auf strukturpolitische Maßnahmen zurück. In Malmö hatte die Gründung der Universität Ende der 1990er Jahre positive Auswirkungen, insbesondere in Form des Zuzugs jüngerer Menschen. Wissensbasierte und kreative Industrien haben maßgeblichen Anteil am wirtschaftlichen Aufschwung. Kopenhagen wuchs in den letzten zwei Jahrzehnten sogar in einem Ausmaß, das in der Stadtgesellschaft kontroverse Debatten über die Gefahren von Verdrängung (*green gentrification*) und die Möglichkeiten einer sozial inklusiveren Entwicklung ausgelöst hat.

Ein zentrales Thema der Stippvisite Kopenhagen/Malmö war indes die tragende Rolle der regionalen Infrastruktur für die Stadt- und Regionalentwicklung. Mit der Eröffnung der Öresundbrücke im Jahr 2000 hatten sich die Rahmenbedingungen für die regionale Entwicklung radikal verändert. Die seitdem kurze Reisezeit zwischen den Kernen beider Städte hat zu einem sprunghaften Anstieg der regionalen Verflechtungen geführt. Das Wirtschafts- und Bevölkerungswachstum in Malmö ist – neben den bereits erwähnten Effekten eines staatlich geförderten Strukturwandels – auch auf die *Spill-over*-Effekte Kopenhagens zurückzuführen. Es ist absehbar, dass beide Städte mehr und mehr zu einer transnationalen Metropolregion zusammenwachsen, die ihre internationale Attraktivität auch über Größen- und Skaleneffekte steigern kann.

Erkennbar sind auch Anzeichen einer raumstrukturellen Arbeitsteilung mit spezifischen ökonomischen Schwerpunkten in beiden Städten. Darüber hinaus ist Malmös Wohnungsmarkt für die von hohen Lebenshaltungskosten geplagte Kopenhagener Bevölkerung zunehmend von Bedeutung. Das von

The enormous growth has long since triggered discussions about an extension of the infrastructure. On the Copenhagen side, the Loop City project has
been discussed for some years, which would change the regional transport
infrastructure just as lastingly as the Öresund bridge at the beginning of
this century. Loop City will extend the radial transport axes ("fingers") that
connect the inner city with the regional towns in the wider surroundings
with a tangential tram system crossing the radials. The explicit aim is to
incentivize growth and network spatial developments in the entire Öresund
region. The project will not only have effects on the everyday choice of in-
traregional means of transport, it also aims to upgrade decentral network
hubs and thus ease the burden on the center of Copenhagen.

The extent to which the project might have an impact as a strategic urban
development initiative through the construction of the city tram out into
the Copenhagen surroundings is still uncertain, however. But the project
shows that many of those who are politically responsible are aware that
a dynamically growing metropolitan region requires a new infrastructural
backbone. The Loop City is therefore part of a context of similar projects
with which European metropolises are reducing the overburdening of their
centers and seeking to overcome a suburban mobility culture that is still
strongly dependent on the car.

The visit was able to show the opportunities presented by a proactive and
integrated settlement and infrastructure development. With their long-
standing innovative transport policy, as well as with new political initiatives
in the further development of green infrastructure and an urban development adapted to climate change, Copenhagen and Malmö have established
themselves as international, pioneering cities. However, the social and
spatial implications of growth in a rather neoliberal political climate—at
least on the Danish side—are more than just scratches on the shiny surface
of a transnational European metropolis.

immer mehr Menschen praktizierte Wohnen in Malmö und Arbeiten in Kopenhagen zeugt von der Entstehung einer integrierten Metropolregion auch in den Köpfen der Menschen. Ob dies in Zukunft neue Konflikte im Sinne einer nach Malmö übergreifenden Gentrifizierungsdebatte nach sich zieht, bleibt abzuwarten.

Das enorme Wachstum hat indes längst Diskussionen über eine Erweiterung der Infrastruktur ausgelöst. Auf Kopenhagener Seite wird seit einigen Jahren das sogenannte „Loop City"-Projekt diskutiert, das die regionale Verkehrsinfrastruktur ebenso nachhaltig verändern würde, wie die Öresundbrücke dies Anfang dieses Jahrhunderts bewirkt hat. „Loop City" wird die radialen Verkehrsachsen („Finger"), welche die Innenstadt mit den Regionalstädten im weiteren Umland verbinden, um ein tangentiales, quer zu den Radialen liegendes Straßenbahnsystem erweitern. Explizites Ziel ist es, räumliche Entwicklungen in der gesamten Öresundregion anzustoßen und zu vernetzen. Das Projekt wird nicht nur Auswirkungen auf die alltägliche intraregionale Verkehrsmittelwahl haben, geplant ist auch die Aufwertung dezentraler Netzknoten und somit eine Entlastung des Kopenhagener Zentrums.

Inwiefern das Projekt über den Bau der Stadtbahn im Kopenhagener Umland hinaus als strategischer Stadtentwicklungsansatz Wirkung entfalten kann, ist jedoch noch ungewiss. Das Projekt zeigt aber, dass vielen politisch Verantwortlichen bewusst ist, dass eine dynamisch wachsende Metropolregion ein neues Infrastrukturrückgrat benötigt. Die „Loop City" ordnet sich damit in einen Kontext ähnlicher Projekte ein, mit denen europäische Metropolen die Überlastung ihrer Zentren mindern und eine noch immer stark autoabhängige suburbane Mobilitätskultur überwinden wollen.

Die Stippvisite hat die Chancen einer proaktiven und integrierten Siedlungs- und Infrastrukturentwicklung aufzeigen können. Mit ihrer seit Langem innovativen Verkehrspolitik, aber auch mit neuen politischen Initiativen in der Weiterentwicklung grüner Infrastruktur und einer dem Klimawandel angepassten Stadtentwicklung haben sich Kopenhagen und Malmö als internationale Vorreiterstädte etabliert. Die sozialen und räumlichen Implikationen des Wachstums in einem – zumindest auf dänischer Seite – eher neoliberalen politischen Klima sind indes mehr als nur Kratzer auf der glänzenden Oberfläche einer transnationalen europäischen Metropole.

Copenhagen, May 2018
Kopenhagen, Mai 2018

Malmö, May 2018
Malmö, Mai 2018

Copenhagen, May 2018
Kopenhagen, Mai 2018

SHAPING OUR LIVING SPACE

LEBENSRAUM GESTALTEN

SHAPING OUR LIVING SPACE! REVIEW AND PREVIEW

BERND SCHOLL

Spatial planners are concerned with living space for people. Since people became sedentary, they have been forced to contend with planning. Land use, landscape changes, and the building of settlements and infrastructure have reflected the respective political, economic, technical, and social circumstances over the centuries, as well as the rise and fall of societies. Specialists have always been needed—some for special tasks and some who took care of how to put the details together. Today the latter are called spatial planners.

We all influence space through our behavior. We decide where we live, when and how we move around, and where we spend our leisure time. We make use of technical developments such as electricity, the railway, or the car. This has effects on space and its future development. It also opens up possibilities for our life, experiences, and behavior. However, spatial developments are sluggish. They proceed over many years and decades, sometimes even longer. Many public and private actors influence them. They incur major costs for investments, operation, and maintenance. Many increasingly specialized subject areas want to contribute their knowledge. Politics and specialists do not often agree about what avenue to pursue.

Key moments

I got to know such aspects during postgraduate studies in spatial planning at the beginning of the 1980s at ETH Zurich. The studies appeared rather abstract to me at the time and far removed from the design tasks that actually fascinated me and in which I wanted to participate. But they exist, those key moments in which it becomes clear in a flash how the abstract and concrete are connected and how theory and practice must work together to be able to master challenging tasks. Such a moment presented itself to me on an excursion during my postgraduate studies. This excursion led us to Vienna and the Neue Donau/New Danube which was just emerging. Neue Donau/New Danube succeeded in making a project with a wide range of uses out of an originally planned twenty-one-kilometer-long technical embankment to contain catastrophic floods of the Danube. Since then— in addition to flood protection—it offers many hundreds of thousands of people a variety of leisure possibilities. The Neue Donau/New Danube was created with swimming water quality, as well as the new Danube island. To do so, tens of thousands of cubic meters of earth were moved, thousands of trees were planted, motorways were replanned and covered, and the island was connected to public transport. I liked this building site. It showed what spatial planning is capable of. From then I was rather motivated to learn

UNSEREN LEBENSRAUM GESTALTEN! RÜCKBLICK UND AUSBLICK

BERND SCHOLL

Raumplaner*innen befassen sich mit dem Lebensraum des Menschen. Seitdem Menschen sesshaft geworden sind, müssen sie sich mit Planung auseinandersetzen. Bodennutzung, Veränderungen von Landschaften, der Bau von Siedlungen und Infrastrukturen spiegeln über Jahrhunderte hinweg das Wesentliche der politischen, wirtschaftlichen, technischen und sozialen Verhältnisse, aber auch den Aufstieg und Niedergang von Gesellschaften. Stets wurden Fachleute gebraucht – solche für spezielle Aufgaben und solche, die sich darum kümmerten, wie die Einzelheiten zusammengefügt werden können. Letztere werden heute Raumplaner*innen genannt.

Wir alle beeinflussen durch unser Verhalten den Raum. Wir entscheiden, wo wir wohnen, wann und wie wir uns fortbewegen und wo wir unsere Freizeit verbringen. Wir bedienen uns dabei technischer Entwicklungen wie der Elektrizität, der Eisenbahn oder des Automobils. Das hat Auswirkungen auf den Raum, seine zukünftige Entwicklung und eröffnet Möglichkeiten für unser Dasein, Erleben und Verhalten.

Aber Raumentwicklungen sind träge. Sie verlaufen über viele Jahre und Jahrzehnte und manchmal noch darüber hinaus. Zahlreiche öffentliche und private Akteur*innen wirken auf sie ein. Große Kosten für Investitionen, Betrieb und Unterhalt sind damit verbunden. Viele zunehmend spezialisierte Fachgebiete wollen ihr Wissen einbringen. Nicht oft sind sich Politik und Fachleute einig über den einzuschlagenden Weg.

Schlüsselmomente

Solche Zusammenhänge hatte ich im Nachdiplomstudium der Raumplanung, Anfang der 1980er Jahre, an der ETH Zürich kennengelernt. Das Studium schien mir damals ziemlich abstrakt und weit von Gestaltungsaufgaben entfernt, die mich eigentlich faszinierten und an denen ich mitwirken wollte. Aber es gibt sie, die Schlüsselmomente, in denen einem schlagartig klar wird, wie Abstraktes und Konkretes zusammenhängen und wie Theorie und Praxis zusammenwirken müssen, damit herausfordernde Aufgaben gemeistert werden können. Ein solcher Moment war für mich eine Exkursion während meines Nachdiplomstudiums. Sie führte uns nach Wien und zur neuen Donau, die gerade Gestalt annahm. Dort gelang es, aus einer ursprünglich geplanten 21 Kilometer langen technischen Entlastungsrinne zur Eindämmung verheerender Überschwemmungen der Donau ein Projekt mit vielfältigem Nutzen zu machen. Es bietet seither – über den Hochwasserschutz hinaus – vielen Hunderttausenden Menschen Möglichkeiten mannigfaltiger Freizeitnutzung. Es entstanden die neue Donau mit Badewasserqualität und die neue Donauinsel. Dazu wurden Zehntausende

the profession of spatial planner. And it was a spatial planning procedural innovation that paved the way to success.[1]

Together with my office partner Rolf Signer, we were able to use the requisite know-how acquired from ETH Zurich from 1987 to around 1990 when planning Frankfurt's application for the Olympic Games in the years 2000 or 2004. In cooperation with the Frankfurt planning office of Professor Albert Speer appointed for the planning, the municipal government set up a high-ranking advisory board following our suggestion, which was called the Olympic Council.

Test plans carried out at the beginning led to the idea of restructuring the river area neglected after World War II into a central and multipurpose urban space. The central idea was to use the application for inward high-rise settlement developments in the main municipal area.[2]

This and other examples encouraged us to publish a book with inspiring examples and important themes on the subject of spatial development. It is intended to foster the courage to shape our living environment.[3]

Core task of spatial development

One of the core tasks of spatial development consists in reducing the expansion of settlement areas—worldwide, but also in Europe and Switzerland. The thrust for this consists, to put it simply, in making use of available settlements instead of extending them to mostly "green meadows." We call this drive "inward development before outward development." It is the minimum strategy for the domestic sustainable handling of ground as a rare resource, the central basis of our living space that cannot be increased. The realization of this strategy is also associated with challenging design tasks. This is to be demonstrated through European and Swiss tasks. We will start in a European context.

1 *New Danube and Danube Island in Vienna*
1 *Neue Donau und Donauinsel in Wien*

Kubikmeter Erde bewegt, Tausende Bäume gepflanzt, Autobahnen umgeplant und überdeckt, und die Insel wurde mit öffentlichen Verkehrsmitteln erschlossen. Diese Baustelle gefiel mir. Sie zeigte, was Raumplanung bewirken kann. Fortan war ich ziemlich motiviert, den Beruf des Raumplaners zu erlernen. Und es war eine raumplanerische Verfahrensinnovation[1], die den Weg zum Erfolg bereitete.[2]

Zusammen mit meinem Büropartner Rolf Signer durften wir das an der ETH Zürich erworbene Rüstzeug 1987 bis etwa 1990 bei der Planung für die Bewerbung Frankfurts für die Olympischen Spiele der Jahre 2000 oder 2004 anwenden. In Zusammenarbeit mit dem für die Planungen beauftragten Frankfurter Planungsbüro von Professor Albert Speer richtete die Stadtregierung auf unseren Vorschlag hin ein hochrangiges Beratergremium ein, das sogenannte Olympia-Konsilium.

Mit zu Beginn durchgeführten Testplanungen entstand die Idee, den nach dem Zweiten Weltkrieg vernachlässigten Flussraum zu einem zentralen und vielfältig nutzbaren Stadtraum umzugestalten. Zentraler Gedanke war, die Bewerbung für hochstehende Siedlungsentwicklungen nach innen im Stadtraum Main zu nutzen.[3]

Diese und andere Beispiele haben uns ermutigt, ein Buch mit inspirierenden Beispielen und wichtigen Themen zur Raumentwicklung herauszugeben. Es soll Mut zur Gestaltung unseres Lebensraumes machen.[4]

Kernaufgabe der Raumentwicklung

2 Urban area Frankfurt am Main
2 Stadtraum Frankfurt am Main

Eine der Kernaufgaben der Raumentwicklung besteht darin, den Siedlungsflächenverbrauch zu senken – weltweit, aber auch in Europa und in der Schweiz. Die dafür geltende Stoßrichtung besteht, vereinfacht gesagt, darin, vorhandene Flächenreserven der bestehenden Siedlungen zu nutzen, anstatt diese auf meist „grünen Wiesen" zu erweitern. Wir nennen diese Stoßrichtung „Innenentwicklung vor Außenentwicklung". Es ist

European corridor developments

On the image one can see two of nine European corridors: the Rotterdam-Genoa corridor and the Hamburg-Athens-Patras corridor with a branch to Istanbul. Corridors are living environments in which trans-European transport networks, as they are called, are supposed to be developed by 2030. The development of the railway is important in order to shift as much freight as possible from the road onto rails and of course also for attractive passenger transport. This is why the Gotthard and Ceneri base tunnel were built in Switzerland, the effective centerpieces of the Rhine-Alpine corridor from Rotterdam to Genoa.

The major transport investments (over 500 billion euros by 2030) are intended to promote the competitiveness of Europe compared to other continents and to foster its coherence. In connection with the railway system, the railway station catchment areas are particularly interesting, because major settlement area reserves are presumed there. This goes together optimally with inward settlement development because of the very good public transport connection. This is referred to as TOD (transport-oriented development).[4] For the Rhine-Alpine corridor, we were able to show for the first time important spatial and railway development aspects, as part of an EU project that was co-initiated by the chair for spatial development at ETH Zurich and that started in 2010. Currently around seventy million people live in the catchment area of the corridor. Along this most important European north-south connection for passenger and freight transport, in the catchment area of the important railway stations we estimate there are land reserves for over seven million people.[5]

These are on an enormous scale, but their activation is endangered. Due to the increase in freight transport driven by progressive globalization and the existing bottlenecks, there can be competition between passenger and goods transport, leading to the sidelining or the impossibility of the development of passenger transport—in Switzerland, as well as in densely populated regions of Germany, the Netherlands, and Upper Italy. This would be counterproductive for the required inward settlement development. The removal of these bottlenecks is therefore urgently necessary to get more trains through, as well as for the unbundling of good transport and passenger transport into the densely populated areas—not only for noise but also safety reasons. In Germany, for example in the Freiburg area, agreements have been made in this regard. Or to give another example: in Switzerland the clarification of the position of a third Jura railway crossing (Basel-Mittelland) is required. Planning costs little compared to building, but one learns a lot in the process. The aim should be to ensure the terrain for the prospective new railway crossing—knowing full well that the realization of such construction works will be long after 2030.

The situation in the Hamburg–Athens–Patras corridor is quite different. In an international work group, we have been working on an overview since 2016 for identifying the challenges of the spatial and railway development

die Mindeststrategie für den haushälterischen Umgang mit der Ressource Boden, der zentralen und nicht vermehrbaren Grundlage unseres Lebensraumes. Mit Verwirklichen dieser Strategie sind auch herausfordernde Gestaltungsaufgaben verbunden. An europäischen und schweizweiten Aufgaben soll dies veranschaulicht werden. Beginnen wir im europäischen Kontext.

Europäische Korridorentwicklungen

Auf der Abbildung sieht man zwei von neun europäischen Korridoren: den Korridor Rotterdam–Genua und den Korridor Hamburg–Athen/Patras mit einem Ast nach Istanbul. Korridore sind Lebensräume, in denen die sogenannten transeuropäischen Verkehrsnetze bis 2030 ausgebaut werden sollen. Der Ausbau der Eisenbahn ist wichtig, um möglichst viele Güter von der Straße auf die Schiene verlagern zu können, und natürlich auch für einen attraktiven Personenverkehr. Deshalb wurden in der Schweiz der Gotthard- und der Ceneri-Basistunnel gebaut, die leistungsfähigen Herzstücke des sogenannten Rhine-Alpine-Korridors von Rotterdam nach Genua.

Die großen Verkehrsinvestitionen (man spricht von über 500 Milliarden Euro bis 2030) sollen die Wettbewerbsfähigkeit Europas gegenüber anderen Kontinenten und seinen Zusammenhalt fördern. Besonders interessant sind im Zusammengang mit dem System Eisenbahn die Einzugsbereiche der Bahnhöfe, weil dort große Siedlungsflächenreserven vermutet wurden. Das passt wegen der sehr guten Erschließung durch öffentliche Verkehrsmittel mit der Siedlungsentwicklung nach innen bestens zusammen. Im englischsprachigen Raum spricht man von TOD (*Transport Oriented Development*).[5]

Im Rhine-Alpine-Korridor konnten wir im Rahmen eines von der Professur für Raumentwicklung der ETH Zürich mitinitiierten und 2010 gestarteten EU-Projektes erstmals wichtige Zusammenhänge der Raum- und Eisenbahnentwicklung aufzeigen. Gegenwärtig leben im Einzugsbereich des Korridors etwa 70 Millionen Menschen. An dieser für den Personen- und Güterverkehr wichtigsten europäischen Nord-Süd-Verbindung existieren

3 Rhine Alpine corridor and Eastern Mediterranean corridor
3 *Rhine Alpine-Korridor and Eastern Mediterranean-Korridor*

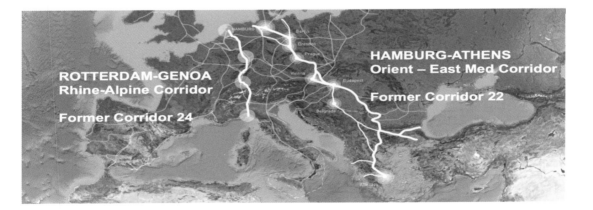

Geschätzte Flächenreserven
CODE 24 | Settlement Development

Ca. 150 Tsd. ha für ca. 6 - 7 Mio. Einwohner

Europaviertel, Frankfurt
ca. 3 - 4 Mrd. € Investment

Einzugsbereich HB Zürich
ca. 4 - 5 Mrd. CHF Investment
(incl. Bahnprojekt)

Arealentwicklung Bovisa,
Milano
ca. 2 - 3 Mrd. € Investment

in this corridor. The initial findings show that one can find significant settlement area reserves at the important railway hubs such as Prague, Vienna, Budapest, Belgrade, Thessaloniki, and Athens.[6] Contrary to the Rotterdam–Genoa corridor, the travel times between different towns are much too long due to the pitiful state of the railway tracks. For example, over eight hours are required for the 400-kilometer-long Budapest-Belgrade stretch. China will now, in connection with its strategy of a new Silk Road, build a high-speed line between these two cities. The development of the ports in Piraeus into a "Rotterdam of the south" has already been started by the Chinese logistics company COSCO, to be able to transport goods from there by railway to the north. So far, a strong European answer to this strategy is lacking. It is urgently needed, however, if we do not want this connection to the strategically significant central area that is so important for Europe to be weakened further. The rapid upsurge at Piraeus port could ease the North Sea ports and therefore lead to a better European balancing of the flow of goods from Asia to Europe—and ultimately also ease the burden on Switzerland. It makes little sense to first transport containers by ship to Rotterdam, transporting some through densely populated areas in the inland areas of the ports and through the Alps to Upper Italy.[7]

The academic cooperation regarding the European spatial and transport development shows that we as specialists are well advised to engage in European discussions. Spatial and transport development are always two sides of the same coin and the railway is the strategic backbone of sustainable spatial development. In reference to the example of the incorporation of the corridor into the city of Patras, as part of a test plan with four teams we were able to gather experiences regarding Greece for the first time. In the end, a robust, cost-effective solution emerged that, contrary to a costly, risky tunnel solution, has a greater prospect of being realized.[8] A field visit

4 *Settlement area reserves on the Rhine-Alpine corridor*
4 *Siedlungsflächenreserven im Rhine-Alpine-Korridor*

im Einzugsbereich der wichtigen Bahnhöfe nach unseren Abschätzungen Landreserven für über 7 Millionen Menschen.[6]

Das sind enorme Größenordnungen, aber ihre Aktivierung ist gefährdet. Durch die von voranschreitender Globalisierung getriebene Zunahme des Güterverkehrs und die vorhandenen Kapazitätsengpässe (*bottlenecks*) kann Konkurrenz zwischen Personen- und Güterverkehr entstehen und zur Verdrängung beziehungsweise zum nicht möglichen Ausbau des Personenverkehrs führen – in der Schweiz, aber auch in dicht besiedelten Regionen Deutschlands, der Niederlande und Oberitaliens. Das wäre für die erwünschte Siedlungsentwicklung nach innen kontraproduktiv. Deshalb ist die Beseitigung dieser *bottlenecks* dringend erforderlich, um mehr Züge durchzubekommen – ebenso wie die Entflechtung des Güterverkehrs vom Personenverkehr in den dicht besiedelten Gebieten; dies nicht nur aus Lärm-, sondern auch aus Sicherheitsgründen. In Deutschland, beispielsweise im Raum Freiburg, sind dazu Vereinbarungen getroffen worden. In der Schweiz ist beispielsweise die Klärung der Lage einer dritten Juraeisenbahnquerung (Basel–Mittelland) erforderlich. Planung kostet im Vergleich zum Bau wenig, aber man lernt dabei viel. Ziel müsste es sein, für die infrage kommende neue Eisenbahnquerung den Raum zu sichern – wohl wissend, dass die Realisierung solcher Bauwerke erst weit nach 2030 erfolgen wird.

Ganz anders sieht die Situation im Korridor Hamburg–Athen/Patras aus. In einer internationalen Arbeitsgruppe erarbeiten wir seit 2016 eine Übersicht, um die Herausforderungen der Raum- und Eisenbahnentwicklung in diesem Korridor zu erkennen. Erste Erkenntnisse veranschaulichen, dass auch an den wichtigen Eisenbahnknoten wie Prag, Wien, Budapest, Belgrad, Thessaloniki und Athen erhebliche Siedlungsflächenreserven zu finden sind.[7] Anders als im Korridor Rotterdam–Genua sind die Reisezeiten zwischen verschiedenen Städte wegen des pitoyablen Zustandes der Gleisanlagen viel zu lang. Beispielsweise werden für die 400 Kilometer lange Strecke Budapest–Belgrad über 8 Stunden benötigt. China wird nun im Zusammenhang mit seiner Strategie einer neuen „Seidenstraße" zwischen diesen beiden Städten eine Hochgeschwindigkeitslinie bauen. Bereits angelaufen ist der Ausbau der Häfen in Piräus zum „Rotterdam des Südens", durch das chinesische Logistikunternehmen COSCO, um von dort Güter in den Norden per Eisenbahn transportieren zu können. Eine starke europäische Antwort auf diese Strategie fehlt bisher. Sie wird aber dringend benötigt, wenn wir nicht wollen, dass diese für Europa so wichtige Verbindung zum strategisch bedeutsamen Mittelraum weiter geschwächt wird. Der rapide Aufschwung im Hafen Piräus könnte die Nordseehäfen entlasten und damit zur besseren europäischen Ausbalancierung der Warenströme von Asien nach Europa und führen – und schließlich auch die Schweiz entlasten. Es ist wenig sinnvoll, Container per Schiff zunächst nach Rotterdam zu transportieren, um einen Teil davon durch dicht besiedelte Räume im Hinterland der Häfen und durch die Alpen nach Oberitalien zu transportieren.[8]

Die akademische Zusammenarbeit im Zusammenhang mit der europäischen Raum- und Verkehrsentwicklung veranschaulicht, dass wir als Fachleute gut

by the International Doctoral College (IDK) led us to this location (see chapter *patras flying visit*).

Test plannning and ideas competition

I have used the term test planning several times. What does it actually mean? Since in difficult tasks nobody possesses conclusive wisdom, it is about achieving the best solution ideas in a short period of time. If there is a difficult central task to solve, we speak of test planning. Ideas competitions are more open and should—through ideas for solutions—also lead to the identification of key tasks. Ideas competitions follow the same methodological principles as test planning.

Several interdisciplinary teams (usually three to four people) work on the same task. They develop and test their ideas independently of each other for the solution of the set task. This results in the required competition of ideas, as one can only assess which are effective solutions and which are not by comparing the suggestions put forward—only in relative and not absolute terms. An assessment committee is appointed for this by the policy executive. In a direct exchange as part of several mostly full-day meetings, everything important is discussed in a direct and critical dialogue between the teams and the members of this committee.

In the competition of ideas, those that have successfully been put forward in the critical discourse win through. This also makes it clear that contrary to competition procedures, there is no victorious planning team. Pieces of the solution puzzle are provided by different teams. The task of the assessment committee is to acknowledge these pieces of the puzzle and ultimately to put them together into a picture that shows the thrust of the future spatial development, and then the party responsible for the policy implementation can be recommended.

Structuring through transformation

For the development of the largest surface reserve in Switzerland at 234 hectares, the Dübendorf airport site, concepts were able to be developed from 2010 to 2012 that are now intended to lead to a nationally significant innovation park.

In the canton Solothurn, concepts were drawn up for the second-largest settlement area reserve in Switzerland, the disused cellulose factory Attisholz with a total area of 110 hectares, which will lead among other things to the settlement of an important company in the pharmaceutical sector, in combination with housing on the Aare. Three years after the completion of the test plans (2012) came the request by the company and the production should go into full operation in 2020. One and a half billion Swiss francs are being invested and 600 highly qualified workers are being hired. The forward-looking purchase by the canton of a strategic area contributed to the development, among many other factors. The ensuring surface area, also on a communal level, can help to achieve the required developments.[9]

beraten sind, uns in die europäische Diskussion einzubringen. Raum- und Verkehrsentwicklung sind immer zwei Seiten derselben Medaille und die Eisenbahn ist das strategische Rückgrat für eine nachhaltige Raumentwicklung.

Am Beispiel der Einbindung des Korridors in die Stadt Patras konnten wir im Rahmen einer Testplanung mit vier Teams erstmals für Griechenland Erfahrungen sammeln. Am Ende kristallisierte sich eine robuste, kostengünstige Lösung heraus, die im Gegensatz zu einer kostspieligen, risikoreichen Tunnellösung größere Aussicht hat, realisiert zu werden.[9] Eine Stippvisite des Internationalen Doktorandenkollegs (IDK) führte uns an diesen Schauplatz (s. Kap. *Stippvisite Patras*).

Testplanungen und Konkurrenz der Ideen

Mehrmals habe ich den Begriff der Testplanung verwendet. Was ist darunter eigentlich zu verstehen? Weil bei schwierigen Aufgaben niemand im Besitz abschließender Weisheiten ist, kommt es darauf an, in überschaubarer Zeit zu den besten Lösungsideen zu kommen. Gibt es eine schwierige zentrale Aufgabe, die zu lösen ist, sprechen wir von Testplanungen. Ideenkonkurrenzen sind offener und sollen – über Lösungsideen – auch zum Erkennen der Schlüsselaufgaben führen. Ideenkonkurrenzen folgen denselben methodischen Prinzipien wie Testplanungen.

Mehrere interdisziplinär zusammengesetzte Teams (meist drei bis vier Personen) arbeiten an derselben Aufgabe. Sie entwickeln und testen ihre Ideen für die Lösung der gestellten Aufgabe unabhängig voneinander. Es entsteht der gewünschte Wettstreit von Ideen, denn: Was zweckmäßige Lösungen sind und was nicht, kann erst im Vergleich vorgebrachter Vorschläge, also nur relativ und nie absolut, beurteilt werden. Dafür wird von der politischen Exekutive ein Beurteilungsgremium eingesetzt. Im direkten Austausch im Rahmen mehrerer klausurartiger, meist ganztägiger Treffen wird alles Wichtige im direkten und kritischen Dialog zwischen den Teams und den Mitgliedern dieses Gremiums erörtert.

In der Konkurrenz der Ideen setzen sich schließlich jene durch, die sich im kritischen Diskurs erfolgreich behauptet haben. Damit wird auch deutlich, dass es im Unterschied zu Wettbewerbsverfahren kein siegreiches Planungsteam gibt. Puzzlesteine zur Lösung werden von unterschiedlichen Teams geliefert. Aufgabe des Beurteilungsgremiums ist es, diese Puzzlesteine zu erkennen und am Ende zu einem Bild zusammenzufügen, das die Stoßrichtung der zukünftigen räumlichen Entwicklung veranschaulicht und dann den politisch Zuständigen zur Umsetzung empfohlen werden kann.

Gestaltung durch Transformation

So konnten für die Entwicklung der mit 234 Hektar größten Flächenreserve der Schweiz, des Flugplatzareals Dübendorf, 2010 bis 2012 Vorstellungen entwickelt werden, die nun zu einem national bedeutsamen Innovationspark führen sollen.

Im Kanton Solothurn konnten für die zweitgrößte Siedlungsflächenreserve der Schweiz, die aufgelassene Zellulosefabrik Attisholz mit 110 Hektar

Outlook

Test planning and ideas competitions are spatial development methods for the long-term shaping of our living environment. They can be significant sources of knowledge for teaching and research.[10] They make it possible to set spatial planning design in motion in a limited time period and with limited means. In strategically important tasks, competition procedures are essential—also because of the consequences of possible errors—in order to sound out the scope of possible solutions and not to overlook anything important. In the same work sequence, qualified rejection leads to the exclusion of unsuitable solutions. I see a great research need for procedural innovations in smaller and medium-sized municipalities, to reach solutions for tricky and strategic tasks for local and regional development by means of more streamlined procedures (and better adapted to the Swiss system).

I am therefore pleased that a procedural innovation came about in an alpine region of Switzerland. In the Urserntal tourism development region in the Gotthard area of the canton Uri (about 2500 inhabitants), which is facing great challenges, the basis for a joint regional development concept is to be established as part of an ideas competition with four municipalities, two corporations, and the canton. The results and findings will be reported.

5 *Attisholz test planning*
5 *Testplanung Attisholz*

Gesamtfläche, Vorstellungen erarbeitet werden, die unter anderem zur Ansiedelung eines wichtigen Unternehmens der Pharmabranche in Kombination mit Wohnen an der Aare führen wird. Drei Jahre nach Abschluss der Testplanungen (2012) kam die Anfrage des Unternehmens und schon 2020 soll die Produktion in Vollbetrieb gehen. 1,5 Milliarden Schweizer Franken werden investiert, 600 hochqualifizierte Beschäftigte werden eingestellt. Zur Entwicklung hat, neben vielem anderen, der weitsichtige Kauf einer strategischen Fläche durch den Kanton beigetragen. Flächenvorsorge, auch auf kommunaler Ebene, kann helfen, zu den erwünschten Entwicklungen zu kommen.[10]

Ausblick

Testplanungen und Ideenkonkurrenzen sind Methoden der Raumentwicklung zur nachhaltigen Gestaltung unserer Lebensräume. Sie können bedeutsame Wissensquellen für Lehre[11] und Forschung sein.[12] Sie ermöglichen es, in begrenzter Zeit und mit begrenzten Mitteln, raumplanerisches Entwerfen in Gang zu setzen. Bei strategisch bedeutsamen Aufgaben sind Konkurrenzverfahren – auch wegen der Tragweite möglicher Fehler – unerlässlich, um die Bandbreite infrage kommender Lösungen auszuloten und nichts Wichtiges zu übersehen. Im selben Arbeitsgang führt qualifiziertes Verwerfen zum Ausscheiden nicht infrage kommender Lösungen.

Großen Forschungsbedarf für Verfahrensinnovationen sehe ich in kleineren und mittleren Gemeinden, um mit schlankeren (und dem Schweizer Milizsystem besser angepassten) Verfahren zu Lösungen für knifflige und strategische Aufgaben der Orts- und Regionalentwicklung zu kommen.

Es freut mich deshalb, dass eine Verfahrensinnovation in einem alpinen Lebensraum der Schweiz zustande gekommen ist. In dem vor großen Herausforderungen stehenden Tourismusentwicklungsraum Urserntal im Gotthardgebiet des Kantons Uri mit etwa 2500 Einwohner*innen sollen im Rahmen einer Ideenkonkurrenz mit vier Gemeinden, zwei Korporationen und dem Kanton die Grundlagen für ein gemeinsames regionales Entwicklungskonzept geschaffen werden. Über Ergebnisse und Erkenntnisse wird an anderer Stelle zu berichten sein.

6 Ideas competition "Urserntal tourism development region"
6 Ideenkonkurrenz „Tourismusentwicklungsraum Urserntal"

Ideenkonkurrenz

«Regionales Entwicklungskonzept (REK) Tourismusentwicklungsraum Urserntal 2040»

Aufgabenstellung

Zurich, September 2017
Zürich, September 2017

Zurich, September 2017
Zürich, September 2017

Zurich, September 2017
Zürich, September 2017

RAILWAY-ORIENTED SPATIAL DEVELOPMENT: STRATEGY FOR INTEGRATED SPATIAL AND RAILWAY DEVELOPMENT IN SWITZERLAND

MAHDOKHT SOLTANIEHHA

The size of urban agglomerations is increasing in most countries as a consequence of the closer integration of regional economies and the associated spatial development of cities and rural areas. However, uncontrolled growth caused by lower land price can lead to low-density developments at the expense of rural and cultural land. Some land use tools and instruments, such as transit-oriented development, try to justify densification with high-quality land use development and good accessibility to public transport in the local scale. However, regional strategic plans and policies often fail to address the issue. Especially planning for functional regions such as "agglomerations" is a complex task of regional strategic planning where the local policies and instruments can no longer be effective beyond the administrative borders.

Currently, 54 percent of the population and 65 percent of the workforce in Switzerland (80 percent working in the tertiary sector) live or work within a radius of one kilometer of a railway station. This number shows the high relevance of the rail network for the distribution of the population and workplaces. The main hypothesis of this research is that the underdeveloped and unfilled land reserves in the catchment area of railway stations can possibly serve as a main driver for more compact settlements in agglomerations. This is of prime importance especially for the densification of small and medium-sized municipalities, as more than 60 percent of the land reserves are available there. In order to incorporate the potential of densification in the railway station catchment areas, a coordinated spatial and transportation policy-making is an essential requirement for a principal strategy of "inward development before outward development," as well as preparation for a new strategy of "railway-oriented spatial development" or ROSD. Implementation of ROSD is possibly confronted with various operational obstacles, including fragmented obstacles. These include, among others, fragmented local administration, general regulations imposed by national and regional authorities, and insufficient planning competence of small and medium-sized municipalities. To identify the complex planning tasks that ROSD must potentially undertake, this study evaluates existing planning tools and suggests a new collaborative tool called Corridor Consilium, which identifies transit corridors as functional regions and explains the planning reasons for the aforementioned problems. A corridor conference can illuminate many relevant aspects, for example, stimulating a collective understanding of the problem, minimizing the impacts of sector-specific planning and conflicting interests and poor planning cooperation, as well as the absence of planning measures for functional regions. A corridor conference thus facilitates decision-making processes to achieve the principal strategy of ROSD especially for small and medium-sized municipalities.

BAHNORIENTIERTE RAUMENTWICKLUNG: STRATEGIE FÜR INTEGRIERTE RAUM- UND EISENBAHNENTWICKLUNG IN DER SCHWEIZ[1]

MAHDOKHT SOLTANIEHHA

Die Größe der urbanen Agglomerationen nimmt in den meisten Ländern als Folge der stärkeren Integration der regionalen Wirtschaft und der zusammenhängenden Raumentwicklung von Stadt und Land zu. Jedoch kann von Kosteneffizienz verursachtes unkontrollierbares Wachstum Entwicklungen mit niedriger Dichte verursachen. Es gibt Bodennutzungstools wie *Transit-Oriented Development*, welche Verdichtung mit qualitativ hochwertiger Bodennutzungsentwicklung und gutem Zugang zu öffentlichem Verkehr rechtfertigen. Allerdings schaffen es ganzheitliche regionale Betrachtungen sowie integrierte Raum- und Transportkonzepte oftmals nicht, kompakte Siedlungen zu veranlassen. Darüber hinaus stellt das Konzept der Agglomeration eine komplexe Planungsaufgabe dar, welche unterstützende Instrumente benötigt.

Momentan leben oder arbeiten 54 Prozent der Bevölkerung und 65 Prozent der Beschäftigten der Schweiz (80 Prozent beschäftigt im Tertiärsektor) im Umkreis von 1 Kilometer zu einem Bahnhof. Diese Zahl verdeutlicht die hohe Relevanz des Eisenbahnnetzes für die Verteilung der Bevölkerung und der Arbeitsplätze. Die Haupthypothese dieser Forschung ist, dass die unterentwickelten und leeren Bodenreserven im Einzugsgebiet der Bahnhöfe möglicherweise als Hauptantrieb für kompaktere Entwicklungsformen in Agglomerationen dienen können. Dies ist speziell für die Verdichtung von kleinen und mittelgroßen Gemeinden von höchster Wichtigkeit, da dort mehr als 60 Prozent der Bodenreserven verfügbar sind. Um die Potenziale der Verdichtung in Einzugsgebieten von Bahnhöfen einzubeziehen, muss eine koordinierte Raum- und Transportgestaltung eine essenzielle Voraussetzung für die Hauptstrategie „Innenentwicklung vor Außenentwicklung" sein – ebenso wie die Erstellung einer neuen Strategie für bahnorientierte Raumentwicklung (*Railway-Oriented Spatial Development*, kurz: ROSD). Für die Implementierung einer ROSD gibt es mehrere operationelle Hindernisse: fragmentierte lokale Verwaltung, allgemeine Auflagen nationaler und regionaler Regierungen sowie geringe Planungskompetenz kleiner und mittelgroßer Gemeinden. Um die komplexen Planungsaufgaben zu identifizieren, welche ROSD potenziell bewältigen muss, evaluiert diese Forschungsarbeit bestehende Planungsinstrumente und schlägt ein neues kollaboratives Instrument namens *Corridor Consilium* vor, welches Transitkorridore als funktionelle Regionen identifiziert und die Planungsgründe der oben genannten Probleme erläutert. Eine Korridorkonferenz kann viele relevante Aspekte beleuchten, zum Beispiel fehlendes kollektives Problemverständnis, sektorspezifische Planung und divergierende Interessen, mangelnde Planungszusammenarbeit sowie fehlende Planungsmaßnahmen für funktionelle Regionen. Somit fördert eine Korridorkonferenz Entscheidungsprozesse, um die Minimalstrategie von ROSD insbesondere für kleine und mittelgroßen Gemeinden zu erreichen.

NONPROFIT HOUSING AND INWARD DEVELOPMENT

ROMAN STREIT

Rising housing costs and the lack of affordable housing present an urgent issue in central urban locations with a high population pressure. Contrary to profit-oriented housing projects, nonprofit construction generally offers lower-priced housing, as the rental rates are set on the basis of the costs for construction, maintenance, and renovation of the properties.

However, the significance of the nonprofit housing sector goes beyond the aspect of affordability. Nonprofit housing also contributes to the spatial planning strategy of inward development, meaning the prioritized guiding of future settlement development towards already built-up areas. Currently in Switzerland, nonprofit housing only comprises a market share of around 5 percent but benefits from highly favorable locations and significant potential for future denser usage. These locations are not only well-connected to public transport but are also often spatially concentrated in areas with a high housing demand, which promotes a district-oriented settlement renewal. Statistics about the existing old as well as newer nonprofit building projects also show their comparably resource-efficient land usage, with the occupants taking up on average significantly less living space than in other rented or owned housing. At the same time, the already effected implementation of constructional densification measures of nonprofit housing reflects many connections with inward development, whereby qualitative, ecological, and social aspects are to be emphasized. The observed acceptance of density allows one to assume a quality-promoting effect of the respective interventions—in many nonprofit organizations, positive majority decisions of the members are a basic condition for enabling their building stock to be comprehensively adapted.

The field of tension between nonprofit housing construction and inward development also presents challenges: firstly, not all the existing sites are suitable for constructional further development, whereby heritage conservation aspects play a central role. Secondly, the framework conditions for a future-oriented further development of the existing substance are not yet given everywhere. A close cooperation culture between authorities and nonprofit housing associations, customized planning processes, and the setting of impulses focused more on growth in housing subsidy schemes provide starting points for the activation of potential among the existing building substance. At the same time, the systematic linking of planning interventions and land policy specifications opens up leeway for a greater use of inward development in order to strengthen the nonprofit housing construction sector in future.[1]

GEMEINNÜTZIGER WOHNUNGSBAU UND INNENENTWICKLUNG

ROMAN STREIT

Steigende Wohnkosten sowie fehlende preisgünstige Wohnangebote stellen in zentralen städtischen Lagen mit großem Bevölkerungsdruck ein hochaktuelles Problem dar. Im Gegensatz zu renditeorientierten Wohnbauakteur*innen bieten gemeinnützige Bauträgerschaften in der Regel günstigere Wohnungen an, da sie ihre Mietpreise auf Basis der anfallenden Kosten für Bau, Unterhalt sowie Erneuerung ihrer Liegenschaften festlegen.

Die Bedeutung des gemeinnützigen Wohnbausektors geht aber über den Aspekt der Preisgünstigkeit hinaus. Viel mehr leisten gemeinnützige Bauträgerschaften einen Beitrag zur raumplanerischen Strategie der Innenentwicklung, also der prioritären Lenkung der künftigen Siedlungsentwicklung auf bereits bebaute Gebiete. Gemeinnützige Wohnungsbestände umfassen in der Schweiz derzeit zwar nur einen Marktanteil von insgesamt rund 5 Prozent, weisen aber eine hohe Lagegunst und ein beträchtliches Potenzial für eine künftig dichtere Nutzung auf. Sie sind nicht nur gut mit dem öffentlichen Verkehr erschlossen, sondern befinden sich auch häufig räumlich konzentriert in Gebieten mit hoher Wohnnachfrage, was eine quartiersorientierte, parzellenübergreifende Siedlungserneuerung begünstigt.

Statistiken zum Altbestand wie auch zu neueren Projekten gemeinnütziger Bauträgerschaften verdeutlichen zudem deren vergleichsweise ressourcenschonende Bodennutzung, indem die Bewohnerschaft im Schnitt deutlich weniger Wohnfläche in Anspruch nimmt als in sonstigen Miet- oder Eigentumswohnungen. Gleichzeitig zeigt die bereits erfolgte Umsetzung baulicher Verdichtungsmaßnahmen gemeinnütziger Bauträgerschaften vielfältige Verknüpfungen mit der Innenentwicklung, wobei qualitative, ökologische und soziale Aspekte zu unterstreichen sind. Die dabei festgestellte Akzeptanz der Dichte lässt eine qualitätsfördernde Wirkung entsprechender Eingriffe vermuten – in vielen gemeinnützigen Organisationen sind positive Mehrheitsentscheide der Mitglieder eine Grundvoraussetzung dafür, dass deren Baubestände umfassend verändert werden können.

Im Spannungsfeld zwischen gemeinnützigem Wohnungsbau und Innenentwicklung werden aber auch Herausforderungen ausgemacht: Zum einen sind nicht alle Liegenschaftsbestände für eine bauliche Weiterentwicklung geeignet, wobei denkmalpflegerischen Aspekten eine zentrale Rolle zukommt. Zum anderen sind die Rahmenbedingungen für eine zukunftsgerichtete Weiterentwicklung der Bestände noch nicht überall gegeben. Eine enge Kooperationskultur zwischen Behörden und gemeinnützigen Bauträgerschaften, maßgeschneiderte Planungsprozesse sowie eine stärker auf Wachstum ausgerichtete Anreizsetzung in Wohnbaufördermaßnahmen stellen Ansatzpunkte zur Aktivierung der Potenziale im Bestand dar. Die konsequente Verknüpfung planerischer Eingriffe und bodenpolitischer Vorgaben eröffnet gleichzeitig Spielräume, die Innenentwicklung vermehrt zu nutzen, um den gemeinnützigen Wohnbausektor künftig zu stärken.[1]

SYNERGIES BETWEEN FORMAL AND INFORMAL PLANNING TO RESOLVE SPATIAL CONFLICTS

THEODORA PAPAMICHAIL

Formal planning instruments and processes have often been unpopular and ineffective for solving complex spatial conflicts like urban sprawl or traffic congestion. Such conflicts turn into complex planning tasks that often exceed the time and funding provided, especially when faced with adversarial interests among different stakeholders and social groups. For example, what happens when a mayor and a railway company do not agree on a common solution for a project of national importance for years? Informal planning as a nonbinding supplement to official planning is often considered highly effective. It includes the principles of collaborative dialogue, diverse networks, trusting relationships and tailor-made processes among stakeholders, delivers problem-oriented solutions and increases public consensus. Since informal planning cannot be taken for granted—especially in countries with rigid planning systems—Greece becomes a great spatial laboratory to explore if and when synergies between formal and informal planning can invite stakeholders to discuss and act together.

Taking, for instance, the multifunctional concept of tourism-oriented railway development in the Peloponnese, the region illustrates a potential in culture, history, landscape, architecture, and tourism infrastructure closely related to a diverse railway network, along with an upward trend in tourism and the strategic position of Greece in transport infrastructure. However, this requires shared action among numerous stakeholders from national, regional, and local planning levels. The concept of synergies between formal and informal planning explores the possibility of a common approach to the reactivation of the railway network as a component of integral public transport, supporting sustainable tourism and spatial development. Interviews with key actors revealed crucial conflicts over this issue, proving the insufficiency of existing formal instruments to support such multidimensional concepts in planning.

Hence, an action-oriented scenario in planning focuses on 1) flexible and adaptable institutional arrangements supportive to various kinds of planning mechanisms, 2) proactive and imaginative planners ready to accept solutions created outside the technical domain of instrumental rationality, 3) the inclusion of numerous stakeholders to exchange various information and different types of knowledge, and 4) problem-oriented solutions. This means that politicians and spatial planners shift their mindsets towards planning processes to improve decision-making in crucial planning tasks. This can boost the socio-economic rehabilitation of the Peloponnese and, in turn, the desired decentralization of supersaturated urban areas like Athens. Although mindshifting is challenging, the concept of spatial synergies among stakeholders, the planning process and the produced content is a potential approach for countries that face complex spatial development tasks.

SYNERGIEN ZWISCHEN FORMELLER UND INFORMELLER PLANUNG ZUR LÖSUNG RÄUMLICHER KONFLIKTE

THEODORA PAPAMICHAIL

Formelle Planungsinstrumente und -prozesse haben sich vielfach als unbeliebt und ineffektiv erwiesen in Bezug auf die Lösung komplexer räumlicher Konflikte wie *Zersiedelung* oder Verkehrsüberlastung. Derartige Konflikte avancieren zu komplexen Planungsgegenständen, die den Zeit- und Kostenrahmen sprengen – und zwar vor allem dann, wenn die konkurrierenden Interessen diverser Stakeholder und sozialer Gruppierungen ins Spiel kommen. Was passiert etwa, wenn ein*e Bürgermeister*in und eine Eisenbahngesellschaft jahrelang keine Einigung finden können bezüglich eines Projekts von nationaler Bedeutung? Die informelle Planung gilt als flankierende Maßnahme zur offiziellen Planung vielmals als hocheffektiv. Sie schließt die Prinzipien des kollaborativen Dialogs ebenso mit ein wie diverse Netzwerke, vertrauensvolle Beziehungen und maßgeschneiderte Prozesse zwischen Stakeholdern, sie liefert problemorientierte Lösungen und führt zu einem Mehr an öffentlichem Konsens. Informelle Planung stellt keine Selbstverständlichkeit dar – vor allem in Ländern mit rigidem Planungssystem. Insofern dient Griechenland hervorragend als Raumlabor, um zu klären, inwiefern und unter welchen Umständen Synergien zwischen formeller und informeller Planung Stakeholder dazu bringen können, zu diskutieren und gemeinsam zu handeln.

Betrachtet man etwa das multifunktionale Konzept der touristisch orientierten Eisenbahnentwicklung auf der Peleponnes, so weist die Region Potenziale in den Bereichen Kultur, Geschichte, Landschaft, Architektur und touristische Infrastruktur auf, die eng an das vielfältige Eisenbahnnetz geknüpft sind – begleitet von einem Aufwärtstrend beim Tourismus und bei der strategische Position Griechenlands in Bezug auf seine Verkehrsinfrastruktur. Das erfordert jedoch das gemeinsame Handeln diverser Stakeholder auf nationaler, regionaler und lokaler Planungsebene. Das Konzept der Synergien zwischen formeller und informeller Planung erforscht die Möglichkeit eines gemeinsamen Ansatzes zur Reaktivierung des Eisenbahnnetzes als Bestandteil des integralen öffentlichen Verkehrs im Sinne eines nachhaltigen Tourismus und einer nachhaltigen Raumentwicklung. In Interviews mit Schlüsselakteur*innen offenbaren sich entscheidende Konflikte bezüglich dieser Thematik, was auf die Unzulänglichkeit bestehender formeller Instrumente im Hinblick auf derart multidimensionale Konzepte in der Planung verweist.

Ein handlungsorientiertes Szenario fokussiert in der Planung daher auf 1) flexible und übertragbare institutionelle Regelungen, welche diverse Planungsmechanismen berücksichtigen; 2) proaktive und fantasievolle Planende, die bereit sind, Lösungen zu akzeptieren, die jenseits des technischen Bereichs instrumenteller Rationalität erarbeitet wurden; 3) das Einbeziehen einer großen Zahl von Stakeholdern, um möglichst viel Informationen und unterschiedlichste Arten von Wissen auszutauschen; 4) problemorientierte Lösungen. Das bedeutet, dass Politiker*innen und Raumplaner*innen ihre Denkweise in Richtung von Planungsprozessen verändern, um bei wichtigen Planungsfragen zu besseren Lösungen zu gelangen. Das kann die sozioökonomische Rehabilitation der Peleponnes vorantreiben – und im Gegenzug die erwünschte Dezentralisierung übersättigter städtischer Gebiete wie Athen. Auch wenn dieses Umdenken eine Herausforderung darstellt, so ist das Konzept der räumlichen Synergien zwischen Stakeholdern, Planungsprozess und produzierten Inhalten ein möglicher Ansatz für Länder, die vor komplexen Aufgaben der Raumentwicklung stehen.

PATRAS
FLYING VISIT
STIPPVISITE
PATRAS

THE TRAIN MUST ARRIVE IN PATRAS!

BERND SCHOLL

Greece is facing significant challenges. The economic crisis ongoing since 2008 is a deep cut into the history of the country. In order to embark on a sustainable development path, investments into the key infrastructures of the country, for example, a modern railway system, are of central importance. However, the upgrading of existing lines in densely populated areas is presenting those involved with great challenges, because a coordinating spatial planning is lacking in Greece. It is therefore key to transfer experiences through know-how partnerships and to arrive at innovative solutions through new ideas and methods.

The aim of the visit was to gain insights into the conditions and conflicts of a country in crisis, based on the example of a current and challenging spatial and railway development task. In accordance with the framework theme of the International Doctoral College (IDK), the intention was to sharpen perception of European tasks and gather knowledge for cross-border projects. The railway connection from Athens to Thessaloniki, as part of the trans-European networks in the Hamburg–Vienna–Thessaloniki–Athens–Patras corridor, provides a wealth of observation material for this. In the development of such networks, the development of railway hubs is of great importance. Patras on the Peloponnese is the southwestern terminus of the corridor and could become an important hub of the railway around the Peloponnese, which was initially renewed with EU funding but was then discontinued due to the economic crisis in 2010.

For the urban development of Patras, the planned connection through a railway line presents extensive opportunities. After the completion, it will be possible to shorten the travel time to Athens from currently four to around two hours. However, a solution for the incorporation of the "last mile" of the railway into the city of Patras was not in sight. The project was originally intended to include the railway in Patras with a longitudinal tunnel through the city and a low-level station in the center. The hope was a free view of the sea and no barrier effect. However, this solution had a high price of one billion euros, with significant realization risks (high ground water level, archaeological finds, etc.). The EU parties responsible for the funding did not consider this solution to be financially viable.

In light of this, in 2013 the Chair for Spatial Development at ETH Zurich, together with colleagues from the Technical Universities in Patras and Athens, took the initiative to sound out alternative possible solutions as part of a joint seminar week with students. Interesting approaches compatible with the city encouraged us to carry out test planning one year later. Three renowned teams from Greece, Switzerland, and Germany, as well as

DER ZUG MUSS IN PATRAS ANKOMMEN!

BERND SCHOLL

Griechenland steht vor großen Herausforderungen. Die seit 2008 andauernde ökonomische Krise ist ein tiefer Einschnitt in die Geschichte des Landes. Um auf einen nachhaltigen Pfad der Entwicklung zu kommen, sind Investitionen in die Schlüsselinfrastrukturen des Landes, beispielsweise ein modernes Eisenbahnsystem, von zentraler Bedeutung. Allerdings stellt die Aufwertung vorhandener Linien die Akteur*innen in dichter besiedelten Landesteilen vor große Herausforderungen, weil eine koordinierende Raumplanung in Griechenland fehlt. Es kommt deshalb darauf an, durch Know-how-Partnerschaften Erfahrungen zu transferieren und durch neue Ideen und Methoden zu innovativen Lösungen zu kommen.

Ziel der Stippvisite war es, am Beispiel einer aktuellen und herausfordernden Aufgabe der Raum- und Eisenbahnentwicklung Einsichten in Randbedingungen und Konflikte eines in der Krise steckenden Landes zu gewinnen. Entsprechend dem Rahmenthema des Internationalen Doktorandenkollegs (IDK) sollte der Blick für europäische Aufgaben geschärft und sollten Erkenntnisse für grenzüberschreitende Aufgaben gewonnen werden.

Die Eisenbahnverbindung von Athen nach Thessaloniki als Bestandteil der transeuropäischen Netze im Korridor Hamburg–Wien–Thessaloniki–Athen–Patras liefert dabei reiches Anschauungsmaterial. Bei der Entwicklung solcher Netze ist die Entwicklung der Bahnknoten von großer Bedeutung. Patras auf der Peloponnes ist der südwestliche Endpunkt des Korridors und könnte ein wichtiger Knoten der um die Peloponnes verlaufen meterspurigen Eisenbahn werden, die zunächst mit EU-Mitteln erneuert, dann aber im Zuge der ökonomischen Krise 2010 stillgelegt wurde.

Für die Stadtentwicklung von Patras ergeben sich durch die geplante Anbindung mittels einer Eisenbahnverbindung weitreichende Chancen. Nach der Fertigstellung kann die Fahrzeit nach Athen von derzeit vier auf nahezu zwei Stunden verkürzt werden. Doch eine Lösung für die Einbindung der „letzten Meile" der Eisenbahn in die Stadt Patras war nicht in Sicht. Ursprünglich war vorgesehen, mit einem Längstunnel durch die Stadt und einem Tiefbahnhof im Zentrum die Eisenbahn in Patras aufzunehmen. Man erhoffte sich davon freie Sicht aufs Meer und keine Barrierewirkung. Allerdings hätte diese Lösung mit über 1 Milliarde Euro einen hohen Preis mit großen Realisierungsrisiken (hoher Grundwasserstand, archäologische Funde etc.). Die für die Finanzierung zuständigen Akteur*innen der EU hielten diese Lösung für nicht finanzierbar.

In diesem Umfeld ergriff 2013 die Professur für Raumentwicklung der ETH Zürich zusammen mit Kollegen der Technischen Universitäten in Patras und Athen die Initiative, im Rahmen einer gemeinsamen Seminarwoche

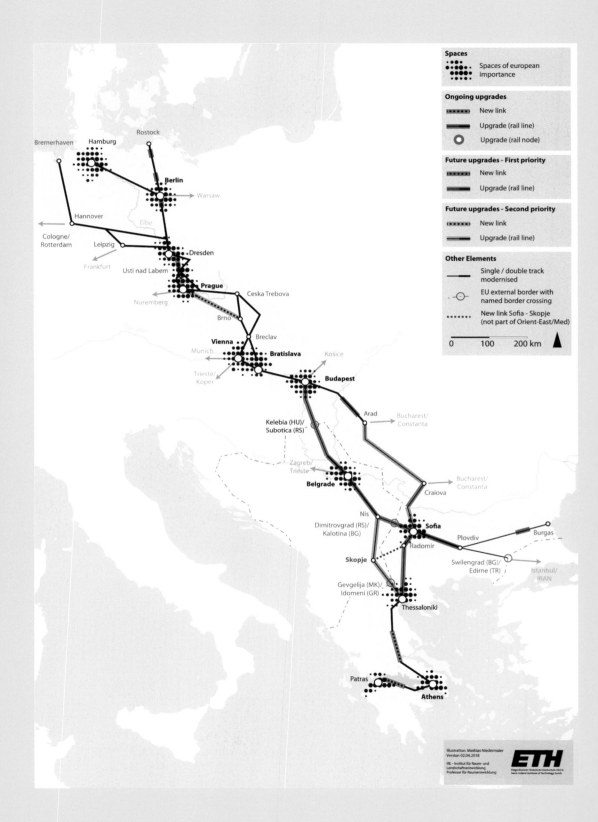

mit Studierenden alternative Lösungsansätze zu sondieren. Interessante stadtverträgliche Ansätze ermutigten uns, ein Jahr später eine Testplanung durchzuführen. Dafür konnten drei renommierte Teams aus Griechenland, der Schweiz und Deutschland und ein internationales Universitätsteam gewonnen werden. Die Stadtregierung, mit dem damaligen Bürgermeister an der Spitze, begrüßte den erstmaligen Einsatz einer Testplanung in Griechenland. Patras verfügte als einer der ersten Städte in Griechenland über eine meterspurige Eisenbahnverbindung (als Teil der Peloponnesbahn); ein Torso dieser Bahn ist in Patras in Betrieb.

Die im Vorfeld der Testplanung abgehaltenen Kommunalwahlen ergaben einen Wechsel an der Spitze der Stadtregierung. Der neu gewählte Bürgermeister vertrat den Standpunkt, dass nur eine Tunnellösung für Patras infrage kommt. Bei einer Tunnellösung bestünde aber die Gefahr, dass das stark frequentierte Verkehrsmittel während der Bauphase über Jahre eingestellt werden müsste. Wir entschieden uns in dieser Lage trotzdem für die Durchführung der Testplanung. Ein hochrangiges Begleitgremium kam nach intensiver Prüfung alternativer Tunnellösungen und eines sogenannten Bypasses zur Empfehlung einer ebenerdigen, schrittweise realisierbaren Lösung. Die Kosten für die Realisierung wurden auf 200–300 Millionen Euro geschätzt, also auf ein Viertel bis ein Drittel der Tunnelvariante – und wären überdies weniger risikoreich.

Im Nachgang zur Testplanung wurde 2016 ein Workshop zur Präsentation und zum kritischen Diskurs mit der interessierten Bevölkerung durchgeführt. Trotz allem konnte, vor allem wegen der kompromisslosen Haltung der Stadtregierung, bis heute der Weg zu einer schrittweisen und stadtverträglichen Lösung nicht gefunden werden. Es besteht die Gefahr, dass die Bahn am Stadtrand von Patras endet, ihre Attraktivität verliert und die so wichtige Aufwertung und Transformation des ehemaligen Bahnhofs Dionysios zum Hauptbahnhof der Stadt unterbleibt.

Die Promovierenden erhielten während des dreitägigen Aufenthaltes interessante Einblicke, sie sollten den bisherigen Prozess kritisch kommentieren und Überlegungen zum weiteren Vorgehen anstellen.

◁ 1 *Spaces of European importance along the OEM Corridor (Orient-East Mediterranean).*
◁ 1 *Urbane Räume von europäischer Wichtigkeit entlang des OEM-Korridors (Orient-East Mediterranean).*

an international university team, were put together for this. The municipal government, led by the mayor at the time, welcomed the first-time use of the test planning method in Greece. Patras was one of the first cities in Greece to have a meter gauge railway connection (as part of the Peloponnese railway); a torso of this track is in operation in Patras.

The local elections held before the test planning resulted in a change at the top of the municipal government. The newly elected mayor represented the standpoint that only a tunnel solution came into question for Patras. However, with a tunnel solution there would be the danger that the heavily used means of transport would have to be halted for years during the building phase. We decided nevertheless to carry out the test planning. A high-ranking accompanying council reached the recommendation, after an intensive examination of alternative tunnel solutions and a bypass, of a ground-level solution that could be realized in different steps. The costs for the realization were estimated as 200 to 300 million euros, in other words a quarter to a third of the tunnel option—and furthermore less risky.

Following the test planning, in 2016 a workshop was carried out for the presentation and critical discussions with interested members of the public. Despite everything, it has not been possible up until today to find the way towards a step-by-step solution compatible with the city, especially because of the uncompromising attitude of the municipal government. There is the danger that the railway will end on the outskirts of Patras and lose its attractiveness, becoming a possible nucleus for urban sprawl and consequently that the so-important upgrading and transformation of the former railway station Dionysios into the main railway station of the city will not take place.

During the three-day stay, the doctoral students received interesting insights. They were encouraged to comment critically on the process up until now and put forward ideas on how to proceed.

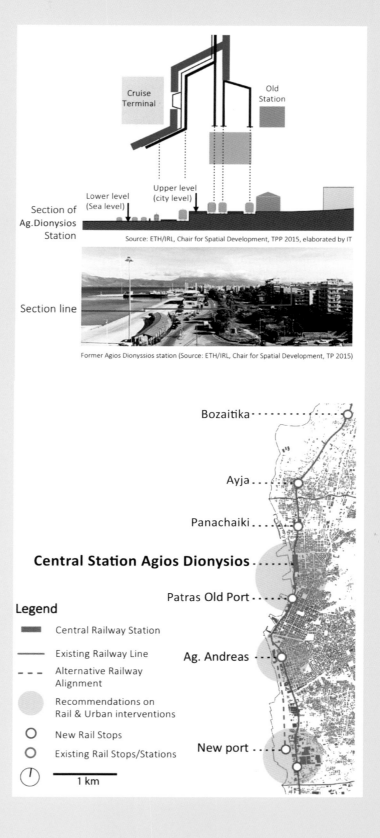

Section of
Ag.Dionysios
Station

Cruise
Terminal

Old
Station

Lower level
(Sea level)

Upper level
(city level)

Source: ETH/IRL, Chair for Spatial Development, TPP 2015, elaborated by IT

Section line

Former Agios Dionyssios station (Source: ETH/IRL, Chair for Spatial Development, TP 2015)

Bozaitika

Ayja

Panachaiki

Central Station Agios Dionysios

Patras Old Port

Ag. Andreas

New port

Legend

- ▬ Central Railway Station
- —— Existing Railway Line
- - - - Alternative Railway Alignment
- ⬤ Recommendations on Rail & Urban interventions
- ○ New Rail Stops
- ◎ Existing Rail Stops/Stations
- 🧭 1 km

2 Solution suggestion for the railway in Patras.
2 Lösungsvorschlag für die Eisenbahn in Patras.

Kalavryta, November 2017

Patras, November 2017

LANDSCAPE AS A COMPLEX SPATIAL SYSTEM IN THE ANTHROPOCENE

UDO WEILACHER

Only those who understand that landscape is a complex spatial system, and how the essence of complexity and the laws of landscape are made up, will be able to participate in shaping landscape in the Anthropocene as a viable network of living environments. The knowledge of these aspects is also the condition for the successful crossing of borders for the targeted activation of spaces in "landscape as a spatial system," in accordance with the leading topic of the doctoral college "Crossing Borders, Activating Spaces."

The key themes "landscape as a spatial system" and "laws of landscape" that are at the center of the opening thesis have been intensively discussed since the beginning of the first International Doctoral College (IDK) Spatial Research Lab in the year 2007.

The findings from these discussions are described in the contributions to both books for the 2012 and 2016 seminars under the titles "We have to learn to perceive landscape"[1] and "New Spatial Images of the Culture Landscape."[2] These document the conviction that landscape must be understood quite differently in the current specialist context than decades ago: "A landscape is not a natural feature of the environment but a synthetic space, a man-made -system of spaces superimposed on the face of the land, functioning and evolving not according to natural laws but to serve a community."[3]

Due to this, the design and planning approaches to the landscape have changed decisively. Today a distinction is no longer made between environment shaped by humans and non-humans, because in the age of the Anthropocene, in which man has an impact on all areas of the environment, this distinction no longer makes sense. The city is therefore also a landscape, a system of spaces—even if of a special nature. As described in 2012, in this landscape the same laws apply as in any other type of landscape. There are almost daily reports in the media about the consequences of disregarding these fundamental laws and in most cases the reporters can all not avoid using the same key word: "catastrophe." The mathematician and philosopher René Thom pointed out in connection with the catastrophe theory he developed in the 1960s that catastrophes are often nothing other than sudden unexpected changes of state.[4] In complex systems such as the landscape, these changes are basically inevitable and therefore it is essential to address complexity in more detail.

Nicht lineare Systeme – berühmtestes Beispiel ist das komplexe Wetter-geschehen – reagieren sehr sensibel auf geringfügige Änderungen in den Anfangszuständen und verändern ihr Verhalten oftmals sprunghaft, also nicht proportional zur Veränderung der Wirkungsparameter. Ein komple-xes System wie die Landschaft neigt durch die Vielzahl und Vielfalt der an ihr beteiligten menschlichen und nicht menschlichen Akteure immer wieder zu solchen nicht linearen Entwicklungen, die mit einfachen Mo-dellrechnungen schlecht zu fassen sind. Murenabgänge in den Alpen zum Beispiel – verursacht durch eine Vielzahl miteinander verflochtener natür-licher und anthropogener Einflussfaktoren, etwa den Klimawandel – zählen zur Kategorie der nicht linearen und irreversiblen Ereignisse in der Landschaft, die häufig auch als Katastrophen bezeichnet werden. Alle Akteur*innen sind lediglich im Rahmen ihres engeren Aktionsrahmens tä-tig, ohne etwas über das Gesamtsystem, in das sie eingebunden sind, zu wissen. Überwiegend sind es die Menschen in der Landschaft, die ihre Par-tikularinteressen verfolgen und damit für nicht lineare Veränderungen ver-antwortlich sind.

Emergenz (lat. *emergere* = auftauchen) bezeichnet die spontane und nicht umkehrbare Ausbildung neuer Ordnungen oder Strukturen in einem Sys-tem, verursacht durch das komplexe Zusammenspiel der Systemkom-ponenten. Emergenz lässt sich, so Beate Ratter, gut am Beispiel eines Verkehrsstaus erklären. „Der Verkehrsstau ist das Emergenzresultat aus der Interaktion vieler Autofahrer. Jeder einzelne Fahrer versucht, ein Ziel zu erreichen, dazu verfolgt er bestimmte Strategien, hier ‚Regeln' genannt. Manche Regeln sind legale Regeln (Einhaltung der Höchstgeschwindig-keit), andere sind soziale Regeln (Verlangsamung der Geschwindigkeit, um andere in die Autoschlange einbiegen zu lassen) oder unsoziale Regeln (Vordrängen vor vermeintlich kleineren oder schwächeren Autos). Auch ohne blockierendes Extremereignis (Unfall, Baustelle etc.) kann es im flie-ßenden Verkehr, dem diese Regeln zugrunde liegen, zu einem Stau kommen. Die Interaktion einzelner Autofahrer, die sich zu Beginn nur rücksichtsvoll, vorsichtig oder egoistisch verhalten, kann zu Behinderungen führen, die sich dann aus nicht ersichtlichen Gründen nach hinten fortsetzen, auch wenn die Autos vorne weiterfahren. Aus der Summe individueller Verhal-tensweisen einzelner separater Verkehrsteilnehmer resultiert der Stau."[8] In urbanen Landschaften zählen zum Beispiel die informellen Siedlungs-strukturen an den Rändern der Megacities zu den Resultaten emergenter Prozesse, die weder planbar noch vorhersehbar sind.[9] Aus dem nicht linea-ren und emergenten Verhalten komplexer Systeme ergibt sich in letzter Konsequenz deren Unvorhersagbarkeit – eine Eigenschaft, die nicht nur in der klassischen Wissenschaft, sondern auch in den planenden Disziplinen zu tiefen Verunsicherungen führt. Der Glaube an die vollkommene Plan-barkeit und Berechenbarkeit von Landschaft und Umwelt wird durch diese Erkenntnis in seinen Grundfesten erschüttert.

these complex happenings, changing the landscape and controlling material cycles to secure our livelihoods. However, we have no ultimate certainty about how this intervention affects life as a whole—the mesh of relationships in our environment is obviously too complex. Nevertheless, ultimately no designer can revoke joint responsibility for an intact environment. A rigid understanding of planning and design, fixated on the production of finished objects and stable end states, must necessarily fail in the face of nonlinear, unpredictable, and emergent realities.

"In light of complexity theory, design is a complexity reduction," the urban sociologist Detlev Ipsen recognized fittingly, thus outlining one of the fundamental dilemmas with which designers must often deal.[11] With their controlling, planning, and cultivating interventions in complex landscape fabrics, humankind has been pursuing another aim for millennia that is just as vital as securing the physical necessities of life. The reduction of spatial complexity is imperative to a certain extent to provide humans with the possibility of orientation. This reduction, which Ipsen speaks of in connection with his explanations of the spatial perception of human beings, must not necessarily go hand in hand with the reduction of complexity of dynamic life processes in the environment, but the probability that this will occur is very high. The fact is that humankind cannot manage without a certain reduction of complexity, either in perception or in everyday communication, because we can neither perceive, nor process, or communicate "world complexity"[12] in its totality. Designing is a complexity reduction that is necessary to a certain extent in order to offer people orientation in a real and figurative sense.

In a manner still applicable today, these fundamental connections were explained very fittingly in relation to the urban living environment by the American urban planner Kevin Lynch in 1969 in his pioneering book *The Image of the City*. "A good environmental image gives its possessor an important sense of emotional security."[13] Lynch pleads for a distinctive design of the urban environment, but his findings are also of central significance in connection with people's orientation in the landscape. A loss of orientation can soon become an existential problem. Too much spatial complexity can thus become a threat—as can too little, as Detlev Ipsen emphasizes. He points out that for people "the search for information, like the search for food, is physiologically determined. … A reduced possibility to seek new, complex information, due to external conditions, leads to a reduction in the attractiveness of a situation. The extreme case of the camera silens, a room which emits no acoustic, visual, or tactile stimuli, leads to death in a relatively short time."[14]

Landscape is the scene of fascinating and complex human-nature interactions and is considered the embodiment of lively complexity. Rigid, linear thinking in this nonlinear, lively context harbors dangers. Designers are faced with a whole host of opportunities that they owe to the knowledge gained from complexity theory. The most important goal is to recognize complexity with its potentially unsettling properties such as nonlinearity,

Herausforderung für die Landschaftsarchitektur

Die kultivierenden Eingriffe des Menschen in die Landschaft waren stets mit einer zweckbestimmten Reduktion der Komplexität von Naturlandschaft verbunden. Man wollte Natur und Landschaft „in den Griff bekommen", und in dieser Tradition stehen letztlich auch Gartenkunst und Landschaftsarchitektur. Noch bis in die erste Hälfte des 20. Jahrhunderts hinein war es das Ziel, die Wirklichkeit dem Plan anzupassen. Die grundlegende Umgestaltung der deutschen Landschaft seit dem 18. Jahrhundert, wie sie in David Blackbourns *Die Eroberung der Natur*[10] eingehend geschildert wird, ist ein anschauliches Beispiel für eine Komplexitätsreduktion durch planvolle Gestaltung, deren dramatische Folgen bis in die Gegenwart ausstrahlen. Heute gelten vielfältige Kultur- und Naturlandschaften als Inbegriff von Komplexität, und die Ökologie lehrt uns, dass in jeder Landschaft eine nahezu unüberschaubare Zahl unterschiedlichster Stoff-, Energie-, Material- und Informationsströme permanent in Bewegung ist, um das Leben in Gang zu halten. Der Mensch greift täglich in dieses komplexe Geschehen ein, verändert Landschaft und steuert Stoffkreisläufe, um seine Lebensgrundlagen zu sichern. Er hat jedoch keine letzte Gewissheit darüber, wie sich sein Eingreifen auf das lebendige Ganze auswirkt – zu komplex seien die Beziehungsgeflechte in unserer Umwelt, heißt es. Doch kann und darf sich letztlich kein*e Entwerfer*in mit diesem Hinweis der Mitverantwortung für eine intakte Umwelt entziehen. Ein starres Planungs- und Entwurfsverständnis, fixiert auf die Herstellung fertiger Objekte oder stabiler Endzustände, muss zwangsläufig an nicht linearen, unvorhersehbaren und emergenten Realitäten scheitern.

„Im Lichte der Komplexitätstheorie ist die Gestaltbildung eine Komplexitätsreduktion"[11], erkannte der Stadtsoziologe Detlev Ipsen treffend und kennzeichnete damit eines der grundlegenden Dilemmata, mit dem sich Entwerfende immer wieder auseinandersetzen müssen. Mit den steuernden, planenden und kultivierenden Eingriffen in komplexe Landschaftsgefüge verfolgt der Mensch seit Jahrtausenden nämlich noch ein weiteres Ziel, das für ihn ebenso lebensnotwendig ist, wie die Sicherung der physischen Lebensgrundlagen. Die Reduktion der räumlichen Komplexität ist bis zu einem gewissen Grad unerlässlich, um dem Menschen die Möglichkeit zur Orientierung zu bieten. Nun muss diese Reduktion, von der Ipsen im Zusammenhang mit seinen Ausführungen zur Raumwahrnehmung des Menschen spricht, zwar nicht zwingend mit der Reduktion der Komplexität dynamischer Lebensprozesse in der Umwelt einhergehen, aber die Wahrscheinlichkeit, dass dies geschieht, ist sehr hoch. Tatsache ist, dass der Mensch weder in seiner Wahrnehmung noch in der alltäglichen Kommunikation ohne eine gewisse Reduktion von Komplexität auskommt, weil er die „Weltkomplexität"[12] in ihrer Gesamtheit weder wahrnehmen noch verarbeiten oder kommunizieren kann. Gestaltbildung ist eine Komplexitätsreduktion, die bis zu einem gewissen Grad erforderlich ist, um den Menschen im eigentlichen wie im übertragenen Sinn Orientierung zu bieten.

emergence, and unpredictability as vital environmental qualities, as an essential law of life. What is derived from this, not only for landscape architecture but for all environmental and spatial planning disciplines, is the demand to be less concerned with the production of finished objects, stable states, and "clean" solutions and more with the development of processes and strategies, with the sensitive design of manifold living environments, which are open to what is unpredictable, emerging, and nonlinear. At the same time they need to be flexible spaces of possibility in regard to people's emotions, intuition, and creativity.

People are to be incorporated more consistently in communication about future developments, planning, and design steps, as they are one of the most effective actors in landscape. People seek orientation in a complex landscape and so spatially effective structures must be ensured where people are in danger of losing direction and orientation. Klaus Mainzer summarizes: "The researching of nonlinear complex systems suggests that we act and react sensitively in precarious and sensitive balance situations. However, those who remain doing nothing, out of fear of chaos, will be overrun by the integral dynamics of complex systems. At the edge of chaos, sensitivity is required but also courage, strength, and creativity for solving problems."[15]

Diese fundamentalen Zusammenhänge hat der amerikanische Stadtplaner Kevin Lynch schon 1960 in seinem richtungsweisenden Buch *The Image of the City*[13], bezogen auf den städtischen Lebensraum, sehr treffend und bis heute gültig erörtert. „Eine gute Vorstellung von der Umgebung verleiht dem, der darüber verfügt, ein ausgeprägtes Bewusstsein gefühlsmäßiger Sicherheit."[14] Lynch plädierte für eine einprägsame Gestaltung der städtischen Umwelt, aber auch im Zusammenhang mit der Orientierung des Menschen in der Landschaft sind seine Erkenntnisse von zentraler Bedeutung. Orientierungsverlust kann für den Menschen rasch zu einem existenziellen Problem werden. Zu große räumliche Komplexität kann auf diese Weise also zur Bedrohung werden – ebenso wie eine zu geringe Komplexität, wie Detlev Ipsen betont. Er weist darauf hin, dass für den Menschen „die Suche nach Informationen ähnlich wie die Suche nach Nahrung physiologisch vorgegeben ist. [...] Eine durch äußere Bedingungen reduzierte Chance, neue, komplexe Informationen zu suchen, führt dazu, dass die Attraktivität einer Situation abnimmt. Der extreme Fall der camera silens, der Raum, von dem weder akustische, optische noch taktile Reize ausgehen, führt in relativ kurzer Zeit zum Tod."[15]

Landschaft ist der Schauplatz ebenso faszinierender wie komplexer Mensch-Natur-Interaktionen und gilt als Inbegriff lebendiger Komplexität. Starres, lineares Denken in diesem nicht linear aufgebauten lebendigen Kontext birgt Gefahren. Entwerfende stehen vor einer ganzen Reihe von Chancen, die sie den Erkenntnissen aus der Komplexitätstheorie zu verdanken haben. Das wichtigste Ziel besteht darin, Komplexität mit ihren möglicherweise verunsichernden Eigenschaften wie Nichtlinearität, Emergenz und Unvorhersagbarkeit als vitale Umweltqualitäten, als essenzielle Gesetzmäßigkeit des Lebens anzuerkennen. Daraus leitet sich nicht nur für die Landschaftsarchitektur, sondern für alle umwelt- und raumplanenden Disziplinen die Forderung ab, sich weniger mit der Herstellung fertiger Objekte, stabiler Zustände und „sauberer" Lösungen zu beschäftigen als vielmehr mit der Gestaltung von Prozessen und Strategien, mit dem sensiblen Entwerfen von vielfältigen Lebensräumen, die dem Unvorhersagbaren, dem Emergenten und Nichtlinearen ebenso als flexible Spielräume offen stehen wie dem Menschen mit seinen Emotionen, seiner Intuition und Kreativität.

Der Mensch ist in die Kommunikation über zukünftige Entwicklungen, Planungs- und Entwurfsschritte stärker und konsequenter einzubeziehen, denn er ist einer der wirkungsvollsten Akteure in der Landschaft. Gleichwohl sucht er in einer komplexen Landschaft nach Orientierung, und so ist immer dort für räumlich wirksame Strukturen zu sorgen, wo der Mensch Gefahr läuft, Halt und Orientierung zu verlieren. Klaus Mainzer resümiert: „Die Erforschung nichtlinearer komplexer Systeme rät uns also zu sensiblem Agieren und Reagieren in labilen und empfindlichen Gleichgewichtszuständen. Wer aber aus Angst vor Chaos im Nichtstun verharrt, wird von der Eigendynamik komplexer Systeme überrollt. Am Rande des Chaos ist zwar Sensibilität gefragt, aber auch Mut, Kraft und Kreativität zur Problemlösung."[16]

Raitenhaslach, March 2017
Raitenhaslach, März 2017

Burghausen, March 2017
Burghausen, März 2017

Burghausen, March 2017
Burghausen, März 2017

Raitenhaslach, March 2017
Raitenhaslach, März 2017

THE TEMPTATION OF WATER— ON THE TRANSFORMATION OF INNER-CITY WATERSPACES

FLORENTINE-AMELIE ROST

Inner-city waterways in European and American metropolises are in a process of transformation: after centuries of a fixed categorization prescribed by use as transport areas, nature areas, leisure areas, or conservation areas, the programming of inner-city waterways is now no longer clearly defined. They are increasingly perceived as *empty urban spaces* or *spaces with potential* and given novel usages by various initiatives or made a focus of development by the urban development authorities themselves. Over the last ten to twenty years, numerous projects have been planned or realized that reprogram water areas either as floating architectures on the water or as urban development and open space planning projects. These projects range from temporary cultural and exhibition buildings, such as the floating pavilions of the Bruges Triennial or the Floating University Berlin, to the floating settlements in various European metropolises and a concentration on the water area, as in the case of the Flussbad Berlin.

With these projects, new requirement and ownership demands are placed on these spaces, which so far, however, have not been formulated and are only implicit in these projects. Many projects cannot be explained with a conventional and purpose-related use of the water only. It is assumed that the motives relate to a changed perception of water in the city and can be found more on a metaphorical level. Water does not seem to be understood anymore as a functional area but also as an association area.

The problem is that waterways are increasingly under development pressure, without these motives, and therefore the altered demands on water areas being specified or being discussed in a negotiation process about the future of these transformation areas.

In addition, the water projects with their constructional manifestation often lose what is assumed here to be one of these motives: the fascination of the dynamics and changeableness of the water.

A disclosure of these motivational reasons is therefore necessary to make the changing coding of the inner-city waterways evident and to be able to develop a new narration for these areas.

DIE VERFÜHRUNG DES WASSERS –
ZUR TRANSFORMATION
INNERSTÄDTISCHER WASSERFLÄCHEN

FLORENTINE-AMELIE ROST

Innerstädtische Wasserflächen in europäischen und amerikanischen Metropolen befinden sich in einem Transformationsprozess: Nach einer jahrhundertelangen festgeschriebenen und klar von der Nutzung vorgegebenen Trennung in Transporträume, Naturräume, Freizeiträume oder Schutzräume ist die Programmierung von innerstädtischen Wasserräumen heute nicht mehr klar festgelegt. Sie werden mehr und mehr als *städtische Leerstellen* oder *Möglichkeitsräume* wahrgenommen und von verschiedenen Initiativen und Akteur*innen neu bespielt oder von den städtischen Stadtentwicklungsbehörden selbst in den Fokus der Entwicklung gerückt.

Seit circa 10 bis 20 Jahren sind zahlreiche Projekte in Planung oder Realisierung, die entweder als schwimmende Architekturen den Raum auf dem Wasser oder als städtebaulich-freiraumplanerische Projekte das Wasser selbst neu programmieren. Die Projekte reichen dabei von temporären Kultur- und Ausstellungsbauten, wie den schwimmenden Pavillons der Triennale Brügge oder der Floating University Berlin, über schwimmende Siedlungen in diversen europäischen Metropolen hin zu einer Konzentration auf den Wasserraum, wie im Falle des Flussbades Berlin.

Mit diesen Projekten werden neue Bedarfe und Besitzansprüche an diese Räume gestellt, die aber bislang nicht formuliert, sondern nur den Projekten implizit sind.

Viele Vorhaben sind alleine mit einer herkömmlichen und zweckgebundenen Nutzung des Wassers nicht erklärbar. Es wird angenommen, dass die Motive mit einer veränderten Wahrnehmung von Wasser in der Stadt zu tun haben und vermehrt auf einer metaphorischen Ebene zu finden sind. Das Wasser scheint nicht mehr nur als Funktions-, sondern auch als Assoziationsfläche verstanden zu werden.

Das Problem ist, dass Wasserflächen zunehmend unter Entwicklungsdruck geraten, ohne dass diese Motive und somit die veränderten Bedarfe an Wasserräume benannt und in einem Aushandlungsprozess über die Zukunft dieser Transformationsflächen diskutiert würden.

Ferner verlieren die Wasserprojekte mit ihrer baulichen Manifestation häufig das, was hier als eines dieser Motive vermutet wird: die Faszination der Dynamik und Unbeständigkeit des Wassers.

Ein Offenlegen dieser Beweggründe ist also notwendig, um die sich ändernde Kodierung von innerstädtischen Wasserflächen sichtbar zu machen und eine neue Narration für diese Flächen entwickeln zu können.

ALPINE INDUSTRIAL LANDSCAPES

MARCELLO MODICA

The common perception of the Alps as mainly a rural and recreational region often leads to considering economic development and associated landscape changes only in relation to agriculture and tourism. However, most of the current environmental, social, and economic key challenges and land use conflicts normally occur in the densely urbanized landscapes of main valleys and foothills. In these contexts, the recycling of derelict industrial land generated by large-scale deindustrialization processes is gaining increasing relevance.

Similar to the surrounding European plains, the Alpine region has experienced a halving of employment in the secondary sector in the period 1975–2015. This decline, which mostly affects traditional heavy and manufacturing industries linked to natural resources, is leaving behind many brownfield sites of relevant size and complexity. At present, 142 sites with an area of over 5 ha have been identified across the entire Alpine region, while another 147 are potentially on the waiting list. For a region where less than one fifth of the land is suitable for permanent settlement, these figures are quite a challenge.

The physical and functional transformation of brownfields is rightly perceived by Alpine communities as a strategic chance to foster socioeconomic development and improve environmental resilience at the local and regional level. However, inherent structural limitations in terms of market pressure, financial support and process management are de facto impeding any attempt of redevelopment to take place. This suggests that intensive, radical, and top-down transformation approaches commonly used in highly dynamic urban contexts are not applicable and replicable in mountain areas. Hence, a more comprehensive, incremental, and flexible transformation strategy needs to be developed.

For this purpose, a *landscape approach* based on structuralist and systemic principles might prove to be extremely useful and relevant. By considering the existing landscape structure of industrial sites in mountainous areas as the result of previous functional interactions between industry and the mountain environment, a sequence of different but complementary systems of built and open spaces can be easily identified. The integrated and gradual reactivation of these systems, driven by specific contextual economic, environmental, and sociocultural needs, can help to set concrete and realistic planning milestones in the complex transformation process of mountain brownfields, thus improving its overall feasibility.

To test this approach, an intensive fieldwork-based analysis has been conducted on four representative Alpine brownfield typologies: a cement plant in Austria, a steel mill in France, a textile mill in Italy, and an aluminum smelter in Switzerland. Following the principles of research-by-design, the resulting methodology is expected to provide a set of cross-typological criteria and transferable operational tools to initiate and support transformation.

ALPINE INDUSTRIELANDSCHAFTEN

MARCELLO MODICA

Die allgemeine Wahrnehmung der Alpen als in erster Linie ländlicher und Erholungsraum führt häufig dazu, dass die wirtschaftliche und kulturlandschaftliche Entwicklung dieser Region lediglich im Hinblick auf Landwirtschaft und Tourismus erfolgt. Der Großteil der ökologischen, sozialen und wirtschaftlichen Herausforderungen und Landnutzungskonflikte tritt in den dicht besiedelten Haupttälern und deren Ausläufern auf. In diesem Kontext und infolge eines umfassenden Deindustrialisierungsprozesses im Alpenraum gewinnt das Recycling von brach liegenden Industrieflächen zunehmend an Bedeutung.

In der alpinen Region haben sich ähnlich wie im angrenzenden europäischen Flachland die Arbeitsplätze im sekundären Sektor im Zeitraum von 1975 bis 2015 halbiert. Dieser Rückgang, der vor allem die traditionelle Schwerindustrie und Industriezweige betrifft, die natürliche Ressourcen verarbeiten, hinterlässt zahlreiche Brachen von entsprechender Größe und Komplexität. Bislang wurden im gesamten Alpenraum 142 Standorte mit jeweils über 5 Hektar Fläche ausgewiesen, 147 weitere Areale befinden sich als potenzielle Konversionsflächen auf der Warteliste. Für eine Region, in der weniger als ein Fünftel der Fläche für eine dauerhafte Ansiedlung geeignet ist, stellen diese Zahlen eine ziemliche Herausforderung dar.

Die physische und funktionale Umwandlung von Brachen wird von den Alpengemeinden zu Recht als strategische Chance zur Förderung der sozioökonomischen Entwicklung und zur Verbesserung der ökologischen Resilienz auf lokaler und regionaler Ebene wahrgenommen. Inhärente strukturelle Beschränkungen in Bezug auf Marktdruck, finanzielle Unterstützung und Prozessmanagement behindern jedoch de facto jeglichen Versuch nachhaltiger Konversion.

Vieles deutet darauf hin, dass die üblichen, radikalen Top-down-Transformationsansätze, wie sie in hochdynamischen städtischen Regionen zum Einsatz kommen, auf Berggebiete nicht übertragbar sind. Folglich gilt es, eine umfassendere, inkrementelle und flexiblere Transformationsstrategie zu entwickeln.

Zu diesem Zweck dürfte sich ein *landschaftlicher Ansatz*, der auf strukturalistischen und systemischen Prinzipen beruht, als außerordentlich nützlich und relevant erweisen. Betrachtet man die gegenwärtige Landschaftsstruktur der Industriestandorte in Bergregionen als Resultat ehemaliger funktionaler Wechselwirkungen zwischen Industrie und Bergwelt, so lässt sich problemlos ein Geflecht unterschiedlicher komplementärer Systeme von bebauten und offenen Flächen identifizieren. Die integrierte, sukzessive Reaktivierung dieser Systeme, welche getrieben werden von kontextspezifischen ökonomischen, ökologischen und soziokulturellen Bedürfnissen, ermöglicht es, im komplexen Transformationsprozess der alpinen Brachen konkrete, realistische Entwicklungsziele zu setzen, und so die Durchführbarkeit der Konversion zu verbessern.

Um diesen Ansatz zu testen, werden auf Basis einer intensiven Feldforschung vier repräsentative alpine Brachflächentypologien analysiert: eine Zementfabrik in Österreich, ein Stahlwerk in Frankreich, eine Baumwollspinnerei in Italien und eine Aluminiumhütte in der Schweiz. Auf Basis der Prinzipien des „Research-by-design" soll die resultierende Methodik eine Reihe typenübergreifender Kriterien und übertragbarer operativer Instrumente zur Initiierung und Unterstützung derartiger Transformationen liefern.

APPENDIX
ANHANG

BIOGRAPHIES

Jonas Bellingrodt

Jonas Bellingrodt (*1980) is a research assistant at the Technical University of Munich at the Chair of Landscape Architecture and Industrial Landscapes. He was responsible as a coordinator for the International Doctoral College "Spatial Research Lab": curriculum 2017–2020. As a landscape architect, he is working as a project manager at the urban planning department of the city of Freising since 2020.

Undine Giseke

Prof. Undine Giseke (*1956) has been a professor at the TU Berlin since 2003 and is head of the Department of Landscape Architecture and Open Space Planning. Since 2013 she has been the dean of studies for the interdisciplinary degree in urban design. She holds positions in numerous advisory bodies and committees and is chairperson of the advisory board of the IBA Heidelberg. As a landscape architect, she co-founded the office bgmr Landschaftsarchitekten in 1987. Her research focuses on landscapes and social-natural connections in the Anthropocene.

Michael Koch

Prof. Dr. Michael Koch (*1950) is an architect and urban planner who lives in Hamburg and Zurich. He is a partner in the firm Yellow Z Urbanism Architecture, Zurich/Berlin. From 1999 to 2018, he was professor of urban development and district planning at the University of Wuppertal, the Hamburg University of Technology, and most recently at the HafenCity University Hamburg. His research and publications focus on the history of urban development and housing, the reorientation of urban planning, urban open spaces, and the connection between transport infrastructures and settlement development. As an independent architect and urban planner, his fields of work have included urban development strategies and projects at the regional and city level in addition to informal planning and the conception and moderation of spatial development processes.

Markus Neppl

Prof. Markus Neppl (*1962) studied architecture at RWTH Aachen University and was co-founder of the student planning group ARTECTA. In 1990, together with Peter Berner, Oliver Hall, and Kees Christiaanse, he founded the office ASTOC architects & planners in Cologne, currently with 100 employees handling numerous urban development projects and buildings of various sizes. In 1999 he was appointed to the chair of urban planning at the TU Kaiserslautern. This was followed in 2004 by his appointment to the chair of urban housing and development at the Karlsruhe Institute of Technology (KIT) in Karlsruhe. From 2008 to 2012 he was dean, and from 2012 to 2019 dean of studies, of the Faculty of Architecture.

BIOGRAFIEN

Jonas Bellingrodt

Jonas Bellingrodt (*1980) ist wissenschaftlicher Mitarbeiter an der Technischen Universität München am Lehrstuhl für Landschaftsarchitektur und industrielle Landschaft. Er ist Koordinator für das Internationale Doktorandenkolleg „Forschungslabor Raum": Curriculum 2017–2020. Als Landschaftsarchitekt ist er seit 2020 Projektleiter am Stadtplanungsamt der Stadt Freising.

Undine Giseke

Prof. Undine Giseke (*1956) ist seit 2003 Universitätsprofessorin an der TU Berlin und Leiterin des Fachgebiets für Landschaftsarchitektur und Freiraumplanung. Seit 2013 ist Studiendekanin für den interdisziplinären Studiengang Urban Design. Sie wirkt in zahlreichen Gremien mit und ist Vorsitzende des Kuratoriums der IBA Heidelberg. Als Landschaftsarchitektin ist sie Mitbegründerin des 1987 gegründeten Büros bgmr Landschaftsarchitekten. Sie forscht zu Landschaften und sozial-natürlichen Verknüpfungen im Anthropozän.

Michael Koch

Prof. Dr. Michael Koch (*1950) ist Architekt und Stadtplaner und lebt in Hamburg und Zürich. Er ist Teilhaber des Büros Yellow Z Urbanism Architecture, Zürich/Berlin. 1999 bis 2018 war er Professor für Städtebau und Quartierplanung an der BU Wuppertal, der TU Hamburg-Harburg sowie zuletzt an der HCU Hamburg. Er forscht und publiziert zu Städtebau- und Wohnungsbaugeschichte, Neuorientierung der Stadtplanung, urbanen Freiräumen und dem Zusammenhang von Verkehrsinfrastrukturen und Siedlungsentwicklung. Freiberufliche Arbeitsfelder sind stadtregionale und städtebauliche Entwicklungsstrategien und -projekte sowie formelle und informelle Planungen sowie die Konzipierung wie Moderation räumlicher Entwicklungsprozesse.

Markus Neppl

Prof. Markus Neppl (*1962) hat Architektur an der RWTH in Aachen studiert und war dort Mitbegründer der studentischen Planungsgruppe ARTECTA. 1990 gründete er zusammen mit Peter Berner, Oliver Hall und Kees Christiaanse das Büro ASTOC architects & planners in Köln, welches mit 100 Mitarbeitenden zahlreiche städtebauliche Projekte und Gebäude in unterschiedlichen Größenordnungen bearbeitet. 1999 wurde er auf den Lehrstuhl für Städtebau an die Universität Kaiserslautern berufen. 2004 erfolgte der Ruf auf den Lehrstuhl für Stadtquartiersplanung und Entwerfen an das Karlsruher Institut für Technologie (KIT) in Karlsruhe. 2008 bis 2012 war er Dekan und 2012 bis 2019 Studiendekan der Fakultät für Architektur.

Markus Nollert

Dr. Markus Nollert (*1977) is co-director of the Spatial Transformation Laboratories at the IRL of the ETH Zurich and founder and partner of the office urbanista.ch. He focuses on the treatment of complex tasks of spatial transformation in multi-actor networks in research and in practice. Core topics include tailor-made planning and learning processes, large-scale designs, and the question of effective methods and instruments for advancing spatial planning. As co-founder of the participation platform Nextzürich and of Urban Equipe, he is also always keen to discover new methods for participation in planning along with possibilities for their dissemination.

Andreas Nütten

Andreas Nütten (*1969) is a lecturer for cultural landscapes in teaching and research at the Institute for Architecture at the University of Applied Sciences and Arts Northwestern Switzerland in Muttenz, canton Basel-Country. His research focus includes the topics "spatial exploration and spatial image" and "Garden City 21—landscape-based development concepts for urban regions." From 2001 to 2006 he was a research assistant at the Institute for Landscape and Garden at the Karlsruhe Institute of Technology. As an architect with a focus on urban development, he has been closely associated with yellow z urbanism architecture in Zurich since 2008, where he has also been a partner since 2019.

Julian Petrin

Julian Petrin (*1968) is an urbanist and urban researcher in the field of large-scale future and strategy processes. With urbanista, a company he founded in 1998 he advises municipalities, companies, and associations throughout Germany on urban development processes. The focus of urbanista's work is on strategies for cities as a whole and for regions and on co-creatively developed visions for the future. In 2009 Petrin founded the internationally recognized Participation Laboratory Nexthamburg. From 2013 to 2015 he was visiting professor for urban management at the University of Kassel. He is a member of DASL and of various advisory boards. Since 2020 he is also teaching as professor for smart city solutions at the Stuttgart University of Applied Sciences.

Walter L. Schönwandt

Professor emeritus Dr.-Ing. Walter L. Schönwandt (*1950), Dipl.-Ing., Dipl.-Psych., was director of the Institute for the Fundamentals of Planning at the University of Stuttgart from 1993 to 2016. He has held visiting professorships in Oxford, Vienna, and Zurich and is a member of the Baden-Württemberg Chamber of Architects, the Academy for Territorial Development in the Leibniz Association (Akademie für Raumentwicklung in der Leibniz-Gemeinschaft, ARL), the Association for Town, Regional, and State Planning (Vereinigung für Stadt-, Regional- und Landesplanung, SRL), the Association of European Schools of Planning (AESOP), the International Association for People-Environment Studies (JAPS), the International Society of City and Regional Planners (ISOCARP), and the Association of Collegiate Schools of Planning (ACSP), in addition to his work as an expert, consultant, and author.

Markus Nollert

Dr. Markus Nollert (*1977) ist Ko-Leiter der Spatial Transformation Laboratories am IRL der ETH Zürich sowie Gründer und Partner des Büros urbanista.ch. Er widmet sich der Behandlung komplexer Aufgaben der räumlichen Transformation in Multi-Akteurs-Netzwerken in Wissenschaft und Praxis. Kernthemen sind dabei maßgeschneiderte Planungs- und Lernprozesse, großmaßstäbliche Entwürfe sowie die Frage nach wirksamen Methoden und Instrumenten für die Weiterentwicklung der Raumplanung. Als Mitbegründer der Partizipationsplattform Nextzürich und der Urban Equipe ist er zudem neuen Methoden der Teilhabe an Planung und deren Vermittlung auf der Spur.

Andreas Nütten

Andreas Nütten (*1969) ist Dozent für Kulturlandschaft in Lehre und Forschung am Institut für Architektur an der Fachhochschule Nordwestschweiz in Muttenz/Basel. Forschungsschwerpunkte sind „Raumerkundung und Raumbild" sowie „Gartenstadt 21 – landschaftsbasierte Entwicklungskonzepte für Stadtregionen". Von 2001 bis 2006 war er wissenschaftlicher Mitarbeiter am Institut Landschaft und Garten an der TH Karlsruhe. Als Architekt mit städtebaulichem Schwerpunkt ist er seit 2008 in enger Kooperation verbunden mit und seit 2019 Teilhaber von yellow z urbanism architecture in Zürich.

Julian Petrin

Julian Petrin (*1968) ist Urbanist und Stadtforscher im Bereich großräumiger Zukunfts- und Strategieprozesse. Mit seinem 1998 gegründeten, 20-köpfigen Unternehmen urbanista berät er deutschlandweit Kommunen, Unternehmen und Verbände in Prozessen der Stadtentwicklung. Schwerpunkte sind gesamtstädtische und regionale Strategien sowie kokreativ erarbeitete Zukunftsbilder. 2009 hat Petrin das international beachtete Partizipationslabor Nexthamburg gegründet. 2013 bis 2015 war er Gastprofessor für Stadtmanagement an der Universität Kassel. Seit 2011 ist er Mitglied der DASL und 2012 wurde er in den Konvent der Bundesstiftung Baukultur berufen. 2020 wurde er als Professor für Smart City Solutions an die Hochschule für Technik in Stuttgart berufen.

Walter L. Schönwandt

Univ.-Prof. em. Dr.-Ing. Walter L. Schönwandt (*1950), Dipl.- Ing., Dipl.-Psych., war von 1993 bis 2016 Direktor des Instituts für Grundlagen der Planung an der Universität Stuttgart. Er hatte Gastprofessuren in Oxford, Wien und Zürich inne, ist unter anderem Mitglied der Architektenkammer Baden-Württemberg, der Akademie für Raumforschung und Landesplanung (ARL), der Vereinigung für Stadt-, Regional- und Landesplanung (SRL), der Association of European Schools of Planning (AESOP), der International Association for People-Environment Studies (JAPS), der International Society of City and Regional Planners (ISOCARP), der Association of Collegiate Schools of Planning (ACSP) sowie Gutachter, Berater und Autor.

Bernd Scholl

Prof. Dr. Bernd Scholl (*1953) was full professor for spatial planning and development at the Swiss Federal Institute of Technology Zurich (ETH) from 2006 to 2018. At the ETH, he was also the delegate for the continuing education programs in spatial planning and in the master's degree program in advanced studies in spatial planning. From 2011 to 2013, he chaired the Network for City and Landscape (Netzwerk für Stadt und Landschaft, NSL). As co-owner of a planning office based in Zurich, he has been involved in numerous urban and regional development projects in Switzerland and abroad since 1987 and has chaired numerous competition juries, test planning processes, and expert commissions nationally and internationally. From 1997 to 2006 he was director of the Institute for Urban Development and Regional Planning at the University of Karlsruhe and full professor for the chair of the same name.

Stefan Siedentop

Prof. Dr.-Ing. Stefan Siedentop (*1966) is managing director of research at the Research Institute for Regional and Urban Development and a professor at the TU Dortmund in the Faculty of Spatial Planning. He holds a doctorate from the Faculty of Spatial Planning at the University of Dortmund, where he also began his studies in spatial planning. At the University of Stuttgart, he held the chair of spatial development and environmental planning and was head of the Institute of Spatial and Regional Planning.

Andreas Voigt

Prof. Dr. techn. Andreas Voigt (*1962) is a spatial planner and associate university professor for local planning at the Institute of Spatial Planning of the Faculty of Architecture and Planning at TU Wien. Since 2013, he has been the research unit head of the TU Wien's Center for Local Planning Research Unit. His research and teaching are focused on sustainable spatial development and spatial simulation in connection with the Spatial Simulation Lab at the TU Wien.

Udo Weilacher

Prof. Dr. Udo Weilacher (*1963), a landscape architect, completed an apprenticeship in gardening and landscaping before studying landscape architecture at the Technical University of Munich in 1986. From 1989 to 1990 he was a student at California State Polytechnic University Pomona in Los Angeles, before completing his degree in landscape architecture at the Technical University of Munich in 1993. He then worked as a research associate and lecturer at the University of Karlsruhe and at the Swiss Federal Institute of Technology Zurich (ETH), where he completed his dissertation with distinction in 2002. In 2002, he was appointed professor of landscape architecture at Leibniz University Hannover, where he also served from 2006 to 2008 as dean of the Faculty of Architecture and Landscape Sciences. Since April 2009, has been professor of Landscape Architecture and Industrial Landscape at the Technical University of Munich.

Bernd Scholl

Prof. Dr. Bernd Scholl (*1953) war von 2006 bis 2018 ordentlicher Professor für Raumentwicklung an der Eidgenössischen Technischen Hochschule Zürich (ETH). Er war dort auch Delegierter für die berufsbegleitenden Fortbildungsangebote im Bereich Raumplanung und im Studiengang Master of Advanced Studies in Raumplanung und von 2011 bis 2013 Vorsitzender des Netzwerkes für Stadt und Landschaft (NSL). Als Mitinhaber eines Planungsbüros mit Sitz in Zürich wirkt er seit 1987 in zahlreichen Vorhaben der Stadt- und Regionalentwicklung im In- und Ausland mit und war Vorsitzender zahlreicher, auch international besetzter Wettbewerbsjurys, Testplanungsverfahren und Expertenkommissionen. Von 1997 bis 2006 war er Direktor des Instituts für Städtebau und Landesplanung an der Universität Karlsruhe und Ordinarius für den gleichnamigen Lehrstuhl.

Stefan Siedentop

Prof. Dr.-Ing. Stefan Siedentop (*1966) ist wissenschaftlicher Direktor des Instituts für Landes- und Stadtentwicklungsforschung und Professor an der TU Dortmund, Fakultät Raumplanung, Fachgebiet Stadtentwicklung. Studium der Raumplanung an der Universität Dortmund, Promotion an der Universität Dortmund, Fakultät Raumplanung. Er war Inhaber des Lehrstuhls für Raumentwicklungs- und Umweltplanung an der Universität Stuttgart sowie Leiter des Instituts für Raumordnung und Entwicklungsplanung.

Andreas Voigt

Prof. Dr. techn. Andreas Voigt (*1962) ist Raumplaner, außerordentlicher Universitätsprofessor für Örtliche Raumplanung am Institut für Raumentwicklung, Infrastruktur- und Umweltplanung der Technischen Universität Wien und seit 2013 Leiter des Forschungsbereichs Örtliche Raumplanung. Die Forschungs- und Lehrschwerpunkte konzentrieren sich auf nachhaltige Raumentwicklung und raumbezogene Simulation auf Basis des Raumsimulationslabors TU Wien (Spatial Simulation Lab).

Udo Weilacher

Prof. Dr. Udo Weilacher (*1963) ist Landschaftsarchitekt. Er absolvierte eine Ausbildung im Garten- und Landschaftsbau, bevor er 1986 Landespflege an der Technischen Universität München studierte. Von 1989 bis 1990 studierte er an der California State Polytechnic University Pomona / Los Angeles und schloss sein Landschaftsarchitekturstudium an der TU München 1993 ab. Danach war er als wissenschaftlicher Angestellter und Lehrbeauftragter an der Universität Karlsruhe und an der Eidgenössischen Technischen Hochschule Zürich (ETH) tätig, wo er 2002 seine Dissertation mit Auszeichnung fertigstellte. 2002 wurde er als Professor für Landschaftsarchitektur an die Universität Hannover berufen und leitete dort von 2006 bis 2008 als Dekan die Fakultät für Architektur und Landschaft. Seit April 2009 ist Weilacher Professor für Landschaftsarchitektur und industrielle Landschaft an der TU München.

NOTES

… Activating Spaces   p. 12
1   Tom Kelley and David Kelley, *Creative Confidence* (New York: Random House, 2013), 190–191.
2   See also Internationales Doktorandenkolleg–Forschungslabor Raum, ed., *Forschungslabor Raum: Das Logbuch* (Berlin: Jovis Verlag, 2012).

Hardware, Software, Orgware:
A Spatial Theory Approach to Large-Scale Design   p. 42
1   See, for instance, Anthony Giddens, *Die Konstitution der Gesellschaft: Grundzüge einer Theorie der Strukturierung* (Frankfurt a. M./New York: Campus, 1988).
2   Henri Lefebvre, *The Production of Space*, trans. Donald Nicholson-Smith (Oxford: Blackwell, 1991), 33.
3   Dieter Läpple, "Essay über den Raum: Für ein gesellschaftswissenschaftliches Raumkonzept," in *Stadt und Raum: Soziologische Analysen*, ed. Dieter Läpple et al., 2nd ed. (Pfaffenweiler: Centaurus-Verlagsgesellschaft, 1992), 157–207.
4   See Manuel Castells, *The Network Society. The Information Age: Economy, Society and Culture*, Vol. 1. (Oxford: Blackwell, 1996).

Designing/Method(s)   p. 50
1   Tristan Lannuzel, Partner of the firm urbanista, Hamburg.
2   Julian Petrin, Partner of the firm urbanista, Hamburg.
3   See Markus Nollert, "Raumplanerisches Entwerfen: Entwerfen als Schlüsselelement von Klärungsprozessen der aktionsorientierten Planung – am Beispiel des regionalen Massstabs" (Dissertation, ETH Zurich, 2013), http://e-collection.library.ethz.ch/view/eth:7302 (last accessed February 24, 2020). Quotes in this paragraph are from pages 16 and 224.
4   See Horst W. J. Rittel and Melvin M. Webber, "Dilemmas in a General Theory of Planning," *Policy Sciences* 4, no. 2 (1973): 155–169.
5   "Within a broad conception, 'Design' is not merely a creative process dealing with the physical context and the design of artefacts. It deals also with the exploration of realities, the development, representation and exploration of visions, concepts scenarios, metaphors and stories, the design of policies and processes, solutions etc., looking for possible 'futures or becoming' in such a way that exchange of information, interpretation and integration of knowledge of a different kind, and visions are generated. As such, design and its products—different kinds of representation and images—become not only a medium for integration of content but also in a way to confront values, visions, and interests, to discuss and negotiate and to deal with power structures." See Jef van den Broeck, "Spatial Design as a Strategy for a Qualitative Social-Spatial Transformation," in *Strategic Spatial Projects: Catalysts for Change*, ed. Stijn Oosterlynck, Jef van den Broeck et al., (London: Routledge, 2011), 88
6   See, for example, Martin Prominski, *Landschaft entwerfen: Zur Theorie aktueller Landschaftsarchitektur* (Berlin, Reimer 2004) and Hille von Seggern, Julia Werner, and Lucia Grosse-Bächle, *Creating Knowledge: Innovationsstrategien im Entwerfen urbaner Landschaften* (Berlin/Munich: Jovis Verlag, 2008).
7   See, for example, Stefan Kurath, *Stadtlandschaften Entwerfen? Grenzen und Chancen der Planung im Spiegel der städtebaulichen Praxis* (Bielefeld: Transcript Verlag, 2011); Thomas Sieverts, "Von der unmöglichen Ordnung zu einer möglichen Unordnung im Entwerfen der Stadtlandschaft," *disP* 169, no. 2 (2007), 5–16.

8   See, for example Nigel Cross, *Designerly Ways of Knowing* (Basel, Birkhäuser, 2006); Wolfgang Jonas, "Design as Problem-Solving? Or: Here Is the Solution—What was the Problem?" *Design Studies* 14, no. 2 (1993): 157–170; Wolfgang Jonas, "Design – Es gibt nichts Theoretischeres als eine gute Praxis: 'Heureka oder die Kunst des Entwerfens'" Symposion IFG, Ulm 2011.
9   See Seggern et al., *Creating Knowledge*, 48.
10   See Anita Grams, Charles Hoch, and Markus Nollert, "Puzzling: How Spatial Planners Compose Plans Together," in *Spatial Planning Matters*, ed. Bernd Scholl (Zurich: vdf Hochschulverlag AG an der ETH Zürich, 2018), 179–181.
11   See Prominski, "Landschaft entwerfen: zur Theorie aktueller Landschaftsarchitektur," 104
12   See Donald A. Schön, *The Reflective Practitioner: How Professionals Think in Action* (New York: Basic Books, 1983); Prominski, *Landschaft entwerfen: Zur Theorie aktueller Landschaftsarchitektur*; Nollert, *Raumplanerisches Entwerfen*.
13   See also Markus Nollert, "The Case of Brig, Switzerland: How 'Moving Simultaneously' Opened New Possibilities for Solving a Muddled Situation: The Case of Brig, Switzerland" in Scholl, *Spatial Planning Matters*, 136–143
14   See Irving John Good, *The Scientist Speculates: An Anthology of Partly-Baked Ideas* (New York, Basic Books, 1965), 9
15   See J. D. Bernal in Good, in *The scientist speculates*, 19.
16   See Rittel and Webber, *Dilemmas in a General Theory of Planning*, 1973
17   See Stephen Kemmis and Robin McTaggart, "Participatory Action Research: Communicative Action and the Public Sphere," in *The Sage Handbook of Qualitative Research*, ed. Norman K. Denzin and Yvonna S. Lincoln, 3rd ed. (Thousand Oaks: Sage Publications, 2005), 559–603.
18   See Jürgen Weidinger, Symposium "Designing Knowledge: Results and Methods of Research by Design in Landscape Architecture," Technical University Berlin, June 22, 2012.

Projecting—Modeling—Visualizing:
A Discussion about Methods   p. 60
1   See Markus Nollert, "Raumplanerisches Entwerfen: Entwerfen als Schlüsselelement von Klärungsprozessen der aktionsorientierten Planung – am Beispiel des regionalen Maßstabs" (Dissertation, ETH Zurich, 2013).
2   See Bernd Scholl "Die Methode der Testplanung – Exemplarische Vernschaulichung für die Auswahl und den Einsatz von Methoden in Klärungsprozessen," in *Grundriss der Raumordnung und Raumentwicklung*, ed. Klaus Borchard (Hannover, 2011), 279–290.
3   Herbert Stachowiak, *Allgemeine Modelltheorie* (Vienna/New York: Springer, 1973), 157.
4   Stachowiak, *Allgemeine Modelltheorie*, 156.
5   Stachowiak, *Allgemeine Modelltheorie*, 157.
6   See also figure 3.
7   Stachowiak, *Allgemeine Modelltheorie*, 131–133.
8   Andreas Nütten, "Raumerkundung und Raumbild," in *Prozesse reflexiven Entwerfens – Entwerfen und Forschen in Architektur und Landschaft*, ed. Margitta Buchert (Berlin: Jovis Verlag, 2018), 160.

Crossing Borders Once Again   p. 72
1   Forschungslabor Raum, ed., *Forschungslabor Raum: Das Logbuch* (Berlin: Jovis Verlag, 2012); Forschungslabor Raum, ed., *Urbane Transformationslandschaften* (Berlin: Jovis Verlag, 2016).

... Räume aktivieren   S. 13
1   Tom Kelley / David Kelley: Creative Confidence. New York 2013, S. 190/191.
2   Vgl. Internationales Doktorandenkolleg – Forschungslabor Raum (Hrsg.): Forschungslabor Raum. Das Logbuch. Berlin 2012.

Hardware, Software, Orgware: ein raumtheoretischer Zugang zum großräumigen Entwerfen   S. 43
1   Siehe u. a. Anthony Giddens: Die Konstitution der Gesellschaft. Grundzüge einer Theorie der Strukturierung. Frankfurt a. M. / New York 1988.
2   Henri Lefebvre: The Production of Space. Oxford 1991.
3   Dieter Läpple: „Essay über den Raum. Für ein gesellschaftswissenschaftliches Raumkonzept", in: ders. et al: Stadt und Raum. Soziologische Analysen (Stadt, Raum und Gesellschaft; 1). Pfaffenweiler 1992 (2. Aufl.), S. 157–207.
4   Vgl. Manuel Castells: The Network Society. The Information Age: Economy, Society and Culture, Vol. 1. Oxford 1996.

Entwerfen/Methode(n)   S. 51
1   Tristan Lannuzel, Partner des Büros urbanista, Hamburg.
2   Julian Petrin, Partner des Büros urbanista, Hamburg.
3   Vgl. Markus Nollert: Raumplanerisches Entwerfen. Entwerfen als Schlüsselelement von Klärungsprozessen der aktionsorientierten Planung – am Beispiel des regionalen Massstabs (Dissertation, ETH Zürich). Zürich 2013, S. 16 und S. 224: http://e-collection.library.ethz.ch/view/eth:7302 (letzter Zugriff: 24.02.2020)
4   Ebd.
5   Vgl. Horst W. J. Rittel / Melvin M. Webber: „Dilemmas in a general theory of planning", in: Policy Sciences, 4(2), 1973, S. 155–169.
6   „Within a broad conception, ‚Design' is not merely a creative process dealing with the physical context and the design of artefacts. It deals also with the exploration of realities, the development, representation and exploration of visions, concepts scenarios, metaphors and stories, the design of policies and processes, solutions etc., looking for possible ‚futures or becomings' in such a way that exchange of information, interpretation and integration of Knowledge of a different kind, and visions are generated. As such, design and it products – different kinds of representation and images – become not only a medium for integration of content but also in a way to confront values, visions, and interests, to discuss and negotiate and to deal with power structures", vgl. Jef van den Broeck: „Spatial design as a strategy for a qualitative social-spatial transformation", in: Stijn Oosterlynck / Jef van den Broeck / Louis Abrechts / Frank Moulaert / Ann Verhetsel: Strategic spatial projects. Catalysts for change. London et al. 2011, S. 88.
7   Vgl. beispielsweise Martin Prominski: Landschaft entwerfen: Zur Theorie aktueller Landschaftsarchitektur, Berlin 2004, und Hille von Seggern / Julia Werner / Lucia Grosse-Bächle: Creating Knowledge. Innovationsstrategien im Entwerfen urbaner Landschaften. Berlin/München 2008.
8   Vgl. beispielsweise Stefan Kurath: Stadtlandschaften Entwerfen? Grenzen und Chancen der Planung im Spiegel der städtebaulichen Praxis. Bielefeld 2011; Thomas Sieverts: „Von der unmöglichen Ordnung zu einer möglichen Unordnung im Entwerfen der Stadtlandschaft", in: disP, 169(2), 2007, S. 5–16.
9   Vgl. beispielsweise Nigel Cross: Designerly ways of knowing. Basel 2006; Wolfgang Jonas: „Design as problem-solving? Or: Here is the solution—What was the problem?",

in: Design Studies, 14(2), 1993, S. 157–170; Wolfgang Jonas: Design – Es gibt nichts Theoretischeres als eine gute Praxis. „Heureka oder die Kunst des Entwerfens". Symposion IFG, Ulm 2011.
10   Vgl. Seggern/Werner/Grosse-Bächle 2008, S. 48.
11   Vgl. Anita Grams / Charles Hoch / Markus Nollert: „Puzzling: How Spatial Planners Compose Plans Together", in: Bernd Scholl (Hrsg.): Spatial Planning Matters. Zürich 2018, S. 179–181.
12   Vgl. Prominski 2004, S. 104.
13   Vgl. Donald A. Schön: The Reflective Practitioner: How Professionals Think In Action. New York 1983; Prominski 2004, S. 104; Nollert 2013.
14   Siehe auch Markus Nollert: „The Case of Brig, Switzerland. How ‚working together' opened new possibilities in organizing", in: Scholl 2018, S. 136–143.
15   Vgl. Irving John Good: The scientist speculates – an anthology of partly baked ideas. New York 1965, S. 9.
16   Vgl. J. D. Bernal in Good 2018, S. 19.
17   Vgl. Rittel/Webber 1973.
18   Vgl. Stephen Kemmis / Robin McTaggart: „Participatory action research: Communicative action and the public sphere", in: Norman K. Denzin / Yvonna S. Lincoln: The Sage Handbook of qualitative research. Thousand Oaks et al. 2005 (3. Aufl.), S. 559–603.
19   Vgl. Jürgen Weidinger: Symposium „Designing Knowledge. Results and methods of research by design in landscape architecture", Technische Universität Berlin, 22. Juni 2012.

Projizieren – Modellieren – Visualisieren: eine Methodendiskussion   S. 61
1   Vgl. Markus Nollert: Raumplanerisches Entwerfen. Entwerfen als Schlüsselelement von Klärungsprozessen der aktionsorientierten Planung – am Beispiel des regionalen Massstabs (Dissertation, ETH Zürich). Zürich 2013.
2   Vgl. Bernd Scholl: „Die Methode der Testplanung – Exemplarische Veranschaulichung für die Auswahl und den Einsatz von Methoden in Klärungsprozessen", in: Klaus Borchard (Hrsg.): Grundriss der Raumordnung und Raumentwicklung. Hannover 2011, S. 279–290.
3   Herbert Stachowiak: Allgemeine Modelltheorie. Wien / New York 1973, S. 157.
4   Ebd., S. 156.
5   Ebd., S. 157.
6   Vgl. auch hierzu Abb. 3
7   Stachowiak 1973, S. 131–133.
8   Andreas Nütten: „Raumerkundung und Raumbild", in: Margitta Buchert (Hrsg.): Prozesse reflexiven Entwerfens – Entwerfen und Forschen in Architektur und Landschaft. Berlin 2018, S. 142–175.

Einmal mehr die Grenzen überschreiten   S. 73
1   Forschungslabor Raum (Hrsg.): Forschungslabor Raum. Das Logbuch. Berlin 2012; Forschungslabor Raum (Hrsg.): Urbane Transformationslandschaften. Berlin 2016.
2   Michael Koch: „Lob des Pragmatismus", in: Forschungslabor Raum 2012, S. 279 ff.
3   Uwe Schneidewind / Mandy Singer-Brodowski: Transformative Wissenschaft: Klimawandel im deutschen Wissenschafts- und Hochschulsystem. Marburg 2013.
4   Michael Koch: „Urbane Transformatoren", in: Forschungslabor Raum 2016, S. 188 ff.
5   David Liebermann, unter: http://disziplinaeregrenzgaenge.de/ (letzter Zugriff: 24.02.2020).
6   Michael Koch / Amelie Rost / Yvonne Siegmund / Renée Tribble / Yvonne Werner (Hrsg.): New urban Professions –

2   Michael Koch, "Lob des Pragmatismus," in, *Forschungs-labor Raum: Das Logbuch*, 279 ff.

3   Uwe Schneidewind / Mandy Singer-Brodowski, *Transformative Wissenschaft: Klimawandel im deutschen Wissenschafts- und Hochschulsystem* (Marburg: Metropolis Verlag, 2013).

4   Michael Koch, "Urbane Transformatoren," in *Urbane Transformationslandschaften*, 188 ff.

5   David Liebermann, http://disziplinaeregrenzgaenge.de/ (last accessed February 24, 2020).

6   Michael Koch et al., eds., *New Urban Professions: A Journey through Practice and Theory* (Berlin: Jovis Verlag, 2018).

7   David Kirsten, "Transdisciplinarity: The Basis for the Increase of Urban Knowledge?" in *New Urban Professions*, 277–279, here, 279.

8   Bernd Kniess et al., "Spatial Agency: From the University of the Neighbourhoods to Building A Proposition For Future Activities or How Urban Design Mobilizes the Performative Plan," in *New Urban Professions*, 193–201.

9   See http://sphhpr.de/2016/05/29/issue-no-2-novas-linhas-de-mobilidade-new-lines-of-mobility-neue-wege-der-mobilitat/; http://sphhpr.de/2015/11/03/issue-no-1-cooperations/ (last accessed June 23, 2020)

10   Andrade Vinicius, "Professional Changes," in *New Urban Professions—A Journey through Practice and Theory*, 15–27, here, 16.

11   Vinicius, Professional Changes, 17.

12   Michael Koch, "… confidere necesse est …," in *New Urban Professions*, 144–146.

A Propaedeutic for the International Doctoral College?   p. 82
1   Mario Bunge, *Philosophical Dictionary* (Amherst, New York: Prometheus Books, 2003), 38.

2   Mario Bunge, *Kausalität, Geschichte und Probleme* (Tübingen: Mohr, 1987), 401.

Border Index—Index of Borders   p. 92
1   Walter Schönwandt, *Planung in der Krise? Theoretische Orientierungen für Architektur, Stadt- und Raumplanung* (Stuttgart, 2002), 71.

2   Schönwandt, *Planung in der Krise?*, 64.

Cultures of Assemblages   p. 104
1   Sonja Windmüller, *Die Kehrseite der Dinge: Müll, Abfall, Wegwerfen als kulturwissenschaftliches Phänomen* (Münster: Lit Verlag, 2004).

2   Undine Giseke, "The City in the Anthropocene: Multiple Porosities," in *Porous City: From Metaphor to Urban Agenda*, ed. Sophie Wolfrum et al. (New York/Basel: Birkhäuser, 2018), 200–204.

3   Gabriele Dürbeck, "Narrative des Anthropozäns: Systematisierung eines interdisziplinären Diskurses," *Kulturwissenschaftliche Zeitschrift* 3, no. 1 (2018): 1–20, here, 4.

4   Dürbeck, "Narrative des Anthropozäns," 7.

5   Walter Siebel, *Die Kultur der Stadt* (Frankfurt a. M.: Suhrkamp, 2015), 30.

6   Siebel, *Die Kultur der Stadt*, 29.

7   Jürgen Renn, "Wissenschaftsgeschichte im Anthropozän," presentation as part of the International Symposium "Wozu Wissenschaftsgeschichte? Ziele und Wege," March 29–30, 2019, https://pure.mpg.de/rest/items/item_3183344_2/component/file_3183699/content (last accessed January 11, 2020), 1–18, here, 4.

8   Timothy Morton, "Zero Landscapes in den Zeiten der Hyperobjekte," *GAM* 7 (2011): 79–87, here, 81.

9   Matthew Gandy, "Rethinking Urban Metabolism: Water, Space and the Modern City," *City* 8, no. 3 (2004): 363–379.

10   Christoph Bernhardt, "Die Vertreibung des Wassers aus der Stadt und der Planung," in *Geschichte der Planung des öffentlichen Raums*, ed. Gerhard Fehl, Gerd Kuhn, and Ursula von Petz (Dortmund: Institut für Raumplanung, 2005), 71–83.

11   Susanne Hauser, "Reinlichkeit, Ordnung und Schönheit:

Zur Diskussion über Kanalisation im 19. Jahrhundert," *Die alte Stadt* 4, no. 19 (1992), 292–312.

12   Susanne Frank, "Die Disziplinierung der weiblichen Körper: Kanalisation und Prostitution in der Großstadtentwicklung des 19. Jahrhunderts," in *Vernunft – Entwicklung – Leben: Schlüsselbegriffe der Moderne, Festschrift für Wolfgang Eßbach*, ed. Ulrich Bröckling (Munich: Fink, 2004), 167–183.

13   Windmüller, *Die Kehrseite der Dinge*, 224 and 231.

14   Kameshwari Pothukuchi and Jerome L. Kaufman, "Placing the Food System on the Urban Agenda: The Role of Municipal Institutions in Food Systems Planning," *Agriculture and Human Values* 16 (1999): 213–224.

15   Hauser, "Reinlichkeit, Ordnung und Schönheit," 302.

16   Hauser, "Reinlichkeit, Ordnung und Schönheit," 294.

17   Timothy Morton, *Hyperobjects: Philosophy and Ecology after the End of the World* (Minneapolis: University of Minnesota Press, 2013), 32.

18   John Tresch, "Anthropotechniken für das Anthropozän," in *Technosphäre*, ed. Katrin Klingan and Christoph Rosol (Berlin: Matthes & Seitz, 2019), 86-103, here, 87.

19   Bernd Scherer and Jürgen Renn, *Das Anthropozän: Ein Zwischenbericht; Zum Stand der Dinge* (Berlin: Matthes & Seitz, 2015); Renn, "Wissenschaftsgeschichte im Anthropozän."

20   Dürbeck, "Narrative des Anthropozäns."

Casablanca—Agriculture as Component of the Emerging Megacity   p. 124
1   Undine Giseke et al., eds., *Urban Agriculture for Growing City Regions: Connecting Urban-Rural Spheres in Casablanca* (London: Routledge, Taylor & Francis, 2015).

Urban Perspectives—Big Plans: Renaissance of the Spatially Oriented Urban Development Plans   p. 142
1   Heidede Becker, Johann Jessen, and Robert Sander, "Auf der Suche nach Orientierung: Das Wiederaufleben der Leitbildfrage im Städtebau," in *Ohne Leitbild? Städtebau in Deutschland und Europa*, ed. Becker, Jessen, and Sander (Stuttgart: Karl Krämer, 1998), 10–17.

2   Kees Christiaanse, "Schnittstelle zwischen Städtebau und Architektur: Projekte in Arnheim und Rotterdam," Becker, Jessen, and Sander, *Ohne Leitbild?*, 367–378.

3   Markus Neppl, "Große Pläne: Prozesshaftes Entwerfen zwischen Städtebau und Stadtplanung" *PLANERIN* 4 (2014): 21–24; Markus Neppl, "Wie zeichnet man ein Leitbild?" in *Auf dem Weg zum Räumlichen Leitbild*, ed. Markus Neppl and City of Karlsruhe (Karlsruhe: KIT Scientific Publishing 2015), 187–194.

4   Christian Holl, "Kein Leitbild ist auch keine Lösung," *Bauwelt* 8 (2015): 8–9.

5   EKI-Dokumentation, Mannheimer Modell, Stadt Mannheim 2009/2013, https://www.mannheim.de/sites/default/files/page/9392/071205_eki-mannheim-konzept. pdf and https://www.mannheim.de/sites/default/files/page/4569/eki-entwicklungkonzept_innenstadt_broschure_2013.pdf (last access for both sites February 25, 2020).

6   Baudezernat Landeshauptstadt Hannover, ed., *Hannover City 2020: Die Vorträge* (Hannover, 2010).

7   Baudezernat Landeshauptstadt Hannover, ed., *Hannoversche Wohnungsbauoffensive: Hannover 2016–2020*.

8   "Dokumentation Stadtteil Kronsrode: Draussen in der Stadt" (2017), https://www.kronsrode.de (last accessed February 25, 2020).

9   Rahmenplan südliche Innenstadt, Rastatt: Barock Stadt Rastatt (2017-085/27.02.2017, Anlage 1, 170322 RP südliche Innenstadt), unter: http://www.buergerinfo-rastatt.de (last accessed February 25, 2020).

10   "Hamburger Bauforum: Offizielles Stadtforum für Hamburg," https://www.hamburg.de (last accessed February 25, 2020).

11   "Kölner Perspektiven," https://www.stadt-koeln.de (last accessed Febuary 25, 2020).

A Journey through Practice and Theory. Berlin 2018.

7   David Kirsten: „Transdisciplinarity: The Basis for the Increase of Urban Knowledge?", in: Koch/Rost/Siegmund/Tribble/Werner 2018, S. 277–279, hier: S. 279.

8   Bernd Kniess / Anna Richter / Christopher Dell / Dominique Peck: „Spatial Agency: From the University of the Neighbourhoods to Building A Proposition For Future Activities or How Urban Design Mobilizes the Performative Plan", in: Koch/Rost/Siegmund/Tribble/Werner 2018, S. 193–201.

9   Vgl. http://sphhpr.de/2016/05/29/issue-no-2-novas-linhas-de-mobilidade-new-lines-of-mobility-neue-wege-der-mobilitat/ sowie http://sphhpr.de/2015/11/03/issue-no-1-cooperations/ (letzter Zugriff: 23.06.2020).

10 Andrade Vinicius: „Professional Changes", in: New Urban Professions—A Journey through Practice and Theory, S. 15–27, hier: S. 16

11 Ebd., S. 17.

12 Michael Koch: „… confidere necesse est …", in: Koch/Rost/Siegmund/Tribble/Werner 2018, S. 144–146.

Ein Propädeutikum für das Internationale Doktorandenkolleg? S. 83
1   Mario Bunge: *Philosophical Dictionary*. Amherst/New York, 2003, S. 38.
2   Mario Bunge: *Kausalität, Geschichte und Probleme*. Tübingen, 1987, S. 401.

Grenzindex – Index der Grenzen   S. 93
1   Walter Schönwandt: Planung in der Krise? Theoretische Orientierungen für Architektur, Stadt- und Raumplanung. Stuttgart 2002, S. 71.
2   Ebd., S. 64.

Verknüpfungskulturen   S. 105
1   Sonja Windmüller: Die Kehrseite der Dinge. Müll, Abfall, Wegwerfen als kulturwissenschaftliches Phänomen (Europäische Ethnologie; 2). Münster 2004.
2   Undine Giseke: „The City in the Anthropocene – Multiple Porosities", in: Sophie Wolfrum et al. (Hrsg.): Porous City – From Metaphor to Urban Agenda. New York / Basel 2018, S. 200–204.
3   Gabriele Dürbeck: „Narrative des Anthropozäns – Systematisierung eines interdisziplinären Diskurses", in: Kulturwissenschaftliche Zeitschrift, 3(1), 2018, S. 1–20, hier: S. 4.
4   Ebd., S. 7.
5   Walter Siebel: Die Kultur der Stadt. Frankfurt a. M. 2015, S. 30.
6   Ebd., S. 29.
7   Jürgen Renn: „Wissenschaftsgeschichte im Anthropozän" (Vortrag im Rahmen des Internationales Symposiums „Wozu Wissenschaftsgeschichte? Ziele und Wege", 29.–30. März 2019), unter: https://pure.mpg.de/rest/items/item_3183344_2/component/file_3183699/content (letzter Zugriff: 11.01.2020), S. 1–18, hier: S. 4.
8   Timothy Morton: „Zero Landscapes in den Zeiten der Hyperobjekte", in: GAM, 7, 2011, S. 79–87, hier: S. 81.
9   Matthew Gandy: „Rethinking urban metabolism: water, space and the modern city", in: City, 8(3), 2004, S. 363–379.
10 Christoph Bernhardt: „Die Vertreibung des Wassers aus der Stadt und der Planung", in: ders. / Gerhard Fehl / Gerd Kuhn / Ursula von Petz (Hrsg.): Geschichte der Planung des öffentlichen Raums (Dortmunder Beiträge zur Raumplanung; 122). Dortmund 2005, S. 71–83.
11 Susanne Hauser: „Reinlichkeit, Ordnung und Schönheit – Zur Diskussion über Kanalisation im 19. Jahrhundert", in: Die alte Stadt, 4(19), 1992, S. 292–312.
12 Susanne Frank: „Die Disziplinierung der weiblichen Körper. Kanalisation und Prostitution in der Großstadtentwicklung des 19. Jahrhunderts", in: Ulrich Bröckling (Hrsg.): Vernunft – Entwicklung – Leben. Schlüsselbegriffe der Moderne. Festschrift für Wolfgang Eßbach. München 2004, S. 167–183.

13 Windmüller 2004, S. 224, 231.
14 Kameshwari Pothukuchi / Jerome L. Kaufman: „Placing the food system on the urban agenda: The role of municipal institutions in food systems planning", in: Agriculture and Human Values, 16, 1999, S. 213–224.
15 Hauser 1992, S. 302.
16 Ebd., S. 294.
17 Timothy Morton: Hyperobjects. Philosophy and Ecology after the End of the World. Minneapolis/London 2013, S. 32.
18 John Tresch: „Anthropotechniken für das Anthropozän", in: Katrin Klingan / Christoph Rosol (Hrsg.): Technosphäre. Berlin 2019, S. 86–103, hier: S. 87.
19 Bernd Scherer / Jürgen Renn: Das Anthropozän: Ein Zwischenbericht. Zum Stand der Dinge. Berlin 2015; Renn 2019.
20 Dürbeck 2018.

Casablanca – Die ökonomische Lokomotive Marokkos S. 125
1   Undine Giseke / Maria Gerster-Bentaya / Frank Helten / Matthias Kraume / Dieter Scherer / Guido Spars / Fouad Amraoui / Abdelaziz Adidi / Said Berdouz / Mohemed Chlaida / Majid Mansour / Mohamed Mdafai (Hrsg.): Urban Agriculture for Growing City Regions. Connecting Urban-Rural Spheres in Casablanca. London 2015.

Urbane Perspektiven – Große Pläne: Renaissance der räumlich orientierten Stadtentwicklungsplanungen   S. 143
1   Heidede Becker / Johann Jessen / Robert Sander: „Auf der Suche nach Orientierung – Das Wiederaufleben der Leitbildfrage im Städtebau", in: dies. (Hrsg.): Ohne Leitbild? Städtebau in Deutschland und Europa. Stuttgart 1998, S. 10–17.
2   Kees Christiaanse: „Schnittstelle zwischen Städtebau und Architektur – Projekte in Arnheim und Rotterdam", in: Becker/Jessen/Sander 1998, S. 367–378.
3   Markus Neppl: „Große Pläne – Prozesshaftes Entwerfen zwischen Städtebau und Stadtplanung", in: PLANERIN, 4, 2014, S. 21–24; Markus Neppl: „Wie zeichnet man ein Leitbild?", in: Stadt Karlsruhe / KIT (Hrsg.): Auf dem Weg zum Räumlichen Leitbild. Karlsruhe 2015, S. 187–194.
4   Christian Holl: „Kein Leitbild ist auch keine Lösung", in: Bauwelt, 8, 2015, S. 8–9.
5   EKI-Dokumentation, Mannheimer Modell, Stadt Mannheim 2009/2013, unter: https://www.mannheim.de/sites/default/files/page/9392/071205_eki-mannheim-konzept.pdf;https://www.mannheim.de/sites/default/files/page/4569/eki-entwicklungkonzept_innenstadt_broschure_2013.pdf (beide letzter Zugriff: 25.02.2020).
6   Baudezernat Landeshauptstadt Hannover (Hrsg.): Hannover City 2020. Die Vorträge. Hannover 2010.
7   Baudezernat Landeshauptstadt Hannover (Hrsg.): Hannoversche Wohnungsbauoffensive. Hannover 2016–2020.
8   Dokumentation Stadtteil Kronsrode: Draussen in der Stadt, 2017, unter: https://www.kronsrode.de (letzter Zugriff: 25.02.2020).
9   Rahmenplan südliche Innenstadt, Rastatt: Barock Stadt Rastatt (2017-085/27.02.2017, Anlage 1, 170322 RP südliche Innenstadt), unter: http://www.buergerinfo-rastatt.de (letzter Zugriff: 25.02.2020).
10 Hamburger Bauforum: Offizielles Stadtforum für Hamburg, unter: https://www.hamburg.de (letzter Zugriff: 25.02.2020).
11 Kölner Perspektiven, unter: https://www.stadt-koeln.de (letzter Zugriff: 25.02.2020).
12 Ebd.

Mittendrin, aber (noch) nicht dabei! S. 169
1   Martin Einsele: Der Oberrhein – eine „andere Metropole" – XVII Triennale di Milano 1988. Karlsruhe 1988.
2   Vgl. dazu auch Ralf Stieber: „Oberrhein – Metropole der Zukunft?", 26.05.1991, unter: https://www.ev-akademie-baden.de/html/oberrhein_metropole_der_zukunft.html (letzter Zugriff: 15.01.2020).

12 "Kölner Perspektiven," https://www.stadt-koeln.de (last accessed Febuary 25, 2020).

In the Midst, But Not (Yet) Part of It!   p. 168
1   Martin Einsele, *Der Oberrhein: Eine "andere Metropole" – XVII Triennale di Milano 1988* (Karlsruhe: 1988).
2   See also Ralf Stieber, "Oberrhein: Metropole der Zukunft?" May 26, 1991, https://www.ev-akademie-baden.de/html/oberrhein_metropole_der_zukunft.html (last accessed January 15, 2020).
3   TMO, Straßburg, http://rmtmo.eu/de/politik/aktuell (last accessed February 27, 2019).
4   On the basis of this paper, the 11th Three-Countries Congress in Strasbourg declared on January 11, 2008: "In the Upper Rhine area between the Jura, Vosges, Black Forest and Palatinate Forest, six million people live on 21,508 square kilometers in an area characterized by a tightly meshed network of dynamic towns with rural areas in between." See here "Joint Declaration for a Trinational Upper Rhine Metropolitan Region: 11th Tripartite Congress, Strasbourg / Déclaration commune pour une Région métropolitaine trinationale du Rhin supérieur: 11ème Congrès Tripartite, Strasbourg," January 11, 2008. https://www.oberrheinkonferenz.org/de/oberrheinkonferenz/downloads.html.
5   EKI-Dokumentation, Mannheimer Modell, Stadt Mannheim 2009/2013, https://www.mannheim.de/sites/default/files/page/9392/071205_eki-mannheim-konzept.pdf and https://www.mannheim.de/sites/default/files/page/4569/eki-entwicklungkonzept_innenstadt_broschure_2013.pdf (last access for both sites February 25, 2020).
6   N. N.: https://www.rmtmo.eu/de/politik/aktuell/newsreader-politik/konferenz-zum-thema-grenzueberschreitender-metropolraum-strassburg-karlsruhe.html, (last accessed January 31, 2019)

Spatial Simulation   p. 178
1   See Andreas Voigt, *Raumbezogene Simulation und Örtliche Raumplanung: Wege zu einem (stadt-)raumbezogenen Qualitätsmanagement* (Vienna: Österreichischer Kunst- und Kulturverlag 2005), 27.
2   Voigt, *Raumbezogene Simulation und Örtliche Raumplanung.*
3   Hartmut Bossel, *Modellbildung und Simulation: Konzepte, Verfahren und Modelle zum Verhalten dynamischer Systeme.* (Braunschweig Wiesbaden: Verlag Vieweg 1994), 36.
4   Voigt, *Raumbezogene Simulation und Örtliche Raumplanung,* 27; Bossel, *Modellbildung und Simulation,* 15.
5   Walter Schönwandt, Peter Wasel, "Das semiotische Dreieck – ein gedankliches Werkzeug beim Planen," in *Bauwelt* 88, no. 20 (1997): 1118; Mario Bunge, *Treatise on Basic Philosophy* (Dordrecht, Boston: Springer, 1974).
6   Mario Bunge, *Epistemologie: Aktuelle Fragen der Wissenschaftstheorie* (Mannheim: Bibliographisches Institut, 1983), 44.
7   Walter Schönwandt, Peter Wasel, "Das semiotische Dreieck – ein gedankliches Werkzeug beim Planen," in *Bauwelt* 88, no. 20 (1997): 1037.
8   Schönwandt and Wasel, "Das semiotische Dreieck," 1037.
9   Schönwandt and Wasel, "Das semiotische Dreieck," 1028.
10 Voigt, *Raumbezogene Simulation und Örtliche Raumplanung,* 22; Hartmut Bossel, *Globale Wende: Wege zu einem gesellschaftlichen und ökologischen Strukturwandel* (München: Verlag Droemer, 1998), 16 ff. and 49 ff.; Kurt Ricica, Andreas Voigt (Eds. for "MA22 Umweltschutz"), *Raumverträglichkeit als Beitrag zur nachhaltigen Raumnutzung. Ein Leitfaden (Teil 1)* (Vienna: Österreichischer Kunst- und Kulturverlag, 1998), 127 ff.
11 Bossel, *Globale Wende,* 51.
12 Bossel, *Globale Wende,* 61.
13 Bossel, *Globale Wende,* 61.
14 Walter Schönwandt, Katrin Vormanek, Jürgen Utz, Jens Grunau, and Christoph Hemberger, *Komplexe Probleme lösen: Ein Handbuch* (Berlin: Jovis Verlag, 2013).

15 Alexander Gosztonyi, *Der Raum: Geschichte seiner Probleme in Philosophie und Wissenschaften* (Freiburg, München: Karl Alber, 1976), 35.
16 Schönwandt/Wasel, "Das semiotische Dreieck," 1128.
17 Voigt, *Raumbezogene Simulation und Örtliche Raumplanung,* 29 ff.
18 Bossel, *Modellbildung und Simulation,* 11.
19 Antero Markelin/Bernd Fahle, *Umweltsimulation: Sensorische Simulation im Städtebau* (Stuttgart: Schriftenreihe 11 des Städtebaulichen Instituts der Universität Stuttgart, 1979), 19 ff.
20 Markelin/Fahle, *Umweltsimulation,* 22 f.
21 Rolf Signer, "'Das Bild geht der Idee voraus': Von Bildern in der Raumplanung," in *Spatial Reseach Lab: The Logbook = Forschungslabor Raum: Das Logbuch,* ed. Nicole Uhrig, Michael Koch, Markus Neppl, Walter Schönwandt, Bernd Scholl, Andreas Voigt, and Udo Weilacher (Berlin: Jovis Verlag, 2012), 51–69.
22 Signer, "'Das Bild geht der Idee voraus,'" 55 ff.
23 Walter Schönwandt: "Grundriss einer Planungstheorie der 'dritten Generation.'" *DISP* 136/137 (1999), 28; Claus Heidemann, *Regional Planning Methodology* (Karlsruhe 1992), 95.
24 https://www.tuwien.at/forschung/schwerpunkte/ (last accessed June 2, 2020).
25 https://simlab.tuwien.ac.at/ (last accessed June 2, 2020).

Activating Spaces—Renaissance of the Silk Road   p. 200
1   See Andreas Voigt, "'Backbone' of the Orient/East-Med Corridor: The Vienna–Bratislava–Budapest–Belgrade Axis," in *Spatial and Transport Infrastructure Development in Europe: Example of the Orient/East-Med Corridor,* eds. Bernd Scholl, Ana Perić, and Mathias Niedermaier (Hannover (= Forschungsberichte der ARL 12), 2019), 231–242.
2   See Milica Bajić-Brković, "Belgrad/Belgrade," in *Internationales Doktorandenkolleg "Forschungslabor Raum": Urbane Transformationslandschaften,* eds. Michael Koch, Markus Neppl, Walter Schönwandt, Bernd Scholl, Andreas Voigt, and Udo Weilacher (Berlin: Jovis Verlag, 2016), 144 f.

Urban Research in Times of Unbounded Urbanization and Major Social Challenges   p. 210
1   Johann Jessen and Stefan Siedentop, "Stadtforschung," in *Handwörterbuch der Stadt- und Raumentwicklung,* ed. Akademie für Raumforschung und Landesplanung (Hannover: Verlag der ARL, 2018), 2465–2476.
2   ILS (Institut für Landes- und Stadtentwicklungsforschung), "Forschungsstrategie 2018+" (Dortmund 2018).
3   Neil Brenner and Christian Schmid, "The 'Urban Age' in Question," *International Journal of Urban and Regional Research* 38, no. 3 (2014): 731–755.
4   Michael Storper and Allen J. Scott, "Current Debates in Urban Theory: A Critical Assessment," *Urban Studies* 53, no. 6 (2016): 1114–1136.
5   Hartmut Häußermann and Walter Siebel, *Stadtsoziologie: Eine Einführung* (Frankfurt am Main/New York: Campus, 2004), 91.
6   Petter Næss, "Built Environment, Causality and Urban Planning," *Planning Theory & Practice* 17, no. 1 (2016): 52–71.
7   Walter Siebel, *Die Kultur der Stadt* (Berlin: Suhrkamp Verlag, 2015), 15.
8   George C. Galster, "The Mechanism(s) of Neighborhood Effects: Theory, Evidence and Policy Implications" in *Neighborhood Effects Research Perspectives,* ed. Maarten van Ham et al. (Heidelberg: Springer), 23–56.
9   Jürgen Friedrichs, "Ist die Besonderheit des Städtischen auch die Besonderheit der Stadtsoziologie?" in *Die Besonderheit des Städtischen: Entwicklungslinien der Stadt(soziologie),* ed. Heike Herrmann et al. (Wiesbaden: VS Verlag für Sozialwissenschaften, 2011), 37.
10 Uwe Schneidewind, "Transformative Wissenschaft: Motor für gute Wissenschaft und lebendige Demokratie," *GAIA* 24, no. 2 (2015): 88. The article is a reaction to

3 TMO, Straßburg, unter: http://rmtmo.eu/de/politik/aktuell (letzter Zugriff: 27.02.2019).

4 Auf der Basis dieses Papiers stellte der 11. Dreiländerkongress in Straßburg am 11. Januar 2008 in einer Erklärung fest: „Am Oberrhein leben zwischen Jura, Vogesen, Schwarzwald und Pfälzerwald auf 21.508 Quadratkilometern sechs Millionen Menschen in einem Gebiet, dessen Merkmal ein engmaschiges Netz dynamischer Städte mit dazwischenliegenden ländlichen Räumen ist." Vgl. dazu: Gemeinsame Erklärung für eine Trinationale Metropolregion Oberrhein: 11. Dreiländerkongress, Straßburg / Déclaration commune pour une Région métropolitaine trinationale du Rhin supérieur: 11ème Congrès Tripartite, Strasbourg, 11.01.2008, unter: https://www.oberrheinkonferenz.org/de/oberrhein konferenz/downloads.html.

5 EKI-Dokumentation, Mannheimer Modell, Stadt Mannheim 2009/2013, unter: https://www.mannheim.de/sites/default/files/page/9392/071205_eki-mannheim-konzept.pdf; https://www.mannheim.de/sites/default/files/page/4569/eki-entwicklungkonzept_innenstadt_broschure_2013.pdf (beide letzter Zugriff: 25.02.2020)

6 O. V.: https://www.rmtmo.eu/de/politik/aktuell/newsreader-politik/konferenz-zum-thema-grenzueberschreitender-metropolraum-strassburg-karlsruhe.html, veröffentlicht am 31.01.2019

Raumbezogene Simulation   S. 179

1 Vgl. Andreas Voigt: Raumbezogene Simulation und Örtliche Raumplanung. Wege zu einem (stadt-)raumbezogenen Qualitätsmanagement. Wien 2005, S. 27.

2 Ebd.

3 Vgl. Hartmut Bossel: Modellbildung und Simulation: Konzepte, Verfahren und Modelle zum Verhalten dynamischer Systeme. Braunschweig/Wiesbaden 1994, S. 36.

4 Vgl. Voigt 2005, S. 27; Bossel 1994, S. 15.

5 Vgl. Walter Schönwandt/Peter Wasel: „Das semiotische Dreieck – ein gedankliches Werkzeug beim Planen", in: Bauwelt, 20, 1997, S. 1118; Mario Bunge: Treatise on Basic Philosophy. Dordrecht/Boston 1974.

6 Mario Bunge: Epistemologie. Aktuelle Fragen der Wissenschaftstheorie. Mannheim 1983, S. 44.

7 Walter Schönwandt, Peter Wasel: „Das semiotische Dreieck – ein gedankliches Werkzeug beim Planen", in: Bauwelt, 19, 1997, S. 1037.

8 Schönwandt/Wasel 1997, S. 1037.

9 Schönwandt/Wasel 1997, S. 1028.

10 Vgl. Voigt 2005, S. 22; Hartmut Bossel: Globale Wende. Wege zu einem gesellschaftlichen und ökologischen Strukturwandel. München 1998, S. 16 ff. und S. 49 ff.; Kurt Ricica, Andreas Voigt (Hrsg. i. A. der MA22 Umweltschutz): Raumverträglichkeit als Beitrag zur nachhaltigen Raumnutzung. Ein Leitfaden (Teil 1). Wien 1998, S. 127 ff.

11 Bossel 1998, S. 51.

12 Ebd., S. 61.

13 Ebd.

14 Vgl. Walter Schönwandt / Katrin Vormanek / Jürgen Utz / Jens Grunau / Christoph Hemberger: Komplexe Probleme lösen. Ein Handbuch. Berlin 2013.

15 Vgl. Alexander Gosztonyi: Der Raum. Geschichte seiner Probleme in Philosophie und Wissenschaften. Freiburg/München 1976, S. 35.

16 Vgl. Schönwandt/Wasel 1997, S. 1128.

17 Vgl. Voigt 2005, S. 29 ff.

18 Bossel 1994, S. 11.

19 Vgl. Antero Markelin / Bernd Fahle: Umweltsimulation. Sensorische Simulation im Städtebau (Schriftenreihe 11 des Städtebaulichen Instituts der Universität Stuttgart). Stuttgart 1979, S. 19 ff.

20 Vgl. ebd., S. 22 f.

21 Vgl. Rolf Signer: „,Das Bild geht der Idee voraus'. Von Bildern in der Raumplanung", in: Nicole Uhrig/Michael Koch/Markus Neppl/Walter Schönwandt/Bernd Scholl/Andreas Voigt/Udo Weilacher (Hrsg.): Spatial Reseach Lab. The Logbook = Forschungslabor Raum. Das Logbuch. Berlin 2012, S. 51–69.

22 Vgl. ebd., S. 55 ff.

23 Vgl. Walter Schönwandt: „Grundriss einer Planungstheorie der ,dritten Generation'", in: DISP, 136/137, 1999, S. 28; Claus Heidemann: Regional Planning Methodology. Karlsruhe 1992, S. 95.

24 https://www.tuwien.at/forschung/schwerpunkte/ (letzter Zugriff: 22.04.2020).

25 https://simlab.tuwien.ac.at/ (letzter Zugriff: 22.04.2020).

Räume aktivieren – Renaissance der Seidenstraße   S. 201

1 Vgl. Andreas Voigt: „,Backbone' of the Orient/East-Med Corridor: The Vienna–Bratislava–Budapest–Belgrade Axis", in: Bernd Scholl/Ana Perić/Mathias Niedermaier (Hrsg.): Spatial and Transport Infrastructure Development in Europe: Example of the Orient/East-Med Corridor. Hannover 2019 (= Forschungsberichte der ARL 12), S. 231–242.

2 Vgl. Milica Bajić-Brković: „Belgrad/Belgrade", in: Michael Koch/Markus Neppl/Walter Schönwandt/Bernd Scholl/Andreas Voigt / Udo Weilacher (Hrsg.): Internationales Doktorandenkolleg „Forschungslabor Raum". Urbane Transformationslandschaften. Berlin 2016, 144 f.

Stadtforschung in Zeiten entgrenzter Urbanisierung und großer gesellschaftlicher Herausforderungen   S. 211

1 Johann Jessen/Stefan Siedentop: „Stadtforschung", in: Akademie für Raumforschung und Landesplanung (Hrsg.): Handwörterbuch der Stadt- und Raumentwicklung. Hannover 2018, S. 2465–2476.

2 ILS (Institut für Landes- und Stadtentwicklungsforschung): Forschungsstrategie 2018+. Dortmund 2018.

3 Neil Brenner / Christian Schmid: „The ,Urban Age' in Question", in: International Journal of Urban and Regional Research, 38(3), 2014, S. 731–755.

4 Michael Storper / Allen J. Scott: „Current Debates in Urban Theory: A Critical Assessment", in: Urban Studies, 53(6), 2016, S. 1114–1136.

5 Hartmut Häußermann / Walter Siebel: Stadtsoziologie. Eine Einführung. Frankfurt am Main / New York 2004, S. 91.

6 Petter Næss: „Built Environment, Causality and Urban Planning", in: Planning Theory & Practice, 17(1), 2016, S. 52–71.

7 Walter Siebel: Die Kultur der Stadt. Berlin 2015, S. 15.

8 George C. Galster: „The Mechanism(s) of Neighborhood Effects. Theory, Evidence and Policy Implications", in: Maarten van Ham et al. (Hrsg.). Heidelberg, S. 23–56.

9 Jürgen Friedrichs: „Ist die Besonderheit des Städtischen auch die Besonderheit der Stadtsoziologie?", in: Heike Herrmann/Carsten Keller/Rainer Neef et al. (Hrsg.): Die Besonderheit des Städtischen. Entwicklungslinien der Stadt(soziologie). Heidelberg 2011, S. 37.

10 Uwe Schneidewind: „Transformative Wissenschaft – Motor für gute Wissenschaft und lebendige Demokratie", in: GAIA, 24(2), 2015, S. 88. Der Artikel ist eine Reaktion auf Armin Grunwald: „Transformative Wissenschaft – eine neue Ordnung im Wissenschaftsbetrieb?", in: GAIA, 24(1), 2015, S. 17–20.

11 Peter Strohschneider: „Zur Politik der Transformativen Wissenschaft", in: André Brodocz/Dietrich Herrmann/Rainer Schmidt/Daniel Schulz/Julia Schulze-Wessel (Hrsg.): Die Verfassung des Politischen. Festschrift für Hans Vorländer. Wiesbaden 2014, S. 175–192.

12 Ebd., S. 182.

13 Jennifer Robinson: „Comparative Urbanism: New Geographies and Cultures of Theorizing the Urban", in: International Journal of Urban and Regional Research, 40(1), 2016, S. 189.

Armin Grunwald, "Transformative Wissenschaft: eine neue Ordnung im Wissenschaftsbetrieb?" *GAIA* 24, no. 1: 17–20.

11 Peter Strohschneider, "Zur Politik der Transformativen Wissenschaft," in *Die Verfassung des Politischen: Festschrift für Hans Vorländer*, ed. André Brodocz et al., (Wiesbaden: Springer VS 2014), 175–192.

12 Strohschneider, "Zur Politik der Transformativen Wissenschaft," 182.

13 Jennifer Robinson, "Comparative Urbanism: New Geographies and Cultures of Theorizing the Urban," *International Journal of Urban and Regional Research* 40, no. 1 (2016): 189.

Shaping Our Living Space! Review and Preview   p. 244

1 My teacher at the time at ETH Zurich and chairman of the planning commission, Jakob Maurer, expounded his experiences over the course of this realization in the book *Das Wiener Modell*, written with his colleague Kurt Freisitzer, a sociologist at the University of Graz. The book remains relevant today, and the principles it presents are considered the root of modern planning procedures, for example, of test planning. See Kurt Freisitzer and Jakob Maurer, *Das Wiener Modell: Erfahrungen mit innovativer Stadtplanung; Empirische Befunde aus einem Großprojekt* (Vienna: Compress, 1985).

2 Julian Wékel, *Zeitzeugen: Vom Museumsufer zum Stadtraum Main* (Darmstadt: TU Darmstadt, 2016).

3 Bernd Scholl, Ana Perić, and Rolf Signer, *Spatial Planning Matters! Inspiring Stories and Fundamenal Topics* (Zurich: vdf Hochschulverlag, 2018).

4 Mahdokth Soltaniehha, "Railway-Oriented Spatial Development" (Dissertation ETH Zurich, 2019); Julian Wékel, *Zeitzeugen*.

5 Hansjörg Drewello and Bernd Scholl, *Integrated Spatial and Transport Infrastructure Development: The Case of the European North-South Corridor Rotterdam–Genoa* (Cham: Springer International Publishing, 2016).

6 Bernd Scholl, "Spaces and Projects of European Importance," in *Spatial and Transport Infrastructure Development in Europe: Example of the Orient/East-Med Corridor*, ed. Bernd Scholl, Ana Perić, and Mathias Niedermaier, Forschungsberichte der ARL 12 (Hannover: Akademie für Raumforschung und Landesplanung, 2019), 14–34.

7 Akademie für Raumforschung und Landesplanung, ed., *Spatial and Transport Development in European Corridors—Example Corridor: Orient/East-Med; Connecting and Competing in Spaces of European Importance*, Position Paper of the ARL 112 (Hannover: Akademie für Raumforschung und Landesplanung, 2019); Scholl, "Spaces and Projects of European Importance."

8 Theodora Papamichail, "Spatial Synergies: Synergies between Formal and Informal Planning as a Key Concept towards Spatial Conflicts; the Case of Tourism-Oriented Railway Development in the Peloponnese" (Dissertation ETH Zurich, 2019).

9 Bernd Scholl, Martin Vizens, and Bernard Staub, *Test Planning: A New Method with a Future* (Solothurn: Kanton Solothurn, Amt für Raumplanung; Schweizerische Eidgenossenschaft, Bundesamt für Raumentwicklung [ARE]; Departement für Umwelt, Verkehr, Energie und Kommunikation [UVEK], 2013).

10 The method of test planning was manifested in "experimental simulations" in the spatial planning studies at ETH Zurich. In various sequences, the participants in the further education offerings in spatial planning run through a test plan with allocated roles. An educational film was made about the Attisholz test plan, led by Anita Grams, a former doctoral student at the college. The film can be accessed at the following link: https://masraumplanung.ethz.ch/forschung/lehrfilme.html (last accessed April 17, 2020). For research on these topics, see Bernd Scholl, "Die Methode der

Testplanung: Exemplarische Veranschaulichung für die Auswahl und den Einsatz von Methoden in Klärungsprozessen," in Klaus Borchard and Akademie für Raumforschung und Landesplanung, *Grundriss der Raumentwicklung* (Hannover: Verlag der ARL, 2011), 330–345; Bernd Scholl, "Test Planning as Means of Solving Complex Problems in Spatial Planning," *disp—The Planning Review* 53 (208): 46–56.

Nonprofit Housing and Inward Development   p. 264

1 Direct link to dissertation: https://doi.org/10.3929/ethz-b-000384492.

Landscape as a Complex Spatial System – Challenges for Landscape Architecture in the Anthropocene   p. 282

1 Udo Weilacher, "Landschaft wahrzunehmen muss gelernt sein," in *Forschungslabor Raum/Spatial Research Lab: Das Logbuch/The Logbook*, ed. Internationales Doktorandenkolleg Forschungslabor Raum (Berlin: Jovis Verlag, 2012), 244–257.

2 Udo Weilacher, "Neue Raumbilder der Kulturlandschaft/ New Spatial Images of the Cultivated Landscape," in *Urbane Transformationslandschaften / Transformation of Cities and Landscapes*, ed. Internationales Doktorandenkolleg Forschungslabor Raum (Berlin: Jovis Verlag, 2016), 266–281.

3 John Brinckerhoff Jackson and Helen L. Horowitz, eds., *Landscape in Sight: Looking at America* (New Haven: Yale University Press, 1997), 304–305.

4 René Thom, *Stabilité structurelle et morphogénèse: essai d'une théorie générale des modèles* (Reading, MA: W.A. Benjamin, 1972).

5 Hans Poser, "Kreativität im Spannungsfeld von Handlung und Komplexität" in *Creating Knowledge: Innovationsstrategien im Entwerfen urbaner Landschaften*, ed. Hille von Seggern et al. (Berlin: Jovis Verlag, 2008), 112

6 See, for instance, Hans-Peter Dürr, *Warum es ums Ganze geht: Neues Denken für eine Welt im Umbruch* (Munich: Oekom, 2009).

7 Beate M. W. Ratter, "Komplexitätstheorie und Geographie: Ein Beitrag zur Begründung einer anderen Sicht," *Mitteilungen der Österreichischen Geographischen Gesellschaft* 148 (2006): 111.

8 Ratter, *Komplexitätstheorie*, 115.

9 See David Byrne, *Complexity Theory and the Social Sciences: An Introduction* (London: Routledge, Taylor & Francis, 1998).

10 David Blackbourn, *The Conquest of Nature: Water, Landscape and the Making of Modern Germany* (London: Jonathan Cape, 2006).

11 Detlev Ipsen, *Ort und Landschaft* (Wiesbaden: VS Verlag für Sozialwissenschaften, 2006), 31.

12 See Niklas Luhmann, *Vertrauen: Ein Mechanismus der Reduktion sozialer Komplexität* (Stuttgart: F. Enke, 1968).

13 Kevin Lynch, *The Image of the City* (Cambridge, MA: MIT Press, 1960), 4.

14 Ipsen, *Ort und Landschaft*, 24.

15 Klaus Mainzer, *Komplexe Systeme und Nichtlineare Dynamik in Natur und Gesellschaft* (Berlin/Heidelberg: Springer, 1999), 26.

Unseren Lebensraum gestalten!
Rückblick und Ausblick   S. 245

1   Mein damaliger Lehrer an der ETH Zürich und Vorsitzender der für die Planungen eingesetzten Kommission, Jakob Maurer, hat mit seinem Kollegen Kurt Freisitzer, einem Soziologen der Universität Graz, die Erfahrungen im Zuge der Realisierung im Buch *Das Wiener Modell* weitergegeben. Das Buch ist bis heute hochaktuell und die dort dargelegten Prinzipien gelten als Wurzel moderner Planungsverfahren, zum Beispiel der Testplanungen.

2   Kurt Freisitzer / Jakob Maurer: Das Wiener Modell. Erfahrungen mit innovativer Stadtplanung. Empirische Befunde aus einem Großprojekt. Wien 1985.

3   Julian Wékel: Zeitzeugen: Vom Museumsufer zum Stadtraum Main. Darmstadt 2016.

4   Bernd Scholl / Ana Perić / Rolf Signer: Spatial Planning Matters! Inspiring Stories and Fundamenal Topics. Zürich 2018.

5   Mahdokth Soltaniehha: Railway-Oriented Spatial Development (Dissertation). Zürich 2019; Julian Wékel: Zeitzeugen. Vom Museumsufer zum Stadtraum Main. Darmstadt 2016.

6   Hansjörg Drewello / Bernd Scholl: Integrated Spatial and Transport Infrastructure Development: The Case of the European North-South Corridor Rotterdam–Genoa. Cham 2016.

7   Bernd Scholl: „Spaces and Projects of European Importance", in: Akademie für Raumforschung und Landesplanung / Bernd Scholl / Ana Perić / Matthias Niedermaier (Hrsg.): Spatial and Transport Infrastructure Development in Europe. Example of the Orient/East-Med Corridor. Hannover 2020.

8   Akademie für Raumforschung und Landesplanung: Spatial and Transport Development in European Corridors – Example Corridor: Orient/East-Med. Connecting and Competing in Spaces of European Importance. Hannover 2019; Bernd Scholl: „Spaces and Projects of European Importance", in: Akademie für Raumforschung und Landesplanung et al. 2020.

9   Theodora Papamichail: Spatial Synergies. Synergies between formal and informal planning as a key concept towards spatial conflicts – the case of tourism-oriented railway development in the Peloponnese (Dissertation). Zürich 2019.

10   Bernd Scholl / Bernard Staub: Test Planning: A New Method with a Future. Zürich 2013.

11   Die Methode der Testplanung hat in der Lehre der Raumplanung an der ETH Zürich ihren Niederschlag in „experimentellen Simulationen" gefunden. In verschiedenen Sequenzen spielen die Teilnehmenden der Fortbildungsangebote in Raumplanung eine Testplanung mit verteilten Rollen durch. Über die Testplanung Attisholz wurde unter Leitung von Anita Grams, einer ehemaligen Doktorandin des Kollegs, ein Lehrfilm erstellt. Der Film ist unter folgendem Link abrufbar: https://masraumplanung.ethz.ch/forschung/lehrfilme.html (letzter Zugriff: 17.04.2020).

12   Bernd Scholl: „Die Methode der Testplanung. Exemplarische Veranschaulichung für die Auswahl und den Einsatz von Methoden in Klärungsprozessen (Methods of test planning. Exemplary illustrations for the selection and use of methods in clarification processes)", in: Akademie für Raumforschung und Landesplanung: Grundriss der Raumentwicklung. Hannover 2011; Bernd Scholl: „Test Planning as Means of Solving Complex Problems in Spatial Planning", in: DISP, 53(208), S. 46–56.

Bahnorientierte Raumentwicklung: Strategie für integrierte Raum- und Eisenbahnentwicklung in der Schweiz   S. 263

1   Mahdokht Soltaniehha: Railway-Oriented Spatial Development; A Principal Strategy for Integrated Spatial and Railway Development in Small and Mid-Sized Communities of Swiss Agglomerations. (Dissertation). Zürich 2019.

Gemeinnütziger Wohnungsbau und Innenentwicklung S. 265

1   Direktlink zur Dissertation von Roman Streit: https://doi.org/10.3929/ethz-b-000384492 (letzter Zugriff: 06.08.2020).

Komplexes Raumsystem Landschaft – Herausforderungen für die Landschaftsarchitektur im Anthropozän   S. 283

1   Udo Weilacher: „Landschaft wahrzunehmen muss gelernt sein / We have to learn to perceive landscape", in: Internationales Doktorandenkolleg Forschungslabor Raum (Hrsg.): Forschungslabor Raum / Spatial Research Lab. Das Logbuch / The Logbook. Berlin 2012, S. 244–257.

2   Udo Weilacher: „Neue Raumbilder der Kulturlandschaft / New Spatial Images of the Cultivated Landscape", in: Internationales Doktorandenkolleg Forschungslabor Raum (Hrsg.): Urbane Transformationslandschaften/ Transformation of Cities and Landscapes. Berlin 2016, S. 266–281.

3   John Brinckerhoff Jackson / Helen L. Horowitz (Hrsg.): Landscape in Sight. Looking at America. New Haven 1997, S. 304–305. („A Landscape is not a natural feature of the environment but a synthetic space, a man-made system of spaces superimposed on the face of the land, functioning and evolving not according to natural laws but to serve a community.")

4   René Thom: Stabilité structurelle et morphogénèse – essai d'une théorie générale des modèles. Reading MA 1972.

5   Hans Poser: „Kreativität im Spannungsfeld von Handlung und Komplexität", in: Hille von Seggern et al. (Hrsg.): Creating Knowledge. Innovationsstrategien im Entwerfen urbaner Landschaften. Berlin 2008, S. 112. („Complexity theories represent a completely new type of theory, even more, they are well on the way to represent a completely new world view whereby everything in the universe has a history, every event is completely unique in its complex connections non-repeatable. These theories attempt to interpret the appearance of self-organizing and of completely new structures. This is exactly what we use to call creativity in the area of human thought and action.")

6   Vgl. z. B. Hans-Peter Dürr: Warum es ums Ganze geht. Neues Denken für eine Welt im Umbruch. München 2009.

7   Beate M. W. Ratter: Komplexitätstheorie und Geographie – Ein Beitrag zur Begründung einer anderen Sicht (Mitteilungen der Österreichischen Geographischen Gesellschaft, 148. Jg.; Jahresband). Wien 2006, S. 111.

8   Ebd., S. 115.

9   Vgl. David Byrne: Complexity Theory and the Social Sciences. An Introduction. London 1998.

10   David Blackbourn: Die Eroberung der Natur. Eine Geschichte der Deutschen Landschaft. München 2008. (Original: The Conquest of Nature. Water, Landscape and the Making of Modern Germany. London 2006.)

11   Detlev Ipsen: Ort und Landschaft. Wiesbaden 2006, S. 31.

12   Vgl. Niklas Luhmann: Vertrauen. Ein Mechanismus der Reduktion sozialer Komplexität. Stuttgart 1968.

13   Kevin Lynch: The Image of the City. Cambridge MA 1960.

14   Kevin Lynch: Das Bild der Stadt. Braunschweig 1989, S. 14. (Lynch 1960, S. 4: „A good environmental image gives its possessor an important sense of emotional security.")

15   Ipsen 2006, S. 24.

16   Klaus Mainzer: Komplexe Systeme und Nichtlineare Dynamik in Natur und Gesellschaft. Berlin/Heidelberg 1999, S. 26.

ACKNOWLEDGEMENTS DANK

The editors would like to thank the following for contributing to the content and financing of this publication:
Für die inhaltlichen sowie finanziellen Beiträge bedanken sich die Herausgeber herzlich bei:

Prof. Fouad Amraoui
Milica Bajić-Brković
Steffen Becker
Jonas Bellingrodt
Fettouma Djerrari
  Benabdembi
Bo Christiansen
Iva Čukić
Lena Flamm
Irini Frezadou
Daniel Galland
Undine Giseke
Anita Grams
Friedbert Greif
Herr Häckl
Manuel Hauer
Max Haug
Leevke Ann-Marie
  Heeschen
Herr Karapanagiotis
Christoph Kasper
Michael Koch
Andreas Kurths
Peter Latz
Marcello Modica
Dominik Neidlinger
Markus Neppl
Mathias Niedermaier
Markus Nollert
Andreas Nütten
Patricia Ott
Uli Paetzel

Theodora Papamichail
Vassilis Pappas
Julian Petrin
Branislav Popović
Radostina
  Radulova-Stahmer
Mario Reimer
Eva Ritter
Amelie Rost
Bernd Scholl
Walter Schönwandt
Isabella Schuster
Reinhard Seiß
Stefan Siedentop
Yvonne Siegmund
Mahdokht Soltaniehha
Rolf Sonderegger
Lisa Stadtler
Matthias Stippich
Roman Streit
Peter Stroms
Martin Thörnkvist
Andreas Voigt
Monika Wächter
Sonja Weber
Frau Weiant
Udo Weilacher
Angelika Weissheim
Isabel Wieshofer
Renate Zuckerstätter-
  Semela

Albert Speer Stiftung
Technische Universität München
Technische Universität Berlin
Technische Universität Wien
ETH Zürich
Ferme pédagogique Dar Bouzza
Université Hassan II, Casablanca
ILS – Institut für Landes- und
  Stadtentwicklungsforschung
Karlsruher Institut für Technologie (KIT)
Stadt Wien
Stadtplanungsamt Karlsruhe
TUM Akademiezentrum Raitenhaslach
Chem Delta Bavaria

PICTURE CREDITS BILDNACHWEISE

8/9: Lena Flamm
18: Udo Weilacher
30/31 u.: Udo Weilacher
31 o.: Markus Nollert
36: Jonas Bellingrodt
48: Julian Petrin
50/51: Urbanista and bureau für RAUM ENTWICKLUNG, 2017/18
54: Markus Nollert, aus: „Raumplanerisches Entwerfen: Entwerfen als Schlüsselelement von Klärungsprozessen der aktionsorientierten Planung" (2013)
57: Markus Nollert, aus: „The Case of Brig, Switzerland. How ‚working together' opened new possibilities in organizing", in: Scholl 2018, S. 136–143.
58: Jürgen Weidinger
62/63: Andreas Nütten
64: Stachowiak 1973, S. 157
66/69/70/71: Andreas Nütten
80/81: Andreas Voigt
104/105: Undine Giseke
106: RapidPlanning Projekt, TU Berlin, Faculty of Landscape Architecture + Open Space Planning, 2018 / RapidPlanning Projekt, TU Berlin, Fachgebiet Landschaftsarchitektur + Freiraumplanung, 2018
111: Jutta Henglein-Bildau
114/115: Udo Weilacher
116/117: Andreas Kurths
118/119: Leevke Heeschen
120/121: Lena Flamm
122/123: Marcello Modica
128/129: Andreas Voigt
130/131/132/133/134/135/136/137/138/139: Marcello Modica
146: StudioUC/mess/ASTOC
147: ASTOC / urbane Gestalt, photo: Langreder / ASTOC / urbane Gestalt, Foto: Langreder
148/149/151 o.: ASTOC
151 u.: urbanista / bureau für Raumentwicklung / ASTOC
154 o.: Udo Weilacher
154 u./155/156/157: Markus Neppl
158/159: Manuel Hauer
160/161: Max Haug
162/163: Radostina Radulova-Strahmer
164: Yvonne Siegmund
166/167: Marcello Modica
172/173/174/175: Udo Weilacher
188/189/190 u.: Andreas Voigt
190 o./191 o.: Isabella Schuster
191 u.: Marcello Modica
192/193: Isabella Schuster
194/195: Mathias Niedermaier
196: Monika Wächter
198/199: Marcello Modica
204 o.: Udo Weilacher
204/205: Marcello Modica
206/207: Udo Weilacher
220/221: Stefan Siedentop

222/223/224/225: Andreas Voigt
226/227: Lisa Stadtler
228: Peter Stroms
230/231: Isabella Schuster
236 o.: Marcello Modica
236 u./237/238/239/240/241: Udo Weilacher
246 l.: Bernd Scholl, 1994, Aktionsplanung
246 r.: Bernd Scholl, 1994, Aktionsplanung
247: Bernd Scholl, 2016
249: ETH Zürich, Professur für Raumentwicklung, 2018
250: ETH Zürich, Professur für Raumentwicklung, 2015
254: ETH Zürich, Professur für Raumentwicklung, 2018
255: Kanton Uri, Amt für Raumentwicklung, 2019
256/257/258 u.: Marcello Modica
258 o.: Udo Weilacher
259/260/261 o.: Marcello Modica
261 u.: Udo Weilacher
262: Mahdokht Soltaniehha
264/265: Roman Streit
266: Theodora Papamichail
268/269: Lena Flamm
272/275: ETH Zurich, Chair for Spatial Development / ETH Zürich, Professur für Raumentwicklung
276/277/278/279: Udo Weilacher
292/293: Lena Flamm
294/295: Andreas Voigt
296/297: Lena Flamm
298/299: Florentine-Amelie Rost
300: Marcello Modica

IMPRINT IMPRESSUM

© 2021 by jovis Verlag GmbH
Das Copyright für die Texte liegt bei den Autor*innen.
Das Copyright für die Abbildungen liegt bei den Fotograf*innen/Inhaber*innen der Bildrechte.
Texts by kind permission of the author.
Pictures by kind permission of the photographers/holders of the picture rights.

Umschlagmotiv Cover: Udo Weilacher
Redaktion Editorial staff: Sonja Weber
Übersetzung Translation: Lynne Kolar-Thompson
Lektorat Copy-Editing: Michael Taylor, Miriam Seifert-Waibel
Gestaltung und Satz Design and setting: Johanna Uhrmann
Lithografie Lithography: Bild1Druck, Berlin
Gedruckt in der Europäischen Union Printed in the European Union

Bibliografische Information der Deutschen Nationalbibliothek
Die Deutsche Nationalbibliothek verzeichnet diese Publikation in der Deutschen Nationalbib-
liografie; detaillierte bibliografische Daten sind im Internet über http://dnb.d-nb.de abrufbar.
Bibliographic information published by the Deutsche Nationalbibliothek
The Deutsche Nationalbibliothek lists this publication in the Deutsche Nationalbibliografie;
detailed bibliographic data are available on the Internet at http://dnb.d-nb.de

jovis Verlag GmbH
Lützowstraße 33
10785 Berlin

www.jovis.de

jovis-Bücher sind weltweit im ausgewählten Buchhandel erhältlich. Informationen zu unserem internationalen Vertrieb erhalten Sie von Ihrem Buchhändler oder unter www.jovis.de.
jovis books are available worldwide in select bookstores. Please contact your nearest book-
seller or visit www.jovis.de for information concerning your local distribution.

ISBN 978-3-86859-573-4